CONTRACT LAW AND SOCIAL MORALITY

When people in a relationship disagree about their obligations to each other, they need to rely on a method of reasoning that allows the relationship to flourish while advancing each person's private projects. This book presents a method of reasoning that reflects how people reason through disagreements and how courts create doctrine by reasoning about the obligations arising from the relationship. Built on the ideal of the other-regarding person, *Contract Law and Social Morality* displays a method of reasoning that allows one person to integrate their personal interests with the interests of another, determining how divergent interests can be balanced against each other. Called values-balancing reasoning, this methodology makes transparent the values at stake in a disagreement, and provides a neutral and objective way to identify and evaluate the trade-offs that are required if the relationship is to be sustained or terminated justly.

Peter M. Gerhart is John Homer Kapp Professor of Law at Case Western Reserve University. Professor Gerhart may hold a record for teaching the most courses in the law school curriculum: twenty-five. His three books exploring the concept of an individual's responsibility to others cover Torts, Property, and Contracts, and implement a process of reasoning that is both deontic and consequential.

Contract Law and Social Morality

PETER M. GERHART
Case Western Reserve University

CAMBRIDGE
UNIVERSITY PRESS

CAMBRIDGE
UNIVERSITY PRESS

University Printing House, Cambridge CB2 8BS, United Kingdom

One Liberty Plaza, 20th Floor, New York, NY 10006, USA

477 Williamstown Road, Port Melbourne, VIC 3207, Australia

314–321, 3rd Floor, Plot 3, Splendor Forum, Jasola District Centre,
New Delhi – 110025, India

79 Anson Road, #06–04/06, Singapore 079906

Cambridge University Press is part of the University of Cambridge.

It furthers the University's mission by disseminating knowledge in the pursuit of education, learning, and research at the highest international levels of excellence.

www.cambridge.org
Information on this title: www.cambridge.org/9781107136762
DOI: 10.1017/9781316480106

First published 2021

A catalogue record for this publication is available from the British Library.

Library of Congress Cataloging-in-Publication Data
NAMES: Gerhart, Peter M., author.
TITLE: Contract law and social morality / Peter M. Gerhart, Case Western Reserve University.
DESCRIPTION: Cambridge, United Kingdom; New York, NY: Cambridge University Press, 2021. | Includes bibliographical references and index.
IDENTIFIERS: LCCN 2020040200 | ISBN 9781107136762 (hardback) | ISBN 9781316501986 (paperback) | ISBN 9781316480106 (ebook)
SUBJECTS: LCSH: Contracts. | Standardized terms of contract. | Contracts – Moral and ethical aspects. | Contracts – Social aspects. | Obligations (Law)
CLASSIFICATION: LCC K840 .G47 2021 | DDC 346.02/2–dc23
LC record available at https://lccn.loc.gov/2020040200

ISBN 978-1-107-13676-2 Hardback

A.T. and a growing family tree.

Contents

Preface

My aspiration in this book is to probe, unpack, and supplement the mental models we use to understand the obligations that arise from promising and contracting. The thesis I advance is straightforward, even if not intuitive. It is this: when people make or exchange promises, they do more than simply bind themselves to a future course of action. They also bind themselves to a method of reasoning about their future course of action, a method that we might call values-balancing reasoning.

I have a second, related claim – when a judge evaluates the legal obligations that arise from promising and contracting, implementing legal doctrine in the context of a dispute, the judge also employs a method of reasoning about the determinants of legal obligations. The judge considers the contextual factors and circumstances that determine how doctrine ought to be applied, which also entails a method of values-balancing reasoning.

Not surprisingly, the method of reasoning that persons ought to use to determine their promissory behavior is the method of reasoning that judges use to implement doctrine. Under the view I present, judges resolve disputes that arise from promising and contracting by using a method of values-balancing reasoning about a person's obligations, and that method of reasoning is the one they believe people should use when people in a promissory, contractual relationship decide how to behave. When people behave as they would if they had used the same method of reasoning as judges, the law's normativity is unified with the normativity of people's own reasoning. When that happens, the distance between law on the books (how people ought to behave) and law on the ground (how people actually behave) shrinks.

What is at stake is not the death, but the disintegration, of contract law. Without an integrating methodology of reasoning about obligations, contract law is in danger of disintegrating under the weight of disparate theories, pluralistic values, obtuse words, specialized doctrine shaped around kinds of contracts, and contradictory doctrine. Are obligations determined by autonomy, reliance, empowerment, consent, or wealth-maximization? If the obligations of promising and contracting are determined by the value of autonomy, which aspect of autonomy matters: freedom from contract, freedom to bind oneself, or the right to rely on another? What justifies a separate restatement for consumer contracts, and will we soon face a restatement for sophisticated business people, and another for small businesses? Are modifications of contracts addressed as a question of consideration or by what is fair and equitable? And what does *fair and equitable* mean? And what about *good faith* and *unconsionability*? As contract design evolves, can contract doctrine adopt to the practice of contracting?

As an antidote to contract law's possible disintegration, I offer a mental model of how people ought to make decisions about their obligations. Mental models help us organize our understanding of complex systems, which is why mental models can help us organize our understanding of promising and contracting. Mental models incorporate a framework within which we can process the multifaceted data that we must organize if we are to create a coherent picture out of the particulars of the moral and legal landscape of promising and contracting. The existing mental models of contracting and promising are well known: doctrinal rules, moral principles, social practices, efficient incentives, and theories of autonomy, reliance, empowerment, consent, wealth, and well-being within cooperative relationships. In this book I suggest a supplementary mental model that I hope will add strength and nuance to these mental models.

I do not pit one mental model against another; I seek not to shift paradigms but to illuminate them, perhaps even to find consilience among them. Instead, I hope to add to our understanding of promising and contracting by articulating a mental model that seems to identify a substructure that supports existing views of promising and contracting. This book is animated by the straightforward claim that we can identify a way of nondoctrinal reasoning about obligations that a reasonable person would use, given the promises and contracts she has made. This method of reasoning determines how we ought to treat each other in the context of promising and contracting.

This approach does not require that we relitigate *The Death of Contract.*[1] That magisterial work assumed that tort law was swallowing contract law because courts were introducing the notion of freewheeling, judicially created obligations into contract law. That is not my view. Instead, I affirm that obligations in contract are derived from, and reflect, the autonomy that promising, contracting parties exercise, so that when legal sources articulate the obligations that flow from promising and contracting their analysis is grounded in choices the parties made. I seek instead to breathe new ideas into contract doctrine by suggesting that reasoning as a reasonable promising party would about the obligations implicit in promising and contracting fills spaces that existing mental models leave unattended. My inquiry is epistemic: By what circumstances and factors do we inform our intuitions about what a reasonable person would do when disputes arise under a promise or contract?

[1] Gilmore (1974).

I present a way of reasoning about relational disputes, what I call values-balancing legal reasoning, that may illuminate the circumstances that determine how disputes are resolved, without necessarily challenging outcomes or doing more than providing a more penetrating understanding of the trade-offs that underlie a dispute. Illumination, not remaking the world, is my goal. If I am able to more clearly identify the important moving parts that allow us to connect the authority of a promise or contract with the resolution of a dispute, I will have succeeded. And I do not seek a complete picture of the complex field; the test of any mental model is not whether it is always right or complete, but whether it is useful.

Values-balancing legal reasoning is embedded in the sources of law that judges use to decide disputes. In any dispute, each party has interests that it hopes to attain in the resolution of the dispute. Those interests, as interests, are largely irrelevant to dispute resolution, but interests can be understood to represent important social values. In any dispute, one party is likely to have a selfish, opportunistic interest, but we do not know which party that is until we fully understand the parties' obligations. Thus, we need first to understand the values each party represents – values such as reliance or freedom from contract. Ultimately, the resolution of the dispute implicates the well-being of each of the parties and the values each party represents; one party argues he should have been able to rely on a counterparty's actions; the other argues that they should not be bound without their consent. The determination of which party's values count, and why, is ultimately a values-balancing choice because it is based on the values that each party presents to the court as a basis for resolving the dispute. One of the parties is taking an incorrect, value-defective position because it has failed to consider adequately the well-being of the other party when reasoning about the arguments and positions it will advance. The loss must fall somewhere and the allocation of the loss is ultimately determined by the values implicated in the dispute. Once the judge determines how the exchange allocated the losses, the judge has given us a new insight into the nature of promissory obligations, and that insight can guide persons in a relationship when they must reason about their obligations. Values-balancing reasoning about promises determines promissory obligations – or so I claim.

Acknowledgments

With too many debts to mention, debts not extinguished by this performance, a special appreciation goes to my colleague Professor Emeritus Ronald J. Coffee, who put me on the path of justificatory analysis, which transformed itself into values-balancing reasoning. Although I never convinced him of Kant's central role, he convinced me of the central role of reason and analytical rigor. My colleague, and sometime coconspirator, Juliet Kostritsky, participated in the robust Coffey, Kostritsky, and Gerhart coffee-klatches. She worked valiantly to show me the preeminence of efficiency analysis, and is not responsible when I stayed. I also benefited greatly from participating in her seminar in Contract Theory and from our many conversations. Another colleague, Dale Nance, allowed me to participate in his Legal Theory seminar and his readings and questions pushed me to think more deeply about the role of reasons in legal theory. Finally, Wendy Wagner has been a constant source of support and good advice.

I have also benefitted from comments received on pieces of this project from presentations I made at several K-Con conferences over the past five years. I especially appreciate the comments I received on an early draft of the book from Mark Gergen, James Gordley, and Victor Goldberg, at K-Con XV in Sacramento. Thanks to Mark for organizing the panel.

Students have been helping with research tasks, including (most recently): Sophia Bilias Hugh Dowell, Young Ko, Andrea Lee, Andy Rumschlag, and Jesse Wynn. I have received wonderful secretarial assistance over the years from, most recently, Ray Utrup, Elisa Tenant, and Malikah Hart.

Introduction

Understanding Implied Obligations: Reasoning and Methodology

REASONING ABOUT OBLIGATIONS

Formidable barriers stand in the way of developing a unifying theory of contracts. When disputes arise, contract terms may fail to provide an unambiguous basis for determining obligations; indeterminate terms, unexpressed but implied obligations, and unaddressed ex post circumstances all require a basis from which we can use the raw material of the exchange, its text and context, to determine each party's obligations. The variety of subject matter, promissory utterances, and relationships based on promising and contracting add layers of complexity to any effort to find a single method for deciphering obligations. We might wonder whether we should ever hope to develop a unified mental map for evaluating promissory relationships as different, for example, as intimate social relationships and detailed provisions for maximizing cooperation over time. The variety is capacious enough to house many kinds of theories, but the realm is diverse enough to suggest the impossibility of a general, coherent theory of contracting and promissory obligations.

Moreover, although it is widely understood that contracting requires the parties to identify and allocate the risks that threaten their relationship's success, and that the allocation of risks determines a party's obligations, it is not always clear how the parties have in fact allocated risks. Risks, and thus obligations, are the subject of the exchange and therefore cannot be assumed to fall one way or the other until we fully understand the exchange's bargaining dynamics. If a party rents an apartment from which to see a coronation parade, one would think that that party would bear the risk of the coronation being cancelled. Yet, if the party informs the owner of the reason for the rental, the risk can easily shift to the owner.[1]

Any approach to promising and contracting must also account for both the person who would take advantage of the other party (the Holmesian bad person) and the person who would do the right thing once they knew what was right in the

[1] *See* Chapter 13 ("Excused Performance and Risk Allocation").

circumstances (the Hartian good person).[2] Indeed, depending on the context, the good and the bad person may inhabit the *same* person. That puts in play the concept of a contract. Are we to think of promising and contracting as a struggle between two parties with proclivities to take advantage of each other, or as mechanisms for achieving collaborative outcomes? And if the answer is that we need to do both, how do we maximize cooperative solutions while inhibiting opportunism or shading? How do we simultaneously encourage and control the power that promises and contracts entail? Should contracting be conceived as an adversarial process by which one party can seek to control the darker angels of the other party, or should contracting be perceived as a process of building trust and shared goals?

Contract law has mechanisms for addressing these questions, of course: gaps fillers, interpretive techniques, and rules concerning consideration, promissory estoppel, excuse, and remedies. And contract theory has plenty of ideas about what contract law does, how it functions, what obligations it entails, and how contract law facilitates cooperation and wealth production. But how are we to choose among those ideas, and on what basis should we make a choice between ideas that seem to offer conflicting visions? Philosophers reason on the basis of moral principles or social practices to determine the obligations that promising and contracting entail. They seek to determine fair or moral obligations from the raw material of promising and contracting. Economists, on the other hand, emphasize that promising and contracting increase wealth. They seek, from the same raw material, to determine efficient incentives. Is the search for justified end points doomed by our choice of starting points?

Before we give in to balkanization (with different theories for various kinds of promises and contracts) or to pluralist surrender,[3] we might turn to a mental model that explores a method of nondoctrinal reasoning about obligations as a possible unifying lens. That is what this book proposes. Starting with the intuition that beneath the diverse views about promising and contracting lies a realm of reasoning that supports, justifies, and explains what we know, this book explores a realm of reason that seems to be common to, and undergird, a wide variety of views about contracting.

Consider the possibility of focusing on how people ought to reason about their obligations, given the text and context of their relationships. We might find

[2] The role of these two prototype persons in legal theory is discussed in Chapter 8 ("Relationality Redux: Law on the Ground and Law on the Books").

[3] Two trends threaten the unity of thought about promises and contracts. One is the trend toward bespoke rules for different kinds of contracts, suggesting that we need different rules for contracts between sophisticated business people and, say, between sellers and consumers. The other threat to the unity of promising and contracting is the trend toward pluralistic theories – theories that highlight various values but fail to provide a way of understanding the relationship between them. *See* Kreitner (2011–2012); Bix (2012). Resort to a pluralistic theory is unnecessary and unwise. Pluralistic theories are essentially anti-theories, denying the idea that we can understand how those values relate to, or ought to be understood in relation to, one another.

a method of reasoning that, because of its properties, displays the hallmarks of moral reasoning about relationships: neutrality, universality, and allegiance to relational expectations. We might also find that the same method of reasoning is used by people who want to minimize costs and maximize the gains from exchange. That is what this book seeks to do. By asking the parties to understand their individual interests in terms of the social values that their personal interests would advance, and then asking the parties to reason about how contested values ought to be balanced behind the veil of ignorance, we can identify which decisions were made with the proper moral and maximizing reasoning. Under this approach, the parties are obligated to subject their private interests to the interests of the relationship by reasoning about the relative weight of contesting values as if they did not know how the resulting rules would affect their private interests.

Consider the situation of parties facing a dispute. Rather than resorting to doctrine as a dispute settlement mechanism, this book offers a method of reasoning as the way of filling the gap of indeterminacy in doctrine and theory. Nondoctrinal reasoning allows the parties to address whether the contractual language is imprecise or incomplete, how the contractual language ought to be interpreted, and what to do when unanticipated events arise. Reasoning helps implement legal doctrine when legal requirements are vague, amorphous, or incomplete.[4] And because not all promises are legally enforceable, reasoning helps appreciate why and when some obligations are relegated to relational settlement.

Consider also the role of nondoctrinal reasoning in resolving disputes. The law provides the basis on which disputes are to be resolved; that basis has to be generalizable to assist in resolving similar disputes. The law's quest is to find the basis for determining obligations when the parties, unable to resolve their disputes, resort to third party dispute resolution. Dispute resolution ought to be faithful to the choices the parties made while providing authoritative guidance for future disputes. Courts face bounded knowledge[5] and conflicting information about the trade-offs the parties made, and the cost of acquiring and processing relevant information is itself a cost of contracting, a cost that is magnified if contracting parties lack confidence in a court's ability to interpret the conflict to reflect their exchange. Courts are in the position of attempting simultaneously to minimize dispute resolution's information and the error costs, which covary.[6] But a sound method of

4 *See, e.g.*, Cohen (2011) at 128 ("[i]t seems fair to say, however, that many if not most contracts are incomplete, or at least the question of their completeness is itself a legitimate question for judicial interpretation.").

5 *See* Williamson (1985) at 44 ("[Bounded rationality] acknowledges limits on cognitive competence" and it is "the cognitive assumption on which transaction cost economics relies."). This assumption assumes that economic actors are "*intendedly* rational, but only *limitedly* so." (quoting Simon (1996) at 45) (emphasis in original). *See also* Crawford (2013) at 512; Harstad & Selten (2013) at 496; and Rabin (2013) at 528.

6 Minimizing error costs requires investment. Schwartz & Scott (2003) at 577 (emphasizing that because contracts are incomplete "firms will attempt to write contracts with sufficient clarity to permit courts to

nondoctrinal reasoning about obligations reduces information costs (by identifying what information is necessary) and error costs (by allowing precise justifications), thus reducing the costs of contracting.

Importantly, the authoritative guidance we expect from judicial dispute resolution is most successful if judges make transparent the method of reasoning that the promising, contracting parties ought to use when addressing a dispute over their obligations. Such transparency helps to align how judges think about obligations with the method the parties ought to use to think about obligations. If parties to a contract use identical methods of reasoning about obligations, they can settle disputes on their own. If the parties cannot settle the dispute, one of them is reasoning in the wrong way, and the court ought to correct that method of reasoning.[7]

This book explores a supplemental method of legal reasoning in three parts. Part I justifies the search for reasoning that undergirds authority and theory. Chapter 1 sets out three characteristics of promising and contracting that seem to characterize promissory obligations: relationality, self-directedness, and contextuality. Relationality emphasizes the interdependence of promissory obligations: a promise is to someone to do something, and the other person reacts to the promise. Promises of the kind that contract law addresses are other-directed. Yet, promises are also self-directed; they seek to advance the private projects of the promisor. This duality identifies the tension of promising: promises are self-directed, but create a form of interdependence that requires other-directed decisionmaking. Promises are also highly contextual: a promise to have lunch with a friend is different from a promise to have lunch with a potential business partner. Reasoning about obligations must be able to take context into account, which begs the question of which contextual details matter, and why they matter.

The remainder of Part I examines various approaches to promising and contracting and finds their implementation to require supplemental reasoning. Chapter 2 presents a legal realist critique of reasoning from authority; it argues that reasoning from authority (legal reasoning) does not fully reveal the reasoning process that is necessary to implement the authority in individual contexts. The chapter does not deny the authority of authority; it locates that authority in nondoctrinal reasoning rather than in command. In addition to pointing out the difficulty of implementing

find correct answers, though with error."); *see also* Posner (2005) (discussing the relationship between negotiating, drafting, interpretive, and enforcement costs).

7 Implicitly, this approach views the common law to be a dispute settlement process rather than a rule-making process. To be sure, the resolution of individual disputes can form the grounds for determining rules to govern behavior, but those rules are rarely stated with sufficient justificatory specificity to govern the contingencies of the next dispute. For that reason, the settlement of relational disputes does not turn on a rule but instead on a way of reasoning about the circumstances that allow the parties and legal decisionmakers to determine how parties in a relationship ought to treat each other. That is what courts do when they settle a dispute, whether they do so by referring to the terms of a promise, legal rules, or the circumstances that determined the outcome of prior disputes. Courts implement rules through reasoning, and that reasoning displays the method of reasoning courts want the parties to use.

legal doctrine and concepts without a supplemental method of reasoning, the chapter makes an important point about contract theory. Because promising and contracting have the quality of relationality, no single value can capture the essence of promising and contracting. Promising and contracting involve the autonomy, reliance, empowerment, consent, wealth, and well-being of at least two people, and those valuable attributes clash. What we value for one party is at odds with what we value for the other party; we care about the autonomy of both parties, and sometimes their autonomy pulls in opposite directions. There must be some basis for deciding whose autonomy, reliance, empowerment, consent, wealth, and well-being matter.

The final two chapters of Part I examine philosophical and economic theories. Although these theories are themselves diverse, they seem to suffer from indeterminacy and therefore from insufficient justificatory and implementary reasoning. Moral principle theories provide a moral justification, but to be implemented, they call for a moral implementary reasoning. Social practice theories, because of their contextuality, can be implemented through the context that reveals the social practices, but they call for a form of reasoning that justifies the morality of practices. Moral principle and practice approaches can both be profitably supplemented with a method of reasoning that contextually examines the source and scope of obligations.

Economic theories are theories of maximization; they capture the relationality and contextuality of promising and contracting. Yet, even if we view economic theories through a broader maximand (say well-being rather than wealth), maximization theories seem to be indeterminate without a supplementary mode of reasoning. Given transaction costs, the ability of bargaining parties to choose from among a range of trade-offs, and inevitable contractual gaps (including gaps from ambiguous language), it is difficult to determine from the existence of a contract the performance obligations the parties agreed to. Only an interpretation that reflects the exchange the parties made will support the institution of contracting and enhance socially valuable transacting.[8] Yet when disputes arise it is because the terms of the contract have run out; then obligations must be determined by identifying how the parties implicitly assigned various risks, their shared but unarticulated assumptions, and the obligations that flow naturally from the choices the parties made. Those issues also call for a method of reasoning about the source and scope of obligations.

Having sought to establish that legal authority and theory would profit from a supplemental method of reasoning, Part II of the book presents the outline of an appropriate method of relational reasoning. The central characteristic of this

[8] Schwartz and Scott note that the "goal of contract interpretation is to have the enforcing court find the 'correct answer.'" Schwartz & Scott (2003). One of the justifications for finding the correct answer is "consistent with an efficiency-based view of contract law" in which "parties contract to maximize the surplus that their deal can create." *Id.* That "goal is unattainable if courts fail to enforce the parties' solution but rather impose some other solution." *Id.*

method of reasoning is that it is nondoctrinal; it does not start with authority, doctrine, or theory. Instead, it displays a method of reasoning about the contest of values implicated in a dispute, suggests a method of choosing among the relevant values, and ends up with a decision that respects both sets of values but reconciles them in a fair and efficient way. I call it values-balancing reasoning.

Values-balancing reasoning posits that a contractual dispute represents a contest between conflicting values, say reliance and freedom to change one's mind. It identifies those values and provides a method for determining how to reconcile them in particular contexts. Because this mental model focuses on how conflicting values ought to be reconciled, the mental model focuses on a process (a methodology) of reasoning rather than on the rules generated by the process of reasoning.[9] Because the mental model takes into account the values presented by two autonomous persons, it serves to supplement and implement approaches that are based on a single value – such as fairness or efficiency.[10] And because the mental model is trans-contextual, I offer it as a possible unifying methodology for understanding contract law.[11]

This mental model claims to be moral reasoning because it recognizes that reasoning is built on values that are universal, neutral, and attentive to relational expectations. The model is maximizing because it recognizes that values must be traded off against each other and that what matters are the consequences of that trade-off for the well-being of two persons. The theory of reasoning purports to identify obligations that are both fair and efficient precisely because they come from a method of reasoning that is both deontic and consequential.

Two key ideas animate this method of reasoning. The first is that it is rational to take into account the well-being of others when making decisions, and thus to make other-regarding decisions. Economic rationality is not limited to self-interest; it is

9 The ideas presented here have many ancestors. I build on the path suggested by James Gordley, namely that contract law involves the Aristotelian concern with "what people should choose to do" once they are in a relationship. Gordley (2001) at 268. Under this conception, contract law "is concerned with how, through voluntary agreements, people are able to get things that help them lead a better life while being fair to others. Consequently it is concerned with the value of what is chosen, with the value of choosing rightly." *Id.* Similarly, I seek to amplify, and provide implementing details for, the philosophical theory of Daniel Markovits (Markovits 2003–2004) that the morality of contracts is determined by the independent value of relationships among people, the collaborative community. He has, for example, captured the spirit of the other-regarding person; the obligation of good faith is neither the duty to act in your contract partner's best interests, nor is it license to act in whatever way would best serve your own. It is, instead, a commitment to the relationship "structured around a shared understanding of a voluntary obligation." *Id.* at 292. Under the view presented here, the obligations of contracting are reciprocal obligations of each party to employ a method of reasoning that is tethered to the terms and context of the relationship.

10 By supplementing theories of fairness and efficiency, I add to efforts to find common ground between these two concepts. *See, e.g.*, Kraus (2000) and Kraus (2007).

11 This discussion was also foreshadowed by Bratman (2006) (developing a theory of shared reasoning to accomplish cooperative activities) and by Shapiro (2011) (developing a theory of law as planning that allows us to see the law of a contract as a process of reasoned planning).

often efficient to rely on others and to internalize their well-being into one's decisions. Humans do not choose between self-interested or altruistic motivations; their self-interest also leads humans to be other-regarding. Indeed, contracting would be difficult if bargaining partners were oblivious to the interests of the counterparty. "Getting to yes" (as it were) is not just an exercise of self-interest; it is an exercise of choices that are other-directed to advance self-directed interests.

The second central idea of Part II is that obligations do not arise by operation of law out of thin air; obligations flow from, and are reflected in, the choices that people make. The obligations that flow from personal choices are then recognized by law. A person is under one set of obligations if a person decides to make fireworks; the person is under a different set of obligations if a person decides to join a monastery. Obligations are self-imposed in the sense that they follow the choices people make. The idea of self-imposed obligations and other-regarding choices are related. The choices one makes often imply the obligation to be other-regarding, the choices are not just self-directed but, because they affect others, are other-directed. That other-directedness is the source of obligations to others. Part II ends by showing how values-balancing reasoning illuminates and explains the relationship between law on the ground and law on the books, the nature of cooperation, the development of trust in relationships, and the dynamic of order without law.

Part III of the book then applies the idea of values-balancing reasoning to enduring doctrinal controversies: formation, performance, the problem of standard terms, doctrines that excuse performance, and remedies. Because values-balancing reasoning is non-doctrinal reasoning, it yields interesting insights about the source and implementation of contract doctrine.

The application chapters in Part III amplify and illustrate the book's Part I claims that reasoning from authority is, without more, an inadequate basis for reasoning about promissory and contractual relationships. They also show the way in which values-balancing, other-regarding reasoning implements legal doctrine. The chapters do something more: they suggest that reasoning about obligations precedes doctrine and that, in fact, doctrine is the concluding point, rather than the starting point. for appropriate reasoning. This allows values-balancing reasoning to focus directly on the issue for which doctrine is giving an answer, and thus, in a sense, to replace doctrine. Under this view, consideration doctrine becomes the answer to this question: At what point can a promisor no longer revoke or modify a promise? Implied obligations, (including good faith) become the answer to this question: When a promisor makes a choice, what kind of obligations are naturally implied by that choice? The doctrine surrounding standard term contracts becomes the answer to the question: Would the counterparty reasonably have expected to encounter these terms? The doctrine of excuse becomes the answer to the question: Given the circumstances of the exchange, which party bore the risk of unaddressed future events? And questions surrounding contractual remedies are driven by this question:

Given the context of the exchange, what implied remedial promises did the parties make?

The application chapters also reinforce the contextuality of promising and contracting. In the approach offered here, we do not seek a hypothetical set of obligations, nor determine what most people, or most reasonable people, would have thought their obligations to be. Those are counterfactual questions that by their nature may differ from the obligations the parties agreed to.[12] We will search, instead, for the obligations that a person reasoning in a values-balancing, other-regarding way would have understood about how the parties divided the risks, the proper interpretation of a disputed term, the implied terms that are binding on the counterparty, and other attributes of contractual obligations.[13]

Several general features of values-balancing reasoning may aid the reader. In the view I present, obligations are not external to the relationship. They do not represent attempts to address distributional values or social ills. Obligations are self-imposed and self-controlled, subject only to the constraint, imposed from a party's choice to invoke the practice of promising, that the parties reason in an appropriate way about their obligations. This may mean, of course, that the parties must take into account the circumstances of the counterparty, but only when other-regarding reasoning suggests that those circumstances are relevant. This book provides no refuge for scholars who would use the law to impose external standards of socially appropriate behavior on contracting parties.

The values-balancing approach also addresses the concern that generalist courts will not successfully interpret obligations. Values-balancing reasoning does not require a special knowledge of the economics of exchange or the art of the deal. The information needed to determine which party is reasoning in a value-balancing way when disputes arise about obligations does not require a court to be steeped in the intricacies of moral hazard or adverse selection, which, after all, are simply labels for intuitive concepts. It requires only the ability to reason about the reasoning that the parties should have used, given the terms of the contract.

Finally, the approach does not subsume contract law within tort law; it conciliates the two doctrinal domains by identifying their substructure of reasoning. The book endorses "the promise principle, which is the principle by which persons may impose obligations [on themselves] where none existed before."[14] And it endorses the principle that in a promissory or contractual relationship the parties get to design the obligations they are willing to assent to; as is often said, the parties legislate their

12 Listwa (2019).

13 As an illustration, if I agree to have lunch with a friend next week, the agreement is not likely to specify the obligations or excuses that accompany that agreement. Yet, the obligations can be inferred from the nature of the relationship and how the other-regarding person would think about the obligations, given the relationship. Under most circumstances, a right-thinking person would understand that if something important comes up the obligation to have lunch is probably excused, but that the agreement comes with an implicit obligation to call the friend so that she can make other plans.

14 Fried (1981) at 1.

own obligations. But in the view presented here, neither the promise principle nor the self-legislation metaphor determine the existence or scope of the obligations that flow from a promise or contract once disputes arise. The scope of any obligation necessarily invokes the proposition that under certain circumstances one ought to consider the well-being of others in a values-balancing way, which I believe to be the unifying principle of private law.[15] Each person in an exchange, in pursuit of its private projects, absorbs burdens that benefit a counterparty. Reasonable people use values-balancing reasoning, and it is that method of reasoning that I believe breathes life into our understanding of how a reasonable person makes reasonable, contextual decisions.[16]

METHODOLOGICAL COMMITMENTS

Because the ideas developed in this book reflect methodological commitments that may not be widely shared, the reader may find a summary of those commitments to be helpful.

There is, I posit, a substructure to the law, a substructure of reason. Given the subject matter of this book, that substructure lies in the method by which persons in a promissory, contractual relationship and lawmakers who evaluate private behavior ought to reason about what people owe each other. The method of reasoning I have in mind is not the method usually associated with legal reasoning. It is a method of reasoning about the factors and values that give rise to obligations, determinants that are nonlegal in the sense that their content does not depend on legal authority (even though the method of reasoning is reflected in legal authority). Consider the distinction between the law's structure from its substructure. The law's structure lies in legal authority, including doctrine, rules, standards, presumptions and, in contract law, a contract's text and context; conventional legal reasoning focuses on reasoning from that authority. The substructure, on the other hand, consists of the method of reasoning that led to the authorities and to structural relationships, a method that the structure may not reveal. Contracts develop from the joint

[15] This is the third (and final) book in my trilogy about the other-regarding person and social morality (what we owe each other). The other two cover tort law (Gerhart (2010)) and property (Gerhart (2014)).

[16] Torts, contracts, and property are differentiated by the source of the obligations to others, not by the scope of the obligations or the method of reasoning that determines the scope. In tort law, the obligation to others comes from creating a risk or standing in relation to someone that makes an actor responsible for the risks the other faces. In property, the source of obligations is the concept of ownership (which creates obligations for both owner and non-owner). In contract law, the source of the obligation is a promise. Yet in all three areas of private law, the existence and scope of any obligation is determined, I maintain, by the obligation to reason in the kind of values-balancing way that I present in this book, which requires each person in a relationship to account in a values-balancing way for the well-being of the person who would otherwise bear an avoidable loss. This principle applies to issues of formation (the existence of a duty), performance (the scope of a duty), and remedy (the losses that could have been, and should have been, avoided).

reasoning of two parties; that reasoning is how the parties structured their relationship. If we understand the shared reasoning from which the contract arose, the contractual substructure, we can more accurately determine the obligations embedded in the contract. Similarly, legal authority comes from some method of reasoning that reflects the reasoning that has guided the evolution of the law's structure.[17] If we can understand the method of reasoning that formed legal authority, the law's substructure, we can more accurately understand how the doctrinal structure ought to be implemented. The authority of contracts and of law is determined by nonlegal factors and those determinants underlie, and help implement, the authority.

Under this view, authority's commands lie not directly in the words of the authority but in the method of reasoning that led to the author's use of the command's words. "Because I said so" is not a sufficient basis for following authority. To implement authority when new disputes arise, we need to extract and replicate the method of reasoning that led to the authority, and then apply the method and content of that reasoning to the dispute that must be decided. This approach turns conventional legal reasoning on its head; rather than start with authority, we start with the factors and values that led to the authority, making the implementation of authority the output of the reasoning (and a new basis for reasoning about how to implement authority).

Implementing this methodology requires a method of identifying the factors and values that determined authority. We do well to put aside what judges say and to concentrate on what judges do. Justice Stevens famously said: "this Court reviews judgments, not opinions."[18] By that Justice Stevens signaled that the law is found in a dispute's outcome (that is, a court's judgment in favor of one party or the other), and not in judicial opinions that seek a doctrine to justify the outcome in terms of doctrine. A dispute's outcome is binding on the parties and on any person similarly situated, but its binding effect depends on reasoning about which persons are in the category of "similarly situated" persons.[19] The judge's opinion can be influential in that subsequent determination, but to have a binding effect on others the law depends on a subsequent finding of similarity, and that depends on how one reasons about similarity, not on prior doctrinal statements.[20]

17 In a state of nature, before law existed, the first legal decision, the one that purported to create authority, must have been grounded on a method of reasoning that did not itself depend on authority. That method of reasoning, if it was worthy of being followed as authority, must have been about the factors and values that the decisionmaker found to be attractive. A role of the dice would not serve as legal authority. Those factors and values must have influenced the implementation of that authority in other cases.

18 *Chevron U.S.A., Inc.* v. *Natural Resources Defense Council, Inc.*, 467 U.S. 837, 842 (1984).

19 Kraus (2008) uses this distinction to understand debates on contract law. Kraus (2007) explores the jurisprudential implications of the distinction between outcomes and judicial explanations. *See also* Steinman (2013).

20 This approach does not deny the power of stare decisis. It simply locates the power of stare decisis in the outcome of cases, not in the rationale that judges provide for the outcome. The power of

Judicial opinions suffer from defects of inductive reasoning, the imperfections that arise when a judge tries to identify a general rule from particular dispute. They also suffer from the problem of deductive reasoning, the difficulty of reasoning from a general rule to a particular conclusion without knowing the determinants of the general rule. Those imperfections give rise to the problems of reasoning from authority that I outline in Chapter 2, the problem of finding a way of reasoning about the particular in the context of a general rule. Take, as an example, the doctrine of consideration. It is one thing for a judge to find a promise unenforceable for lack of consideration, and quite another to explain why the promise was unenforceable for lack of consideration. Too often judicial justifications amount to a declaration (rather than a justification) and often a tautological declaration; a judge will say that a promise was unenforceable for lack of consideration because there was no consideration, without explaining the method of reasoning that led to that conclusion. By contrast, if we could answer the question of why the judge determined that there was no consideration, without clothing the outcome in doctrinal garb, we would have a window that allows us to observe how the decision's authority should be implemented in other contexts. Judges seem to have a well-honed intuition about justified outcomes, but seem less skillful at justifying their results in nondoctrinal terms that identify the factors and values that determined their outcome.

If outcomes are the appropriate unit of analysis to determine what the law requires or enables, an appropriate methodology for legal reasoning is to examine a series of cases that seem to address similar kinds of problems and sort them by their outcomes; some on one side of an issue (say, finding consideration) and some on the other (say, finding no consideration). Then, focusing on the circumstances that seem to differentiate one case from another, a process of reverse engineering allows us to identify the factors that appear to explain the divergent outcomes.[21] This provides only a conjecture, of course, for the outcome of the next dispute may give us a different view of the determinants that matter. But the process of developing conjectures and testing them against seemingly different disputes (hypothetical or real) increases confidence that we can identify the nondoctrinal determinants that seem to influence judicial outcomes.

precedent comes in determining whether a subsequent case is like a prior case so that the outcome of the prior case serves as precedent. The determination of the "likeness" of cases depends not on doctrine but on the facts and circumstances (the nondoctrinal determinants) that are relevant to the outcome.

21 The approach here is aligned most closely with Ronald Dworkin's interpretive theory of "constructive elaboration." Dworkin (1986) at 49–56. Like other theories of reasoning, the idea of values-balancing reasoning seeks to achieve the goal of treating like cases alike, achieving justifiable outcomes, and ensuring the coherent pursuit of worthy objectives. *See, e.g.*, Fried (2012)(arguing that a theory of law must have substantive content that only a consequentialist theory can supply); Jody S. Kraus, in Villanueva (2002) (recommending a "vertical" understanding of the relationship between the deontic and the consequential).

Facts alone, however, are not enough to explain similar-looking cases that have different outcomes. Something more guides a judge's intuition. Values matter, and, in particular, it matters how judges balance values against each other. Disputes arise because people have interests that clash. But, as I explain in Chapter 5, that clash can be understood as a clash of values rather than a clash of interests. Arguments about competing interests invoke competing principles, each of which represents a value that is important to society. That is why a methodology of outcomes leads to a methodology of value-balancing. The methodology of value-balancing asks how a person or legal decisionmaker who takes the values that animate promising and contracting seriously will reason about the implications of those values for the resolution of a dispute.

Values-balancing legal reasoning is *legal* reasoning because it portrays the reasoning that seems to inform a judge's intuition when judges decide private disputes, given the institutional constraints of private law dispute resolution. It is *values-balancing* because it takes seriously the moral principles that underlie any private dispute, deploying a method of reasoning that allows decisionmakers to compare moral values raised by disputing parties. It is values-balancing because it employs a method of reasoning that gives moral weight to disparate values raised in a dispute in a way that minimizes the moral sacrifice required by an exercise of comparative moral values.

The values-balancing methodology is reflected in theories of cooperation. When parties exchange enforceable promises, they reach an equilibrium – a balance of burdens and benefits that each party finds to be in its private interest. But this equilibrium comes under pressure as new circumstances challenge the expectations that formed that equilibrium. Sometimes the equilibrium is so changed that one or both parties desire to withdraw from the exchange. In other instances, the parties can adjust their expectation to new realities. Either way, it is reasoning about how the coordination of private interests can create value and stabilize through changing circumstances.

Fortunately, humans seem to have a built-in methodology for identifying a new equilibrium, when they must adjust their original relationship to new circumstances. If we did not have that methodology, voluntary cooperation would be limited. In fact, most performance disputes are settled as part of identifying what the relationship entails. Some disputes are settled because private parties have built into their relationship the norms of cooperation that will refocus the equilibrium as circumstances change. Some are settled because the parties set up private governance mechanisms for settling disputes and adjusting obligations to new realities. But many are settled because people invest in the relationship and understand the adjustments that must be made for the sake of the relationship. As a result, parties to a commercial relationship often act as if the authority of contract terms and contract law are irrelevant to the relationship.[22]

22 Macaulay (1963).

When faced with unexpected circumstances parties in a relationship are able to recognize adjustments they must make in their own expectations in order to minimize the counterparty's burdens. Cooperation is possible because people of goodwill reason with a fairness norm that allows them to restore a relationship to equilibrium when circumstances change and they must understand their obligations in light of the promises they have made. The fairness criterion is contextual because it takes into account the circumstances the parties face. The fairness criterion is also universal because it follows a version of the Golden Rule that is itself universally followed across religions and cultures: do unto others as you would have them do unto you if you had their private goals and preferences. This is what I call other-regarding reasoning, the recognition that our own well-being depends on the well-being of others. The other-regarding fairness criterion allows people to understand the consequences of their behavior and to reason about their behavior in a way that reflects an ex ante bargain. People are willing to accept the burdens of additional costs so that the partner in the relationship can avoid unnecessary cost, and so that the relationship continues to produce the joint benefits that were originally anticipated. Values-balancing reasoning implements that fairness criterion.

Because cooperation depends on how people reason about their relationship, our analytical focus shifts from how people behave to how people reason about their behavior. Although this seems to be at odds with the idea that the law functions to control behavior, telling people what they should do or refrain from doing, reasoning and behavior are connected in an important way. Whether a particular behavior meets legal norms is contextual, and therefore not authoritatively determined by a rule of behavior. Killing another is improper behavior unless done in self-defense (or when done in service of the state). As Justice Cardozo reminded us, driving at ninety miles an hour means one thing if done on the street and another if done on the racetrack.[23] As a result, the law must evaluate behavior by asking whether a person thinking reasonably about her behavior in a particular context would behave the way she did. A contract calls not just for certain behavior but also for a certain way of reasoning about one's behavior given the contract's terms and context.

Importantly, I am not arguing that a promisor must actually use the appropriate reasoning for the court to find her behavior to be appropriate. Instead, I am arguing that she must act as if she had used the appropriate reasoning. The determination of appropriate behavior depends on evaluating how a person who reasoned appropriately would have behaved, even if the person decided how to behave by flipping a coin. That is why motivations are irrelevant to the law when the behavior is of the kind that is required under law. My point, however, is this: the law expects people who make promises and contracts to behave as if they had thought in a moral way

[23] *Palsgraf* v. *Long Island Ry. Co.*, 162 N.E. 99, 100 (N.Y. 1928).

about their obligations, and the law determines what behavior is required under a promise or contract by examining how a person in that situation would have behaved if the person had used moral reasoning. That is the role of the reasonable person – to set a basis for evaluating the reasoning that determines which behaviors people should follow.

The values-balancing, other-regarding methodology has implications for how we understand the concept of law.

- By focusing on the law's reasoning substructure, the methodology allows us to break down doctrinal boundaries that form the law's structure. Doctrinal boundaries are historically determined and haphazard. Judges decide disputes; theorists put them into categories. If judges or theorists do not correctly define the determinants of a category, they may define meaningless doctrinal boundaries. Some theorists then seek to seal off one category from another, even if the categorical boundaries turn out to be artificial in light of the factors and values that actually determine how judges settle disputes. We are told that a contract is defined by the fact that parties had an opportunity to bargain over their commitments, but this seems to separate, artificially, contracts from unbargained-for obligations, like simultaneous exchanges or the terms and conditions of software use. Yet, if we denominate the field as covering all exchanges, then it is difficult to exclude from the field obligations imposed in tort under product liability, which are obligations derived from exchange relationships. Perhaps what binds contract law with other private law doctrines is neither bargaining nor exchange, but the concept of reasoning in a values-balancing way about obligations to others.
- Additionally, values-balancing reasoning embodies the potential to successfully integrate deontic and consequential reasoning. The decades-long debate about the relative merits of these two categories – those that rest on moral conceptions and those that rest on the consequences of action – is largely resolved by values-balancing reasoning. It is possible for moral theory to take consequences seriously without resorting to the simple additive devices of consequential theories. Reasoning morally about consequences is not an oxymoron because the method of moral reasoning that satisfies the requirements of moral thought (the deontic and universal) is separate from its contextual implementation (which takes consequences into account in a moral way). A theory of values-balancing legal reasoning recognizes and embraces values on which morality and law are founded, and yet it is contextual because it shows, without loss of moral weight, how those values are balanced against each other in particular contexts.
- Unlike other views about the morality of promising, the views expressed in this book do not assume that the moral obligations are self-evident or absolute.[24]

[24] Shiffrin (2007) (assuming that a promise requires performance and that breaking a promise is immoral, begging the issue of what obligations a promise entails).

Instead, it assumes that moral behavior reflects the moral reasoning that determines what behavior is appropriate in the circumstance. It affirms the moral command that promises should be kept, but seeks to identify the obligations of promising in order to implement that moral command. It thus affirms the Holmesian view that "law is the witness and external deposit of our moral life."[25] It does, however, explain why and when moral obligations are not also legal obligations.

- The theory here locates the authority of authority not in what authority commands but in the reasoning that authority authorizes. The reasoning that led to the authority provides a good reason to obey authority; the fact that authority commands does not. When authority's command is worth following, it is because the authority reflects the way people ought to reason about their obligations to others. This approach denies that legal normativity has some special qualities that are different from the normativity of good moral reasoning about obligations to others.[26] The idea that law commands or enables behavior is affirmed only insofar as the law commands or enables a method of reasoning about one's ideal behavior. Among other things, this means that the way people successfully think about their obligations is not distinct from, but is reflective of, the method of reasoning that legal requirements impose on a relationship. Law on the ground is less distant from law on the books than is normally assumed.
- The approach here also explains the drawbacks of pluralistic or compartmentalized theories; they seem to deny the unity of relational obligations because they focus on obligatory behavior, rather than behaving as if one had used obligatory reasoning. Because the morality of behavior is context specific, obligatory behavior may well change with the context, even when the appropriate method of reasoning does not. Promissory and contractual commitments, no matter what the contextual features, have one thing in common: each requires the parties to think in a moral way about the obligations implied by promising and contracting, given the contextual circumstances they face. In this way a theory of values-balancing reasoning provides the unified and unifying theory of promising and contracting that no other theory is able to provide.

25 Holmes (1897) at 459.
26 Hershovitz (2014–2015).

PART I

Grounds for a Supplemental Approach

Part I establishes the need for a supplemental approach to promising and contracting. Chapter 1 outlines the three characteristics of promising and contracting that ground the analysis here: relationality, self-directed aims, and contextuality. The first two characteristics reveal the tension between self-interest and relational interests that law must bridge. The third recognizes the myriad of contexts in which that tension can occur, given the variety of promises and their circumstances. Chapters 2 through 4 then show the way we can clarify the law if we supplement existing theories with values-balancing reasoning. Chapter 2 summarizes the inadequacy of reasoning from authority, concepts, and theory. Chapter 3 summarizes moral principle theories and social practice theories of promising and shows the gaps that we can fruitfully fill with values-balancing reasons. Chapter 4 endorses the relationality and contextuality of economic analysis but finds gaps in the way economists identify and balance the values at play in any dispute.

1

Individuals and Relationships

This book's principal idea – that promising and contracting implicate a method of reasoning about one's private interests in the context of a relationship that advances the private interests of another person – reflects several characteristics of promising and contracting: relationality, self-directedness, and contextuality. Relationality and self-directedness reveal the tension between private and relational goals. Contextuality recognizes the many permutations that relationships can take. Accounting for each characteristic is the challenge of any approach to promising and contracting.

This structural framework is not new: in any relationship, each party will take on burdens that allow the other party to receive the benefits of the collaborative enterprise. Yet a party approaches the relationship only as a means to her own ends; the relationship is not an end in itself. Each party wants to maximize the returns to her private, self-directed projects; each party treats the other party's commitments as an input to achieving her own private projects, assessing the probabilistic contribution of the other party to the value of her project. Neither party has precise information about the private projects of the other party, nor will each party disclose such information unless that disclosure will induce cooperation. Each party tries to minimize the costs of its private projects, but is limited because reducing the costs of one's private projects means reducing the benefit for the other party's private projects (which would work against the collaboration).

As a result, each party faces the tension between her own self-directed interest, which is to minimize the burden of collaboration, and her ability to get the benefits of collaboration by satisfying the legitimate interests of the counterparty. It is therefore helpful to understand how the parties reason about the joint interests that flow from their separate, self-directed projects, the content of the obligations implied by the collaborative enterprise, and how each party's self-directed projects create relational tension even after a deal has been reached.

Because obligations are understood from the terms the parties deployed to express their relationship, as well as the content of implied terms that reflect the exchange context, the search for obligations also requires us to examine the terms the parties might have, but did not, choose. Promissory disputes are born, and develop, out of the tension between individual and joint interests and choices. When that tension is successfully addressed, the parties' interests in their relational well-being outweigh a party's interests in her individual well-being; then promises and cooperative adjustments in the relationship can build trust and collaborative behavior. However, when the tension between self-interest and relational interest is not successfully addressed, when one of the parties finds her individual interest to be more important than her relational interest, either social or legal forces must intercede if the relationship is to be preserved. Promissory relationships fail when one or both of the parties places her individual, self-directed interests above the interest the relationship represents.

Transaction cost economics identifies the barriers to bargaining over, and performing obligations; it provides a source of wisdom about the tensions that beset relationships, both ex ante (before a deal is struck) and ex post.[1] But transaction cost economics captures only the bilateral barriers to successful relationships. Tensions also arise from changes in the environment in which bargaining and performance takes place. Each party understands its own projects in connection with the projects of the other party, but each also understands its projects in the context of environmental factors they cannot control.

Potential tensions within a relationship are heightened by gaps in promissory terms, unexpressed expectations, personal proclivities, and personal values in the face of a changing world that upsets the expectations of one or both parties. Contracts and promises are notoriously incomplete as statements of obligation. The parties may fail to articulate assumptions that adhere in the promise; the lure of moving forward with private projects often outweighs the benefits of negotiating more determinate solution; risks may be unanticipated; the world will almost certainly change after a promise or contract is made; contracting parties sometimes have strategic reasons for leaving the terms of a relationship ill-defined.[2]

Given the tensions between private and joint projects, each party must choose between flexibility to meet developing contingencies and the obligations previously embedded in their relationship. Each party must choose between the relationship in

[1] Williamson (1985) at 20. As Oliver Williamson explained:

> Transaction costs of *ex ante* and *ex post* types are usefully distinguished. The first are the costs of drafting, negotiating, and safeguarding an agreement. This can be done with a great deal of care, in which case a complex document is drafted in which numerous contingencies are recognized, and appropriate contingencies are recognized, and appropriate adaptations by the parties are stipulated and agreed to in advance. Or the document can be very incomplete, the gaps to be filled in later by the parties as the contingencies arise. Rather, therefore, than contemplate all conceivable bridge crossings in advance, which is a very ambitious undertaking, only actual bridge-crossing choices are addressed as events unfold.

[2] Sanga (2018).

its present and potential future iterations and her own private projects. Flexibility, accommodation, modification, and improvisation enable the relationship to be maintained, but when the strain on one party's private projects is too great, the relationship will end (with or without legal dispute resolution). Even when anchored in a relative precise set of terms, the relationship, and its obligations, can change.

As this framework shows, three characteristics of promissory and contractual relationships determine the relationship's future course: relationality, self-directed aims, and contextuality.

1.1 RELATIONALITY

Although ubiquitous in the contracting literature, the term "relational contract" appears to have lost a stable meaning. Ian McNeil first applied the term to contracts that lasted over a period of years and required the parties to adjust their relationship to changing circumstances, such as franchise agreements.[3] He thought it important to distinguish those long-term contracts from contracts for the sale of widgets, around which traditional contract doctrine had developed. He focused on the time dimension; nonrelational contracts had known and fixed performance dates in discrete increments, while relational contracts evolved over time.

However, as contract theory developed, the idea of relational contract came to be applied, especially in the law and economics literature, to any contract with incomplete terms, which significantly broadens the concept. Contracts with completely specified terms are rare and can be executed without dispute. Exchanges with incomplete terms are more prevalent; even a one-time exchange in a retail store has incomplete terms because it is accompanied by implied warranties and by payment issues (when a check or stolen credit card is used). Moreover, even discrete transactions have a time dimension because a retail store is likely to seek repeat customers and reputational goodwill. Digital exchanges are often have incomplete terms; when accompanied by detailed standard terms, the very existence of the detailed terms is likely to raise relational disputes. As in long-term franchise agreements, a contract with an open term (or one with too many terms) requires the parties to make a choice between their loyalty to the relationship and their self-directed goals.

The term relational contracts has also come to express the idea that contractual obligations can be enforced informally, not through the formal litigation process.[4] In this sense, contracts are relational because the relationship itself imposes a centrifugal force that refines and enforces obligations.

Because all promises and contracts involve a relationship between two or more persons, and because relationships themselves are at stake when disputes arise, we might view "relationality" to be the central characteristic of promising and

3 Macneil (1977–1978).

4 Jennejohn (2018) at 21–22 (summarizing literature); *see also* Goetz & Scott (1981); Gil & Marion (2012) at 140 (relational contracts cannot be enforced by third parties and therefore must be self-enforcing).

contracting. By their nature, promises and contracts give one person power over another, creating expectations that require cooperation rather than defection if the expectations are to be fulfilled. They also require each party to accept burdens in terms of performance burdens and forgone opportunities. Promising and contracting implicate the well-being of at least two persons, the health of the relationship between them, and the many characteristics the parties display, including their background and individual make-up, levels of trust, prior dealings, past experience, social standing, shared or disparate values.

Relationality thus expresses the central moral core of promising and contracting. As Daniel Markovits has argued: "Promises generally, and contracts in particular, establish a relation of recognition and respect – and indeed a kind of community – among those who participate in them, [and this, in turn allows us to] explain the reasons that exist for making and keeping promises and contracts in terms of the value of this relation."[5]

Relationality also recognizes that relationships rise or fall at the intersection of voice and exit.[6] Voice allows the parties to reason with each other about what each gains from the relationship, how the relationship serves each party's private goals, and what the parties can do to reduce the burdens and increase the benefits of cooperation over time. Exit allows the parties to assess what they are giving up by cooperating, the opportunity costs of cooperation. Potential exit is also a communicative device that signals to the other party that the burdens and benefits of cooperation are no longer in equilibrium. Voice and exit represent the two options that define the relationship: either reason through the problems in the relationship or leave the relationship.

1.2 SELF-DIRECTED AIMS

An important aspect of the relationality of promises and contracts, as I have already indicated, is that neither party views the relationship as an end in itself; for both parties, the relationship is a means to an end. The aim of promising and contracting is to enlist another person in one's private projects by offering something of value to the other person. With the possible exception of the institution of marriage, promises and contracts are used to form the relationship but are not the point of the relationship.[7] And because the relationship is a means to an end, an offer may be rejected when it does not meet the private projects of the offeree (given the offeree's

5 Markovits (2004) at 1420.

6 Hirschman (1970).

7 This depiction is contested. *See* Kraus & Scott (2009) (suggesting that the contractual ends are embodied in the contractual objectives, and that the contractual terms are the means to that end). In the view presented here, the relationship is the means by which each party achieves its private ends and the terms of the contract are the means to preserve those ends. The distinction is important because the idea that the relationship is the end also suggests that the parties had an intent in the words they choose, and that the intent is accessible by some means other than considering the private projects

other options). Yet even during negotiations, obligations to others may arise to protect the private projects of one of the parties. And even when binding relationships are formed from promises and contracts, the inherent tension between the private projects of the individuals and the goals of the relationship as a unifying institution threatens to destabilize the relationship and invite disputes that must be resolved.

This feature has important implications for understanding contracts. Each contractual party is seeking to maximize its benefits from the relationship and to minimize the burdens; in that way the parties maximize their private contractual surplus. Neither party is especially interested in increasing the contractual surplus except to the extent that such an increase will increase its private surplus from the contract. As I have already indicated, it is difficult for one party to increase its surplus without simultaneously decreasing the surplus of the other party. A party dissatisfied with the contractual surplus allocated to its private projects may look for ways outside the exchange to increase its private surplus.

Because each party views a potential or already formalized relationship from the standpoint of the party's own projects, it faces the losses that arise from risks to its private projects. It must determine whether there are barriers that put its private projects at risk and it must negotiate the terms of the contract with those barriers in mind, determining which inputs from other people will reduce the risks to its private projects, and what commitments to make in light of the risk that its private projects will fail even when all inputs are delivered as expected. A person opening a grocery store and making commitments to suppliers will consider the possibility that the store might fail for reasons unrelated to the performance of its suppliers.

When a party assesses the risks its private projects face, the party understands those risks as a reflection of its private goals. The party will adjust its negotiating goals to reflect the kinds of risks that the party is willing to take, so that the expected burdens of its promises remain less than the expected benefits. The self-directed expectation that parties bring to the negotiation determines what risks they face in the exchange and how they want to negotiate in light of those risks. The risks may never be identified, for they may be implied by the private goals of each party and not made explicit. But they are nonetheless risks that fall within the basic assumptions the parties make when they bargain.

We can therefore understand the process of bargaining to entail not only the risk of nonperformance by a counterparty but also the identification of risks that each party faces in completing its own private projects. Private projects' risks fall naturally on the party that is trying to advance its private projects. If A leases land from B for growing crops, A knows that she faces the risk that crop prices will go down, or that

of one party in relation to the private projects of the counterparty. The idea of joint intent, in turn, suggests that one who would interpret the contract from outside the bargaining struggle can find contractual intent merely by examining what the parties were trying to accomplish, without considering how the parties sought to accomplish those ends. This misses the contextuality of the exchange.

the cost of harvesting the crops will go up, along with many other risk-creating contingencies. Those are risks that naturally fall on A, for they are risks that A naturally accepts as the cost of reaching its private objectives. We can therefore understand the process of bargaining to be built around each party's expectation of the risks it naturally accepts as the cost of reaching its private projects.

Naturally, these private project risks can be shifted to the counterparty if the parties negotiate for that shift (which generally means that the party bearing the private party risks must offer something of value to the counterparty). That means that the party that naturally bears the risk must make the private project risks a part of the negotiation; otherwise risks associated with a party's private projects can be said to be one of the contract's implicit assumptions. The self-directed aims of each party generate assumptions about the risks and rewards each party faces before negotiations start, and those assumptions become a basis for shaping other obligations unless the party bearing those risks makes them a part of the negotiation.[8]

Although the existence of a contract proclaims the parties' joint intention to act collaboratively, it does not eliminate their independent interests and therefore does not eliminate disputes that arise from those interests. The equilibrium reached in an exchange – the source of the parties' common interests – is constantly challenged by changes in their environments, the changing options each person has, their fear that the counterparty will shirk her obligations, and by the divergent interests and opportunities from which the parties started the process of relationship building. The common interest from the cooperative relationship does not put an end to their use of the exchange for their private interests.

Relationships are, therefore, constantly evolving, their equilibrium points fluctuating between the opposing forces of the independent, self-directed aims and the joint interests of two parties. For simple exchanges, the relationship may be held together by the potential for future exchanges. When the relationship seeks a common output rather than an exchange (say, in a joint venture), the relationship is held together by the potential of that joint output, which provides a sense of unity that draws the cooperating actors together. When cooperation is designed to produce outputs that are independent of each other (such as the private, self-directed goals of contracting parties), cooperation requires that each party continually consider adjustments to meet the private projects of the counterparty if the relationship is to continue.

Importantly, once the parties have agreed to a set of terms governing their relationship, the relationship is governed by those terms, but alternative terms that could have been agreed upon drop away; they are terms rejected by at least one party. Those rejected terms (the obligations not accepted) reveal the scope of the

[8] The idea that risks naturally fall on one party or the other, depending on the expectations of the parties under the circumstances, is further developed in Chapter 13 ("Excused Performance and Risk Allocation").

obligations that were accepted, for the rejected terms provide evidence of how the parties distributed the risks to their private projects and the exchange.

Because promise and contracting integrate relationality and self-directed aims, we see the irony of contracting – to enter into and sustain a relationship, a person must care about the well-being of the counterparty, for a person must improve that well-being in order to harness the counterparty's private projects. That means that independent reasoning of each party, as implemented through self-governance, the power of social reputation, or legal coercion, is the force that keeps the institution of contracting afloat. Indeed, as I claim in this book, the obligation to take into account the well-being of the counterparty is the basic obligation from which, because of contextuality, obligations are derived.

1.3 CONTEXTUALITY

The obligations created by promising and contracting depend on who communicated what to whom, under what circumstances, and how that communication was, or should have been, understood. A promise to meet for lunch next week means one thing between social friends, and another between commercial bargainers. Relationships, like snowflakes, are unique, and they change over time in response to their environment. They can morph into ice or into mush, depending on the environment. Even parties that have dealt with each other for years under standard-term contracts may find that new circumstances require them to consider adjustments in their obligations. The weight given to facts is contextual – change a fact and you can change an outcome – but even when the facts do not change, they take on different meanings in different settings. Finally, as many have observed, promising and contracting cover a large variety of relationships, some commercial and some social, in a wide variety of settings. Even within the category of commercial promises, a theory of promising and contracting must account for the diversity of leases, consumer contracts, employment contracts, and insurance contracts. Given this contextuality, any attempt to understand promissory obligations as a unified whole depends on a method of nondoctrinal reasoning that addresses contextuality.

The contextuality of contracting is not doubted.[9] But the implications of that contextuality may not be fully appreciated. As already noted, parties bargain over the benefits they will provide to their counterparty's private projects. This means that the

9 Schwartz & Scott (2016) at 1527 ("a 'context' is an economic environment populated by agents with the same or similar contracting preferences. A context may be as small as the parties to a particular contract. but commonly is larger"). Although most contract scholarship seeks to adopt assumptions that suppress the contextuality of contracts in order to fuel a rule-based approach, some scholarship recognizes the kind of radical contextual analysis that makes rule-based regimes difficult to manage and suggests the need for systems based on reasoning. Eggleston, Posner & Zeckhauser (2000). As I highlight in this book, even parties with similar contracting preferences will not necessarily come to the same set of terms because the trade-offs they make depend on what each is willing to give up to get what their private projects need, given their options.

parties bargain over risks and performance obligations that reduce risks. But because risks and performance obligations are fungible, they can be made the subject of an exchange and shifted for a price; one party can accept a risk that would otherwise belong to the private projects of the other party as long as they are compensated by favorable terms along some other dimension of bargaining, including the price.

As a result, the obligations that arise from promising and contracting are, except in obvious cases, highly indeterminate. When parties bargain, they bargain over a range of possible terms and conditions, seeking the trade-offs that best accommodate their private projects. The outcome of those negotiations is highly unpredictable, depending, as it does, on each party's taste for risks and options for achieving the party's private projects. Once the bargain is made and the terms are selected, and other potential terms (the terms the parties could have but did not agree on) fall away, the equilibrium terms the parties have chosen govern the relationship; yet the relationship must be known by the agreement the parties could have made, but did not make.

Of course, the parties may, and often do, work out disputes between themselves, adjusting their expectations to new realities, effectively reaching an adjusted equilibrium of expectations. When they do, it is because each party's benefit from continuing the relationship (or anticipated future relationships) induces them to make adjustments when the potential benefits of those adjustments outweigh the costs of ending the relationship. Clearly, the parties address contractual uncertainty by reasoning their way out of it; they deploy a method of reasoning about how to treat other people that allows them to restore the equilibrium of the contract or promise. But when the parties cannot work things out, they need a neutral and independent arbiter to make the obligations implied by the promise or contract determinate. That is the role of legal decisionmakers – namely to determine and enforce the obligations of the parties by requiring the parties to do what they would have done had they reasoned in a values-balancing way about their obligations.

Law is open-textured enough to accommodate the contextuality of promising and contracting, but the open-textured nature of legal doctrine means that legal doctrine must be supplemented by a method of reasoning about doctrine's implementation in order to make the law determinate. As I demonstrate in the next chapter, the acontextuality of positive law is no match for the contextuality of promising and contracting.

1.4 CONCLUSION

The self-imposed obligations of promising and contracting depend on the language a person uses to express future intentions. But that language takes its meaning from the nature of the relationship, each party's self-directed goals, and the way parties act and interact over time as their environment changes. The many unstated contingencies that can affect a promissory or contractual relationship require the parties to assume unexpressed obligations that reflect relationality, self-directed goals, and context. It is those characteristics of promising and contracting that make a method of non-doctrinal reasoning about the well-being of others an attractive and flexible way of addressing promissory obligations.

These characteristics also emphasize the difficulty of identifying and addressing the obligations that arise from relationships. The diversity and contextuality of promising and contracting suggest that we need an approach that can identify which contextual details matter. Contextuality also challenges the idea of generality and rule-based obligations that the law otherwise relies on. The self-directed aims of the parties suggest that joint intentions are difficult to identify and even more difficult to sustain in the face of a changing environment. And relationality suggests that the relationships themselves take on a life of their own in a changing environment that must transcend the environmental changes.

2

Authority's Limits

The relationality, self-directedness, and contextuality of promising and contracting overwhelm the mental maps that we often use to understand the obligations of promising and contracting. In this chapter, I explore the gaps that I seek to supplement with the ideas in this book

As the last chapter established, tensions and disputes are inevitable in the performance of promises and contracts. Their successful resolution depends on the flexibility of the parties; and if the parties cannot resolve the tensions and accommodate each other's private projects, the dispute's resolution depends on the certainty and predictability of the system of dispute resolution they resort to. Although it is commonly assumed that a rule-based system provides the needed certainty and predictability, I question that assumption and offer value-based reasoning as an alternative source of predictability and certainty. A rule-based system itself leaves gaps that must be filled, which I suggest is the function of values-balancing reasoning. When gaps exist in the implementation of the relevant authority, successful dispute resolution depends on both parties adopting a method of reasoning about the authority's instructions that allows the parties to reach the conclusion that the authority itself would reach.

In this chapter, I explore the nature of authority, the role of rules and standards, the role of theory, and the idea of rules of good faith as means of helping the parties determine their obligations in a way that is faithful to the terms of their relationship. The underlying theme is this: if the parties understand how conflicting values have been reconciled in previous, analogous disputes, they can understand how legal authorities expect the parties to reconcile the conflicting values that gave rise to their disputes. But when the words of authority provide incomplete answers to how the dispute ought to be resolved, the parties must know *why* the authorities resolved disputes the way they did in order to usefully implement the authorities.

2.1 REASONING FROM AUTHORITY

As Joseph Raz has emphasized in his writing, an important characteristic of legal authority is that it is content-neutral and opaque;[1] authority tells a legal decision-maker what to do but not why the decisionmaker should do what the authority requires or enables. This is a seemingly satisfactory state of affairs when the authority is specific, as when a legal authority describes the minimum age to be President of the United States, when a chess club (a private authority) adopts a rule allowing members to bring up to three guests to a chess tournament, or when a contract (another legal authority) specifies that delivery is to be on March 30 at 5:00 p.m. come hell or high water. But when the authority is less specific, the opaque and content-neutral character of the authority keeps the authority from itself justifying one outcome of a dispute over another. If the legal authority says that a promise "justifiably relied on" may give rise to an obligation, or if a private authority says that members of the chess club may bring a reasonable number of guests, or if a contractual authority says that delivery must be within a reasonable time, the fact that we can identify what the authority requires linguistically tells us little about why the authority requires one thing and not something else. The content-neutrality and opaqueness of authority robs the authority of its justificatory power and therefore keeps the authority from successfully resolving disputes.

Of course, the formality of reasoning from authority has properties that some find to be attractive – namely, authority's supposed neutrality and efficiency. But the supposed neutrality and efficiency of reasoning from authority can create a trap that hides the values important to the law from the justificatory glare of identification and evaluation. And the claimed efficiency of reasoning from authority confuses ease of application with an application that is justified given the values at stake. If the law's values are hidden, those who are subject to the law can hardly know whether they are being treated justly. Many a child has rebelled when a parent has issued a directive and justified it by saying, "because I said so." If the normativity of the law is based on command rather than on reasoning that right-thinking people can understand and accept, the state must increase sanctions to give its authority weight. The gaps that opaque and amorphous authority cannot fill are magnified when, as is the case of promising and contracting, disputes are highly contextual and relational.

It might be thought that the normative force of an authority comes from the pedigree of its author. This characteristic of authority is also its weakness. When the reason for the command is opaque to those who must interpret it, the command lacks normative force. Because an authority often tells its audience what to do but not why one should do what the authority commands, it is difficult to implement unless one brings to bear on the authority a method of reasoning that gives the authority contextual meaning. Without knowing the normative grounds for the

[1] Raz (2009) at 201–219.

command, the scope and meaning of even a partially determinate command are unclear.

When an authority is vague rather than specific, being able to reason about the authority's content is important; the very fact that the authority is opaque and content-neutral requires that the authority be given contextual meaning by reasoning about the determinants of the authority in a way that is neutral and acceptable. The belief that one can reason from authority by deduction, analogy, and precedent is highly misleading. One cannot reason by deduction until the major premise of the deduction is justified, and one must reach outside the major premise to provide its justification. Reasoning by analogy fails unless one is secure in the characteristics that make one dispute like a prior dispute that has itself been justified. That is why we can agree that under our system of precedent, a case "on all fours" with a prior case ought to have a similar outcome, yet disagree about whether the prior outcome is justified and which characteristics make cases "on all fours" with each other.

Authority is determined by some method of reasoning. If that reasoning is not self-evident from the authority, authority becomes discretionary. One cannot reason from authority when the authority does not reveal the basis on which the authority was determined. Amorphous doctrine is not a unique characteristic of promising and contracting, of course, but it is a great impediment to traditional notions of legal reasoning. Even a cursory view of the Restatement of Contracts (Second) shows the limitations of that authority for anything but a framework for additional reasoning, reasoning that is not self-evident from the Restatement. Restatement provisions await implementation, and I offer values-balancing reasoning about the provisions as an appropriate methodology.

Opaque and amorphous authorities also risk damage when not accompanied by appropriate implementing reasoning. Formal reasoning gives rise to the danger of literalism, a brand of textualism that leads implementation away from an authority's original justification. When a consumer agrees to the seller's terms and conditions by accepting, without reading, a long list of standard terms, does that constitute a meeting of the minds that incorporates those terms and conditions as a part of the contract? Words like *consent* and *assent* lose their original meaning when applied to standard terms that the consumer neither reads nor comprehends. [2] If the practice of contracting changes, but the literal meaning of legal authority fails to accommodate those changes, the justifications for the original authority may be deformed in their implementation.

In other words, the methodological commitment of this book is that obligations come from a methodology of reasoning *about* authority rather than a method of reasoning *from* authority. Authority is itself determined by the method of reasoning that makes the authority authoritative. A contract's content is determined by the

[2] Kar & Radin (2019). Issues raised by consumer contracts are discussed in Chapter 12 ("Consumer Contract and Standard Terms").

reasons that led each party to agree to achieve that party's private projects by enlisting the help of another person. Legal doctrine is determined by the method of reasoning that led a judge to resolve a dispute in one way rather than another, for it is the nondoctrinal reasoning that judges use to settle disputes that gives rise to legal doctrine. And theory is determined by the question the theorist is asking, and, if it is a moral theory, by the reasoning that allows the theory to be implemented in various contexts. It makes sense then to turn to methods of reasoning that underlie how people should treat each other – the ones that determine the content of contracts, legal doctrine, and theory – when searching for a method of reasoning that determines obligations within a relationship.

2.2 RULES AND STANDARDS: THE LIMITS OF LEGAL DOCTRINE

Rules are important as sources of law, and they settle many potential disputes.[3] When they clearly apply, they do not demand a complex method of reasoning to be implemented. But when rules function as standards, as they sometimes do, they require a method of reasoning to guide their implementation.

In fact, much of the contract doctrine consists of rules and standards that leave a gap between their words and their contextual implementation.[4] Even the distinction between rules and standards has an insecure, wavering boundary. Rules are a matter of form; but they often function as if they were standards. Assume that legal doctrine embodies the rule that a contracting party ought to keep her promises. As long as there are exceptions to the rule – as is true when performance is excused – the rule acts as a standard. Even if the rule requiring performance were true in a large array of circumstances, the rule would not itself settle disputes as long as performance might be excused. The law does not deal with what is generally true; it deals with what is true in the dispute that must be settled, and a rule that is accompanied by exceptions begs for a method of determining when those exceptions should be implemented.[5] And, of course, any rule requiring performance also forces us to determine what performance requires.

Rules also act as standards when rules are formulated using words whose meaning is not fixed; contract doctrine is filled with such words. The law of promising and contracting has a particular problem with respect to its use of rules. Many rules are so-called default rules – that is, rules that apply unless the parties agree otherwise. While default rules, if precise, can function to settle disputes, they fail to settle disputes about whether the parties have opted out of the default rules. When legal

3 *See generally* Alexander & Sherwin (2001).

4 The relative value of rules and standards is the subject of a large and diverse literature. *See generally* Kennedy (1976), Kaplow (1992), and Nance (2006).

5 It does no good to resort to doctrinal words to describe the grounds for excuse, such as words like "commercial impracticability;" those words also require a method of reasoning before being implemented

decisionmakers are deciding whether a dispute should be settled by referring to a default rule, the rule ceases to be a rule, for then some method of reasoning must be used to determine whether an opt-out or the default rule applies. If legal decisionmakers require the parties to agree expressly to an opt-out provision, legal decisionmakers add to the cost of contracting and risk turning default rules into real, but misguided rules.[6] If, on the other hand, legal decisionmakers easily infer that the parties have opted out of default rules, they need to explain the basis of that inference and provide a method of determining the implied obligations that remain.

Supplementing imprecise rules and standards with values-balancing reasoning aligns the normativity of reasons and the normativity of rules. People of goodwill know how to reason about their obligations; they can determine how to make the necessary trade-offs between their private projects and the needs of a relationship. They can reason about how to change their behavior in response to a changing environment. For all but the most specific rules, the normativity of a contract term or contract doctrine depends on how we reason about the values that the words reflect, the values that animate contract law, not on linguistic meaning alone.

It is sometimes thought that standards can be understood by referring to rules, which can themselves be implemented by rules that are themselves implemented by additional rules. This, however, starts a reductionist spiral that robs the law of any justificatory foundation; if every rule is justified by a rule, and no rule is itself justified, the law loses its normative force. Alternatively, the reductionist approach to rules threatens to create a rule for every context, and this either destroys the generality of the law that is necessary to the rule of law or results in amorphous generalities that fail to specify whether the outcome of disputes is just.

2.3 THE GOOD FAITH EXAMPLE

Consider the rules/standards dichotomy in the context of the methods by which scholars have attempted to understand the obligation of good faith. Contracting parties must perform their contracts in "good faith"[7] – an ineffable standard that seems to defy an operational definition. Good faith is an implied term of every relationship, and it protects the institution of contracting by protecting the trust that

6 If the parties want to opt out of the default rule, but must do so expressly, they must bargain over the rule that is appropriate to their exchange and one of the parties will lose from the bargaining. If parties assume, but do not express, a set of obligations that are contrary to the default rule, a legal decision-maker requiring an express opt out would overturn the terms of the exchange.

7 According to the Restatement (Second) of Contracts §205: "every contract imposes upon each party a duty of good faith and fair dealing in its performance and its enforcement." The good faith requirement is required in the sale of goods and other commercial transactions by §1–304 of the UCC. Good faith is defined in the UCC as: "honesty in fact and the observance of reasonable commercial standards." UCC. §1–201(b)(20). The implementation of these words begs for a method of reasoning about the obligations the words imply. The good faith standard also applies in the formation of contracts, but there it is implemented differently, given the discretion that parties have before relationality attaches. This book does not address good faith in the formation of contracts.

makes cooperative relationships viable. Yet its content cannot be determined from a simple restatement of its meaning, and, in fact, good faith takes on different meanings depending on whether the requirement applies to contract formation, performance, or enforcement. The concept of good faith begs for a method of reasoning about what the term requires of people when people think about their obligations.

As things stand, the open-ended texture of the good faith concept is one of contract law's enigmatic features. Some see the concept's vagueness as a barrier to contracting, an infringement on the autonomy of the parties, or an invitation to courts to adjust contracts to reflect bargaining power and post-contract developments.[8] Under this view, good faith allows courts to "intervene" in contractual disputes to impose terms that the parties never bargained for.[9] For others, the good faith requirement builds needed flexibility into the law and encourages contracting by allowing the parties to trust that judges will contextualize the parties' obligations to make sure that they reflect fair dealing and honesty. In the words of E. Allen Farnsworth, "the elasticity and lack of precision of the concept allows courts to develop the meaning of the term in light of unforeseen and new circumstances and practices."[10] To some, the rule of good faith transfers power from the parties to the courts; to others, it provides a guarantee of fidelity to the exchange that is integral to the concept of contracting.

Because it is opaque, the good faith requirement hovers ominously over contractual relationships. When performance issues arise under the contract, each party must act in good faith, which, in the absence of a clearly articulated method of reasoning about good faith, seemingly allows each party to use extra-contractual leverage to heighten, rather than reduce, disagreements. When one contracting party claims that the other party is acting in bad faith, how does a legal decision-maker know whether either party's position is made in good faith?

The field is well-traversed, but scholars of good faith share one common trait – they believe that the law must be understood by means of a test, definition, or rule that can determine whether a party has performed its obligations in good faith. Yet these efforts to control the good faith inquiry by appealing to authority are universally incomplete. They either replace one standard with another standard, or they atomize and contextualize the standard in ungeneralizable ways. That is why I recommend that we protect the institution of contracting by viewing good faith

8 Dubroff (2006), Feinman (2015), and Dobbins (2005).

9 Goldberg (2006) at 95.

10 Farnsworth (1963) at 670. The good faith requirement addresses some of the most intractable interpretive questions. May a lender cut off a line of credit to a borrower or will a court say that doing so is acting in bad faith? May a seller close a production line and stop selling to a contractual buyer, or will a court say that the closure was done in bad faith? When contracting parties agree to agree in the future about their relational obligations, what role does the good faith obligation play in controlling or guiding their subsequent behavior? What obligations can be inferred through the good faith inquiry about the unarticulated obligations of the exchange?

to embody a method of values-balancing reasoning that each party is obliged to use in determining its promissory obligations.

Commentators agree that the good faith requirement must be comprehensible, faithful to a contract's terms, evenhanded, yet contextually flexible. If the authority is too amorphous, it provides no guidance and leaves the legal standard untethered from the deal the parties made. If the authority is too contextual, it threatens to segment the idea of contracts into little boxes that are unconnected to a universal idea of cooperative exchange. And if the good faith requirement is unresponsive to context, it may be applied in a way that upsets the bargaining equilibrium chosen by the parties.

How then is the legal system to implement the good faith standard when, as Robert Summers has said, no verbal formula can capture the many contexts in which good-faith is likely to be an issue?[11] Yet, the idea that we need an "operational standard"[12] is also misleading if, by that, we mean a standard that functions as a rule. Instead, as I argue in this book, the law needs a mental map that provides a method of reasoning that fulfills the need for the good faith concept to be comprehensible, faithful to the exchange, evenhanded, and contextual.

The problem is that scholarly attempts to encapsulate good faith invariably use undefined words or concepts that cannot be applied without a supplemental method of reasoning. For example, the idea that good faith entails the absence of an intention to harm a legally protected pecuniary interest[13] requires a method for determining the scope of legally protected pecuniary interests and a definition of intent. Similarly, the separate idea that good faith can be defined by the expectation of the parties[14] requires a method for determining whether the parties had shared expectations and, if not, which party's expectations would prevail over the other's. Dictionary definitions weigh themselves down with vague, undefined words; definitions themselves beg for a way of reasoning about the definition's meaning and implementation.

Definitional problems are not successfully addressed by changing the terms of the inquiry. Economic approaches to good faith often suggest that good faith seeks to prohibit opportunistic behavior.[15] Because this approach highlights the fact that a contracting party who acts in bad faith is getting an unearned benefit, this approach points us in the right direction. But the substitution of opportunism for good faith does not solve the problem of determinacy because the concept of opportunism is also inadequately defined.[16] We can agree with Oliver Williamson that bad faith is "self-interest seeking with guile"[17] and that it is the "calculated efforts

11 Summers (1968); Summers (1982).
12 Burton (1980) 94.
13 Burton, (1984) at 372–373, n. 17.
14 Yee (2001).
15 Muris (1980) Kostritsky (2007–2008).
16 Shell (1991).
17 Williamson (1975).

to mislead, distort, disguise, obfuscate, or otherwise confuse."[18] And we can agree with Timothy Muris that bad faith results when one contracting party transfers wealth from the other contracting party.[19] Yet we need a methodology for identifying when those circumstances have occurred.

Steve Burton suggests that bad faith is the use of contractual discretion to recapture opportunities foregone in the exchange – that is, to get a benefit that one had already bargained away.[20] This standard helpfully captures the idea, which is implicit in the bargaining model developed in Chapter 1 – namely, that a contracting party should not get unearned benefits – but it begs for a method that identifies the opportunities a party gave up when signing the contract. Moreover, it seems unduly narrow because it seems not to account for later-arising circumstances that were not within the contemplation of the parties but affect their relationship.[21]

Robert Summers suggests that good faith can be defined by its mirror image, bad faith, that bad faith can be understood in categories, and that reasoning from those categories allows the parties and legal decisionmakers to distinguish between good and bad faith performance.[22] This approach has promise as long as the prohibited conduct is an open category (to preserve the universality of the good faith requirement). But this approach too, is founded on words that cannot be applied in context without a supplemental methodology of reasoning. We must, under the Summers categories, determine when a party has been "slacking off," when a person has "evaded the spirit of the deal" and so forth. Perhaps we would get further if we abandoned our fixation with law as a system of rules, and saw law instead as an institution of reasoning, and specifically as a system of values-balancing legal reasoning. We might then successfully facilitate, in a way that legal rules do not, the determination of which promissory behavior is impermissible. As yet, no scholar, it seems, seeks to understand the good faith requirement through a method of reasoning that the parties ought to use to determine their obligations. That is a pity; once the law is understood to be a system of practical reasoning about one's obligations, the impenetrable haze that covers the good faith requirement will lift and we can achieve the goals of fidelity to the terms of the exchange, reasonable predictability, and evenhandedness. Or so I hope to show.[23]

2.4 THE LIMITS OF LEGAL CONCEPTS

Legal analysis sometimes revolves around concepts, which play an important (but restricted) role in reasoning about obligations. Concepts like offer and acceptance,

18 Williamson (1985).
19 Muris (1980).
20 Burton (1980 & 1981).
21 This point we made in Summers (1982).
22 Summers (1982) at 828 and Summers (1968) at 235–237.
23 *See* Chapter 11 ("Performance Obligations: The Values-Balancing Approach").

consideration, promissory estoppel, unconsionability, impossibility, and expectations govern our thinking about the existence and scope of obligations. Yet, the role of concepts in the legal analysis is problematic. As others have pointed out, an important distinction exists between a concept's structural function and its normative content.[24] Structurally, concepts play an organizing role, creating a mind map that allows us to break the complexity of contractual obligations into segments that provide an organizing, normative framework. But the content of the concept is a different matter; how we fill the framework by implementing the structural function is not necessarily governed by structure itself. Indeed, as I argue here, the structural function of concepts shows us the conclusions we seek to reach, but not the method of reasoning we use to reach those conclusions. Believing that the structural function of a concept can also determine the normative content of the concept mistakes the existence of an obligation with its content. As I will argue in this book, knowing that a person has an obligation to another does not by itself tell us the content of that obligation.[25]

The structural function of legal concepts is uncontroversial. Concepts serve to demark the categories of thought that legal analysis must touch base with. They serve as boundary markers that are necessary because legal analysis does not naturally fall into neat categories. The idea of obligation is multifaceted, not unitary, which means that the various facets of obligation must be demarcated so that when analyzing one facet of a problem, reasoning does not spill over into a different facet of obligations. But the concepts that serve as boundary markers do not necessarily tell us where the boundary markers should be placed.

Perhaps the example of tort law would illuminate this point.[26] In tort law, the relevant concepts are duty, reasonable care, causation, proximate cause, and harm. Each of those concepts denotes a facet of one person's responsibility for the well-being of another that is relevant to determine a person's obligations in tort. The concepts structurally separate the idea of responsibility in tort into analytical categories. The concept of duty determines when an actor has a responsibility to another, the concept of reasonable behavior determines the scope of that duty, the concept of causation determines the necessary conditions for responsibility, the concept of proximate cause (harm within the risk) determines limitations on responsibility because an actor is not required to take all possible consequences into account when making decisions, and the concept of harm denotes those losses for which the law will require the injurer to pay compensation.

Similarly, in contract law, the concept of offer and acceptance connotes the meeting of the minds that is a prerequisite to enforceable obligations, the concept of consideration denotes the kind of response that turns the offeror's promise into an obligation, the concept of good faith determines the scope of performance and

24 Balganesh & Parchomovsky (2015).

25 A contrary view is presented in Smith (2012).

26 *See generally* Gerhart (2010).

repair obligations, the concept of promissory estoppel denotes the binding effect of promises that bring about a change of position of another party, and the concept of harm denotes the losses for which one who breaches a promise or contract is responsible.

Although the structural function of concepts is noncontroversial, what is controversial (and thus far relatively unexplored) is the method by which to determine the content of those concepts. In particular, it is not clear whether the content of the concept is determined by, or inherent in, the concept, or whether the content is determined by reasoning about the nondoctrinal circumstances that determine the concept's content, referencing only the idea of the concept. What is at stake is whether a concept is an input to determining its own content or whether a concept's content is determined by independent inputs.

Many scholars, perhaps most, believe that a concept provides its own content; that a concept has a content that can be discovered by reasoning about the concept *from* the concept, using the concept as its own implementing source of reasoning. Under this view, a concept like consideration – the entity that makes a promise legally enforceable – defines itself and provides its own predetermined basis for reasoning about the implementation of the entity.[27] Consideration is then the input into, and the output of, the concept. This view gives concepts a kind of rule-like sovereignty over legal reasoning.

That is not my view; for me, the concept is important as an output, and the output serves the structural function of maintaining a marker for the function denoted by the concept. The input is determined by factors that lead to the conclusion that consideration is present, but those factors respect the circumstances that tell us when a promise *should* be enforceable. They are the factors that are relevant to the conclusion that the concept of consideration wants us to determine; they are determined by the need to reach a conclusion that fits the structural function of the concept, but they are independent of that conclusion. Under this view, the concept of consideration embodies the conclusion reached by evaluating factors that are relevant to determining whether a promise ought to be revocable. The analysis of relevant factors simply tells us, as an output, that those factors are such that consideration ought to be found.

I am not alone, of course. Professor Fried, for one, suggested thirty years ago – albeit in a slightly different context – that the concept of consideration can be manipulated to reach the result the court wants.[28] His view apparently was that

[27] That appears, for example, to be the view of Robin Kar; his theory of empowerment assumes, and depends on, the existence of an entity called consideration. Kar (2016). If consideration were a fixed entity that determines its own content, then we can say that it functions as an empowering device and the empowering theory is a truism. But if the circumstances that determine whether a court will find return consideration for a promise are determined by independent factors that address the question of revocability, then the empowerment theory depends on those factors and not on the concepts of consideration itself.

[28] Fried (1981) at 19.

consideration was a concept without content (because of the difficulty of determining which promises should be enforceable and which should not be). But if this is correct, if the content of the concept of consideration is not determined by the concept, then we need a supplemental mode of reasoning to determine which promises are enforceable and which are not. That, I believe, is the role of values-balancing legal reasoning.[29]

2.5 THE LIMITS OF THEORY

Two kinds of theories dominate the literature on promises and contracts. Essentialist theories fail to capture the contextuality and relationality of promising and contracting. Relational theories have not yet fully addressed the value-based issues embedded in interpersonal relationships. Both kinds of theories can be strengthened with the methodology presented by this book.

2.5.1 *Essentialist Theories*

Essentialist theories seek to identify what is essential about the institutions of promising and contracting. These theories, therefore, rest on an important value that is advanced when we recognize and meet our obligations – values of autonomy, reliance, empowerment, consent, and wealth maximization. Yet, essentialist theories run out of steam as theories of obligations because they can capture neither the contextual nor the relational nature of promising and contracting. It is true, of course, that "self-authorship" of a meaningful life expresses an important moral value, but values do not by themselves create moral obligations and moral obligations do not arise to protect everything of value. Sometimes important values are made subservient to other values. The moral values underlying promising and contracting are relational values; they include values of autonomy in relation to other people, the value of reliance on other people, and the consent given to specific people. We can easily accept the idea that the obligations are derived from human will without knowing what turns a promise into a moral or legal obligation. Likewise, we understand that obligations arise out of an expression of consent to be bound, but that does not tell us the scope of a person's consent. Protecting reliance is an important moral value, but only in relation to the source being relied on.

Similarly, we might consult Professor Fried's idea of contract as promise, but we are then in the uncomfortable position of determining what to do when (in Professor Fried's felicitous phrase), "the promise runs out." Then, we need both a theory of when promises "run out" and a theory of what to do next. We can plug that hole by conceding, with Justice Cardozo, that obligations are imposed by law, but that raises

[29] My own view on the determinants of a promises enforceability is given in Chapter 9 ("Legal Enforceability: Formation").

the question of the basis on which the law imposes obligations. After the promises run out, what determines whether a judge decides that an obligation exists? Moreover, saying that law imposes obligations begs the issue of the nature and properties of law, which is by no means settled.

In other words, a striking aspect of essentialist theory is that it fails to encompass the relational nature of promising and contracting. Essentialist theories are unitary, focusing on one side of a relationship or the other. Indeed, contract theory seems to vacillate between the two poles of a relationship, substituting new names for old concepts. Theories of autonomy focus on the promisor but are easily reformulated as theories of reliance (focusing on the promisee), which then allows theories of autonomy to be transformed into theories of consent to be bound (the promisor again). The problem is that what is essential in contracting and promising is not a single value but the values important to the relationship that leads to obligations, and those generally invoke several values that require reasoning about how to minimize conflicts between those values.

Supporters of essentialist theories expect theory to be general rather than contextual, and to highlight values of promising and contracting rather than a methodology of reasoning about the values of promising and contracting. Theory is, almost by definition, perceived to require a general and universal statement of principles, values, or rules rather than a contextual assessment of moral action. They seem to say that theory is *supposed to be* general; it cannot simply chart particular instances of moral action; it must provide some general and universal statement about the way that particular instances of morality derive from or create, an overarching theme. For this reason, theory requires us to reduce our understanding of law or morality to its essence and that essence implies a single value, a general and universal principle, or a rule.

This book challenges that view by exploring the following question: What if we view the essence of promising and contracting to be a method of reasoning that seeks to recognize and balance the values that are implicated by the practice of promising and contracting? Could we find a method of reasoning about reconciling values that avoids the indeterminacy of pluralism and single-value theories?

2.5.2 *Relational Theories*

Other theories of promising and contracting are relational theories in the sense that they take seriously the relationship between promisor and promisee. Moral principle theories develop, on a contractarian basis, principles to govern promissory relationships. Theories of social practice suggest that the practices society follows are binding on a person who invokes those practices. In the next chapter, I point out the gap in those theories. Moral principle theories beg for an implementing method that is consistent with the principle, while social practice principles beg for a way of evaluating the values that make the practice moral. As I then explain in Chapter 4, economic theories are both relational and contextual. I find them, however, to be insufficiently moral, having no neutral way of undertaking the interpersonal comparison of well-being that economic theories demand.

2.6 CONCLUSION

This book is born from the limits of reasoning from authority that I have tried to sketch in this chapter. To be sure, I make no claim that authority is irrelevant, and certainly no claim that the authority of contractual terms is irrelevant. My claim, rather, is that the idea of reasoning *from* authority is limited. The limits of language, the need to implement the meaning of language in the context of a dispute, the obligations that are only implicit in promises, the relationality and contextuality of promising, and the need to consider the well-being of two parties, lead me to suggest the need to supplement our understanding of authority with a method of reasoning *about* authority, and I advance values-balancing reasoning as a suitable supplement.

At bottom, my intuition is this: authority does not exist as an independent entity. Authority itself, including the authority of contractual terms, is determined by some form of values-balancing reasoning. Otherwise, it would not serve as authority (except through coercion). The parties to a contract reasoned about their individual and collaborative objectives; a judge reasoned about a dispute not settled by authority. If we can replicate the method of reasoning that led to the authority in the first place – that is, if we can reason about the determinants of authority – we can come closer to identifying the determinants of authority's correct normative implementation.

3

Promises and Obligations

Promises do not themselves create binding moral obligations; promises are not "an independent source of a distinct moral duty."[1] Not all promises must be kept; a person making a promise may, under the right circumstances, change her mind. Even when promises are morally or legally enforceable, the requirements of a promise – what one is morally bound to do and the requirement of repair – may not be easily inferred from the promise's terms. And promissory-like obligations can arise even in the absence of a promise when we can imply consent to be bound from people's behavior.

Because promises and obligations are distinct moral and juridical categories, a person's claim about the obligations created by the promise does not arise from the fact that a promise was made. A gap exists between the act of promising and the source of moral and legal obligations (and concomitant claims against the promisor) that result from the act of promising. As I hope to show in this chapter, a mental model of the kind I offer helps us determine why and how a promise – the expression of the present intention to do something – creates an obligation to behave in a certain way.

Consider the two major theories that scholars have advanced to explain the moral obligations that arise from promising: (1) moral principle theories of the kind propounded by T. M. Scanlon[2] and (2) practice theories of the kind advanced by Hume[3] and Rawls.[4] Much of the philosophy of promising rotates around these two kinds of theories and the contest between them. The first kind of theory, moral principle theory, provides a moral source for obligations because it is based on a hypothetical agreement between reasonable persons concerning the moral

[1] Ronald Dworkin (2011) at 304. The statement that promises are not an independent source of a distinct moral duty is not inconsistent with the statement that promises are the source of obligations in contract law. The moral duty created by promises comes from a relationship induced by the promise, which means that obligations rest on promises as their source, but that their content is determined by the relationality of promises.

[2] Scanlon (2001) at 86; Scanlon (1990) (earlier version of Scanlon (2001)). *See generally* Scanlon (1998).

[3] Hume (1739), Book III, Pt. II, Ch V.

[4] Rawls (1971) at 344–350.

principles that should govern their relationship, taking into account the values that people would endorse as worthy of respect in their own lives. This kind of theory suffers from generality that leaves contextual details unaccounted for. The second kind of theory, the social practice theory, describes how people act in a culture where promising leads people to accept and implement obligations, but it cannot explain why it is that the way people behave creates a moral obligation to behave in that way. This kind of theory is contextual because it focuses on how people normally act, but it appears not to bridge the divide between "is" and "ought," and therefore is value-less.

This chapter examines these two types of theories and identifies the gaps that keep them from being fully realized theories of promising and contracting. It identifies how the mental model I propose can help implement and contextualize moral principle theories and identify the values that are imminent in social practice theories.[5]

3.1 MORAL PRINCIPLE THEORIES

The quintessential moral principle theory is that of T. M. Scanlon. He argues that the morality of promising is controlled by principles that are derived from a method of reasoning about the obligations that we owe each other. Scanlon invokes a thought exercise, one that requires reasoning about a principle that we would agree on to determine how to treat each other based on how we would like to be treated. Hence, Scanlon's principles depend on the reasoning of a reasonable person, but his focus is on the principles that should govern a persons' behavior. He posits that we should act only on the basis of principles that no reasonable person could reasonably reject, a form of hypothetical contractualism that would regulate social interdependence.[6] That requires a neutral evaluation of how we ought to treat each other, taking into account both a reasonable person's interest in being free from claims by others and a reasonable person's desire to be able to secure collaborative behavior from others. As Scanlon says, these principles do not assume the preexistence of a practice of promising; they depend only on the ability to communicate

5 A question separate from the question of how a promise gives rise to an entitlement is the question of how we conceive of the entitlement in terms of legal theory. Alan Brudner and Jennifer M. Nadler are certainly correct to emphasize that the obligations created by promises are rights-based, in the sense that the creation of the promisor's obligation to the promisee gives the promisee a right against the promisor to enforce the promise. Brudner & Nadler (2013) at 185. But that is not a theory that explains the existence or content of a promisor's obligations, or the correlative right of the promisee. Similarly, Steven Smith is clearly correct that the promisor's obligation can be understood to be correlated with a property right in the promisee. Smith (2004). Again, however, the question I address is the existence and content of the promisor's obligation that determines the promisee's property right.

6 Needless to say, the approach here bears a strong resemblance to that of Scanlon. His approach searches for principles that can guide behavior; mine looks for a way of reasoning to implement those principles.

future intentions in a way that influences the recipient of the communication. They require, in other words, a communicative practice but not a social practice.

Such theories explain many of the puzzles that surround the institution of promising. They explain how obligations arise from communication. Because a moral principle rests on a communicative practice that creates a protectable expectation in the promisee or that induces the promisee to change her behavior,[7] moral principle theories explain why an obligation arises at the moment of communication, and why moral principles immediately entitle the recipient to make a claim against the promisor. The terms of a moral principle determine how the change in position that the promise induces determines the content of the promisee's legitimate claim against the promisor at the moment the promisee changes his position in the way described by the principle. Because the principles are the product of consent to a principle that a reasonable person would accept whether the person was the promisor or the promisee, the principles make consent their source and create the promisee's entitlement at the moment the promise (or other communicative practice) of a certain type occurs. The logic of consent implies consent to the creation of an immediate entitlement in the promisee.

Despite their power, moral principle theories do not fully address all moral disagreements because they do not provide a full guide for interpreting and implementing the principles in the particular contexts in which moral dilemmas arise. Scanlon's moral principles are general, while their implementation is contextual; because they are general, the principles necessarily incorporate words whose meaning is unknown outside of the core context that served as the foundation for the principles in the first place. We need not question the principles themselves; they provide a sound basis for identifying the general moral obligations that follow from promising. But they need to be supplemented by a method of reasoning that is itself morally grounded if the principles are to be implemented and applied in a way that is consistent with the morality of the principles themselves.

The principles, at key points, employ words whose meaning depends on the context in which the principles are to be applied. They contain exceptions that are broad and amorphously worded. Putting aside the contest between moral principles and social practice principles, and the possibility that Scanlon's moral principles might themselves depend on social practices, one can see that Scanlon's principles are abstract enough to require some method of implementing reasoning. Take, for example, Scanlon's principle of "unjustified manipulation," Principle M, which is his version of an estoppel principle.

> In the absence of special justification, it is not permissible for one person, A, in order to get another person, B, to do some act, X (which A wants B to do and which B is morally free to do or not do but would otherwise not do) to lead B to expect that

7 I have occasion in Chapter 7 ("The Source of Obligations") to elaborate on the idea of reliance that animates the values-balancing approach.

if he or she does X then A will do Y (which B wants but believes that A would otherwise not do) when in fact A has no intention of doing Y if B does X, and A can reasonably foresee that B will suffer significant loss if he or she does X and A does not reciprocate by doing Y.[8]

One can see the ways in which this principle's implementation depends on further reasoning. The principle operates "in the absence of special justification," and it turns on an actor's lack of "intention" to do the thing promised. It also depends on it being "reasonably foreseeable" that the other will suffer a loss and that the loss will be "significant." Each of these words takes its meaning from the context of the relationship and each needs to be interpreted in that context. Each, therefore, requires a method of reasoning to understand its meaning in context. Among other aspects of this principle, the question of "special justification" depends on reasoning about the excuses for breaking a promise that B would find to be acceptable under the circumstances. B's expectations in light of A's promise depend on a method of reasoning about how expectations are formed, their reasonableness, and how person A ought to understand those expectations. And whether B's loss is significant depends on how we define "loss" and whether the loss includes emotional as well as pecuniary loss.[9]

Undoubtedly, the principles are developed with prototypical cases in mind, and they can be applied to those prototypical cases with seeming ease. But the principles themselves are general and elastic enough to require a method of reasoning (of some variety) to determine what the principles' terms require in particular contexts. For those who believe that one can reason from the words of a principle to its particular implementation – for those who believe that the words used in principles generate their own rules of implementation – the meaning of the words may be all we need. But, in my view, the words of moral principles do not define themselves; the context of their implementation does. Words must be interpreted in a particular context, and the principles depend on a method of reasoning to determine the obligations of promising under the principles. To me, moral principles are applied to specific contexts by a method of reasoning that draws from the values that led to the principle in the first place.

It is relevant to recognize *why* the disjunction exists between the principles and their implementation. Because the principles depend on unanimous consent by reasonable people, agreement to the principle does not necessarily represent an agreement to the principle's implementation. From the standpoint of moral principles, the intuition driving the ideas here is the inadequacy of any moral principle that is not accompanied by reasoning to implement that principle.[10] Moral

8 Scanlon (2001) at 88–89.

9 Scanlon himself describes circumstances that can override a moral principle: special circumstances unanticipated in forming the principle but known to potentially exist, and reasons that can justify us in setting aside a moral principle, the latter encompassing contexts in which the moral principle was never thought to apply.

10 Alexander & Sherwin (2001) at 12.

principles are general; their implementation particular. We might all agree with the moral principle that one should not torture children. But that principle does not determine which practices, in fact, constitute torture; outside of prototypical cases, the moral principle fails to cover the range of disputes about how children ought to be treated. One can agree with the prototypical cases prohibited by the principle without also agreeing about what constitutes torture; the meaning of the word *torture* depends on some method of reasoning, contingent on social practice or moral understanding, that is not itself revealed by the principle. Put another way, even a moral principle that would be adopted by the unanimous consent of reasonable people can lead to divergent understandings of what the principle means when implemented in a particular context. The principle of unanimous consent requires only that all people agree that the principle is reasonable in one implementation, without necessarily agreeing that it is reasonable in other implementations. If all people agree that it is immoral to waterboard children, each may assent to the hypothetical principle without also assenting to the principle that smoking around babies is immoral. In fact, to get unanimous consent, the only requirement is that each reasonable person assent to one implementation of the principle, even if others would not agree to any implementation but her own.

Reasoning about the implementation of moral principles such as those developed by Scanlon does not mean that one must abandon the values that determined the moral principles. It simply means that reasoning must be able to recognize the moral values underlying the principles and use those moral values to shape specific responses to contextual details. It is not enough to reason toward a general principle; reasoning must lead to an implementation of the principle that would itself draw wide consent.

It could be that we could implement moral principles by looking to social practices. We might think it possible to examine social practices to determine whether, as Scanlon's principle requires, A knows that B wants to be assured that person A will do X. If, in the context of social practices, person A normally knows that B wants to be assured of A's commitment, then we could rely on that social practice to find that this condition has been met. But that interpretive strategy only results in a moral implementation of the principle if the practice itself represents behavior that we would call moral. That approach, therefore, suffers from the defect that characterizes social practice theories, the fact that social practices may not be moral practices.

We might also ask whether moral reasoning can be done by a person who has not engaged in the practice of promising and whether moral reasoning varies between societies that employ different promissory social practices. In order to determine whether a particular accommodation of interests is reasonable, we must ask whether the analyst must refer to how people usually treat each other, or whether the analyst can rely on abstract ideas alone. The theory of values-balancing reasoning that I propound allows the implementation of moral values to be influenced by moral social practices as a way of contextualizing moral principles. But it requires that those social practices themselves result from values-balancing reasoning that can determine when social practices can also be considered to be moral practices. I turn to that question next.

3.2 SOCIAL PRACTICE THEORIES

Social practice theories emphasize that communities develop the practice of promising to foster trust and facilitate cooperative relationships. These theories posit that resort to a social practice gives rise to the obligations inherent in the practice.[11] If the social practice is to call a luncheon partner as soon as the promisor knows that she cannot keep her promise to have lunch, then that practice creates the obligation to make the call (in the absence of a sound excuse for not making the call, which would also be determined by social practices). The right thing to do is determined by the social practice and the obligation to do the right thing is determined by the use of social practice to facilitate relationships of trust and cooperation. The fact that one has resorted to the practice is the source of the obligation to abide by the norms of the practice.

Social practice theories address several central questions about promising. Most notably, the practice of promising is rich in details that make social practices highly contextual. Although social practices evolve over time and leave some questions unanswered, their contextual detail provides a rich source of information about how actors normally behave. Because they focus on what people normally do, social practice theories can take into account fine-grained practices that account for context. And because social practices respond to social rewards and sanctions, and to the promisor's own moral and social sentiments, the line between approved and disapproved behavior is not difficult to discern. Social practice theories also explain how social practice can raise a promisee's expectations and what those expectations are likely to be, which are important determinants of obligations.

But social practice theories are less successful at articulating why and when social practices give the promisee an enforceable moral or legal claim against the promisor. The central problem is the difficulty of evaluating whether what *is* (the practice) is also an *ought*. Social practices perform many valuable social functions, of course, and many theories of social practice emphasize the important function that social practices perform. But the value of social practice as a morally sound device for bringing about social cohesion depends on the morality of the social practice, and the morality of the social practice is not demonstrated by the practice's stability and longevity. A long-standing social practice could be a habit or a

[11] *See* John Rawls (1971) at 344–350 and John Finnis (1980) at 304. David Hume called fidelity to promise an "artificial virtue," meaning that promising was not a practice that arose from human nature (because promising was not a natural instinct for survival), but he did not directly address the extent to which promises create obligations by virtue of the practice of promising.

convenience that cannot create an obligation. Social practices are not morally self-validating. Social practice theorists who seek to explain how and why a promisee's expectations turn into an entitlement stress the social value of social practice, but they lack a theory of what the promisor owes the promisee. As a result, social practice theories do not explain why they are moral theories; they fail to convincingly explain why the behavior we usually exhibit is what we ought to do and why a social practice is one worth endorsing. Social practices may, in fact, be immoral.[12]

In other words, the central flaw in social practice theories of any variety is that they focus on the favorable outcomes that social practices produce rather than on the values that generate and sustain those favorable outcomes and generate moral obligations. Sometimes a favorable outcome is expressed in terms of the trust that promise-keeping creates.[13] At other times, the value of social practices is expressed in terms of the value of the will or autonomy of the promisor that promise-keeping affirms; because promises are an expression of the will, sovereignty, or intentions of the promisor, the intent to create the obligation is the source of the obligation,[14] especially when an individual is engaging in a social practice that endorses such obligation-enabling acts.[15] These social practice theories are grounded on the expressory value of promises that are themselves valuable. And sometimes social practice theories are expressed in terms of the common good that promise-keeping produces.

Because social practice theories focus on the good social outcomes that practices produce, they are purely instrumental and provide no reason why a practice gives rise to moral obligation unless an actor has a legal obligation to contribute to good social outcomes, and that is doubtful. Many practices of value do not create obligations for an actor. Charitable giving serves a valuable social function, but the value of the practice creates no obligation to make charitable contributions. Indeed, both law and morality draw on the distinction between altruism, which is valued but not obligatory, and other-regarding reasoning, which, as I hope to show, is required morally and legally. One has no moral or legal obligation to confer a benefit on another in the absence of a special relationship with the other, but once the appropriate relationship is formed, an actor has an obligation to be other-regarding.[16]

We understand the moral obligations that social practices create only if we determine that moral values gave rise to and justify the practice. In the view I

12 Nor are norms necessarily efficient. Kraus (1997).

13 Charles Fried (1981).

14 John Finnis (1980) at 288. James Gordley writes in the Aristotelian tradition that keeping promises reflects the virtue of making right decisions, ones that are justified not on instrumental grounds but on grounds of human flourishing. Gordley (2001).

15 *See generally* the essays in Benson (2001). Atiyah puts it in terms of having reasons for the obligation to exist, and links this with the doctrine of consideration. Brudner (2013) is skeptical. If promise theories see the right to be arising from the promise and therefore as unilateral, this ignores the idea of a promisee having a claim against the promisor.

16 For an elaboration of this distinction, see Gerhart (2014) at 109–122.

present, a social practice creates a moral entitlement only if the values that underlie the practice are values that are themselves morally salient and justified. It is not what we do, or what we accomplish, that creates an obligation to act in one way rather than another. It is *why* we do what we do that provides the basis for turning the social practice of promising into an entitlement to be treated one way rather than another.

The idea that social practices create moral obligations seems to be looking through the wrong end of the telescope and to confuse inputs and outputs. The idea that social practices provide socially beneficial outputs fails to recognize that moral values often shape social practices (and are therefore inputs into the practice) and that those values provide the practice's social benefits. The view that obligations are created because the practice of promising is a valuable practice – that it provides something important to the promisor, the promisee, or the general public – assumes that valuable practices create their own obligations, simply because they create value. That views promissory obligations to come from the output of the practice of promising, rather than from the values that generate the practice. But valuable practices do not create obligations by virtue of their value. We cannot assume that people do what it is valuable to do because they are, or feel, obliged to do so. People may be motivated by social approval, which supplies a kind of external motivation that validates practices because of the good they produce. External influences on behavior cannot easily be correlated with morally obligatory behavior, for external forces are equally consistent with morally bankrupt behavior.

But the value-producing view is not a necessary interpretation of the way that social practices give rise to obligations. If we turn the telescope around and examine the inputs into social practices, we see that social practices create obligations when people ascribe to the values and method of reasoning that makes the social practices moral.

Naturally, if a social practice follows, or is consistent with, a moral principle, the practice provides a moral way of acting. To be sure, that obligation may, as T. M. Scanlon argues, come from the moral principle and not from the social practice, but the social practice at least expresses and reinforces the moral pull of the principle. But how, exactly, does a moral principle generate an obligation in ways that social practice cannot generate one? We can, it would seem, accept the idea that moral principles do not depend on social practices without rejecting the idea that social practices can also reflect values that create moral obligations. Here is why.

First, consider the way in which moral principles create obligations. As we have seen, moral principles describe obligations, but they do not have some magic power to create obligations that practices do not. Moral principles create obligations because they are the product of moral reasoning and because the reasons that support the principles express sufficient moral force to allow the principles to act as an expression of obligations that come from reason. It is not the principles that lead to obligations, but the moral reasons reflected in the principles that lead to obligations. Those moral reasons reflect the reasoning from which the principles are derived, as well as the reasons the principles display for behaving in one way rather than another. The normativity of principles comes from the reasoning that led to the principles and from the reasoning the principles give for implementing the principles.

Moral social practices are different only because the reasoning that led to the practice, and the reasoning that leads people to engage in the practice, are not as evident or explicit as they are with moral principles. By their nature, social practices arise without a prior blueprint for action. There is no predetermined way to act; no philosopher king to justify, guide, or evaluate the practice. By their nature, social practices arise from social interactions, the invisible hand of countless human interchanges.

But social practices, and especially moral social practices, can reflect a set of values that people use to guide their behavior – a set of reasons for acting and a method of moral reasoning about how to behave. Practices evolve in the way they do as a reflection of the values that the practices themselves are expressing. For example, when a community develops the practice of forming a queue at a bus stop, the community is expressing the value of a certain form of fairness – namely, the fairness of first possession. Those who get to the bus stop first ought to have priority to get on the bus. And if the practice develops that older adults or a parent with a young child are able to move to the front of the queue, *that* practice develops from, and reflects, the values that the group has (implicitly and silently) "decided" to give to people who need, or appear to need, special accommodation.

In this way, social practices reflect social reasoning, a kind of collective working out of an aggregate of individual reasoning about how people ought to behave. That reasoning may reflect values of self-regard or power that we would not accept as moral reasoning under the method of moral reasoning we adopt. The practice might, for example, reflect the reasoning that white people, being thought superior to others, should be allowed to enter the bus first. That, being an unacceptable reason, would make the social practice an unacceptable and immoral social practice.

But other practices do reflect reasons and reasoning that we would find to be morally appealing under the method of moral reasoning we adopt. We would call those moral social practices, precisely because they reflect a method of reasoning that we can justify as itself moral. When an actor notifies a future luncheon partner that he is unable to keep his commitment to have lunch, that practice is done out of a sense of other-regarding morality that marks the practice as a moral social practice. The actor has balanced the value of his time and effort with the value of alerting that friend, a balance of values that we would endorse as obligations of the relationship.

Because *moral* social practices are grounded in moral reasons and values, and ascribed to because of those moral values, the values underlying the practice can create a moral obligation reflected in the practice.[17] Social practices give actors

[17] Brudner captures this sense when he says that people give up their subjective inclination in favor of a principle that can be willed into universal law. He associates this with the view that social practices

reasons for action when the actor has accepted the morality of the reasons that gave rise to the social practice, and it is precisely those reasons that provide reasons for acting. The obligatory nature of moral practices and principles comes from the values and methods of reasoning that the principle or practice embodies. Those values and methods of reasoning have the same force (and may well be identical) whether the values are formed from prior reasoning about the right way to do things or from the evolution of social forces that express those values. It is all about the method of reasoning (express or implicit) that gives rise to the principle or the practice.

That is why I say that the mistake in social practice theory has been to understand practices as a description of what people do rather than as an indication of *why* people do what they do. Practices ought to be known and evaluated by the reasons people engage in the practice. One cannot derive an is from an ought, of course, but if one knows the values-balancing reasons that led to the practice, one can identify the reasons why people ought to follow the practice – and therefore the way in which practices give rise to obligations. The morality of social practices, in other words, depends on the method of reasoning that an individual uses to determine whether to adopt the social practice as a basis for acting in one way rather than another. The moral strength of a practice depends on the moral strength of the reasoning that binds an actor to the practice. The common good is the output of a process in which all decisions reflect the right reasons, which are the inputs into the practice. And it is those right reasons that are the source of the obligation to follow the practice.[18]

This understanding of the morality of social practices helps to unify the diversity of moral views posited by P. S. Atiyah. He drew a distinction between the internal and the external moral view: the first being the moral view that a person uses to determine the right thing to do, and the second being the moral view that reflects what people take to be right about their practices.[19] This distinction, however, disappears once we accept that social practices can reflect a person's internal moral view because that person has understood and evaluated a social practice on

can lead to the common good, and with the idea that supporting the common good is a reason for the obligation. We should, however, distinguish between two meanings of the "common good." When people act from the reasons that they would accept as universal in that context, they are acting in accordance with reasons that every reasoning person should accept as universal. But universal acceptance of a reasoned principle is acceptance of a moral method of reasoning, not acceptance of an outcome that is, for some instrumental reason, good.

18 This analysis makes sense of John Rawls's notion that an actor who engages in a practice would be a free-rider if the actor took the benefits of the practice without bearing its costs. The moral reasons that support a practice reflect a division of the burdens and benefits of the practice that is itself moral (by virtue of the reasoning that supports the morality of that division of burdens and benefits). An actor who expends energy to get to the bus stop early in order to get to the front of the line (the benefit of the practice) must accept the burden (if that is the practice) of allowing an elderly person to go to the front of the line.

19 Atiyah (1981).

the basis of the values that others have for thinking that the practice they follow is, in fact, the right and moral practice. Assume that a newcomer to a community enters a line at a bus stop where the practice is to allow physically impaired individuals to go to the front of the line and enter the bus first. The newcomer can evaluate the moral basis for that practice, and internalize it as one that the newcomer wants to accept and endorse. Under those circumstances, the internal moral point of view and the external point of view merge into a point of view that represents the acceptance of the values that underlie both the internal and the external view.[20]

On the other hand, if the stranger enters a line at a bus stop where the practice is to allow white people to go to the front of the line, the newcomer can follow the practice (because of social pressure) without accepting the moral values underlying the practice. The disjunction between the internal and the external view of morality will contribute to the evolution of the practice in a morally sound way. But in all cases, it is the reasoning that leads to acceptance or rejection of the social practice that determines whether the social practice is also a moral practice.

3.3 CONCLUSION

I advance the idea that legal decisionmakers evaluate behavior by comparing an actor's behavior to the behavior that would be adopted through an ideal, reasonable method of reasoning; this idea allows us to supplement existing theories of the morality of promising. For practice theories, it means that the obligations arising from the practice of promising can be morally justified on the basis of the reasoning that a moral actor should use when deciding whether to adopt the practice. As we have seen, what matters for social practice theories is neither the practice's existence nor its benefits; what matters is the reasons a social practice is adopted and followed. Those reasons are revealed when we adopt a moral method of reasoning about the decisions under that practice. For moral principle theories, which depend on a method of reasoning about right and wrong, reasoning means that the principles can be implemented in context by asking whether the actor in question behaved as a person would if the person used the correct method of reasoning when deciding what to do under moral principles.

Under this view, promissory practices and principles do not provide distinct and competing forms of reasoning about promissory obligations. Both theories are founded on a view of how ideal actors who would behave morally ought to reason about the decisions they make. For practice theories, the method of reasoning about an actor's decisions informs a legal actor's evaluation of the practice's morality. For moral principle theories, the appropriate method of reasoning is both the source of the moral principles and the method by which the principles are applied in

[20] One might easily develop a theory of the evolution of social practices that sees changes in social practices to be driven by internal moral views about the immorality of the social practice, which then spreads to others who think morally about how the practice ought to change.

particular contexts. Underlying both theories is a method of reasoning about one's obligations that fulfills the potential of each theory, showing that the two theoretical approaches are not, in fact, distinct and separate. When the reasons that support ideal behavior are the appropriate reasons, moral social practices align with moral principles.

4

Maximization and Cooperation

Economic theory is attractive because it is relational and contextual. It posits that the practice of promising increases society's wealth by allowing an actor to rely on others to do tasks more efficiently than the actor could do alone. The interdependence created by promising and contracting increases wealth by protecting legitimate expectations, facilitating reliance, and developing trust (each of which conserves resources, lowers the cost of making and enforcing contracts, and builds social capital). Economic theory is relational because it posits that wealth is created by the interaction of at least two actors. It is contextual because it defines wealth creation in a way that points us to wealth maximization's contextual determinants – namely, the burdens and benefits of interdependent decisions. Because it takes the promising or contracting relationship seriously, the economic approach is able to model the way in which each actor has, through voluntary action, received gains that are at least equal to that actor's burdens.

Economic theory shares with other theories of contracting an important perspective on the function of exchange. The economic approach recognizes that in an interpersonal relationship, both parties can be made better off by promising and contracting. Putting to one side the question of what values the practice of promising and contracting maximize, an economic approach emphasizes that successful exchanges constitute positive sum games: the idea of an exchange, and the justification for governmental enforcement, is that both parties become better off. That is the beauty of enforcing contracts; when parties have entered the contract voluntarily, society has no need to question the terms of an exchange freely bargained for. The exchange, and its enforcement, affirm the autonomy of freely choosing, self-actualizing persons and therefore affirm something special about human beings. The consensual exercise of autonomy empowers both parties to pursue their private projects by relying on a counterparty's promises. In this sense, maximizing wealth is the twin cousin of maximizing autonomy. When economic theory takes the form of defining incentives that align human behavior with ideal behavior, it correctly suggests, as do other theories, that the law should be understood as centering around the search for the ideal, and that the law functions to bring reality closer to the ideal.

However, economic analysis faces three barriers that require a supplemental method of reasoning of the kind that I advance in this book: the question of terminology, the question of multiple efficient equilibria, and the question of determining contractual obligations over time.

4.1 WHAT IS MAXIMIZED?

The idea of wealth maximization has deterred many from appreciating the positive features of the economic approach. Fortunately, wealth maximization is not a necessary characteristic of the economic approach. The economic approach is no less powerful if we substitute for "wealth maximization" a term that has stronger moral overtones. We might, for example, talk about maximizing human flourishing, human capacity, or human autonomy; we would then posit that the obligations of promising and contracting reflect the institution's ability to maximize human flourishing, capacity, or autonomy, given the relationality of promising and contracting. Or we might, as I do in this book, talk about the potential for promising and contracting to maximize human well-being, a term that signifies that the persons involved in the practice of promising or contracting exercise the autonomy to define what they find to be valuable and therefore what they consider to be wealth.

In other words, an important distinguishing feature of economic theory is not what it maximizes but *that* it maximizes; it takes seriously the values of both parties to a transaction and highlights the trade-offs that must be evaluated in order to maximize well-being. Unlike theories of autonomy, consent, or reliance, it does not focus only on values important to one party to the transaction; it recognizes that both parties gain from the exchange but that the amount of their gain depends on their willingness to surrender something that they value – their autonomy, consent, or reliance costs. Economic theory recognizes the relational nature of promising and contracting.

What rightly gives people pause about maximizing wealth (well-being) as a moral theory is that it provides an insufficient basis for deciding what counts as wealth, whose wealth matters, and what circumstances determine when one person's wealth must be sacrificed so that another's wealth may be increased. When disputes arise about the obligations created by a promise or contract, maximization is a zero-sum game; one person's well-being can be increased only if another person's well-being is decreased. Just as tort law requires that a driver take reasonable precautions, which imposes a cost on drivers to decrease the risks they impose on others, society will be unable to maximize anything if society has no mechanism for determining which party must bear costs so that the other party's legitimate expectations are fulfilled. For the reasons I explain in this chapter, economic theory has not supplied a satisfactory way of undertaking maximizing evaluations.

Economists suggest that we can identify a party's obligations by determining which obligations will maximize the benefits (or minimize the costs) of exchange, but this is an empty vessel. It is one thing to say that when an exchange is successful it maximizes well-being, or to say that each party takes on burdens for the benefit of the other party (the necessary trade-off). It is quite another thing to think that the fact of maximization determines what obligations the parties agreed to in an exchange. That is because of the problem of multiple equilibria, the allocation of risks, and the time dimension of contracting. I discuss these problems in Sections 4.2, 4.3, and 4.4.

Moreover, it is still another thing to say that when one party's contractual performance leaves a counterparty worse off than before, that we can ignore that loss on the theory that in general exchanges maximize well-being. Losses are not morally neutral, and if the loss was caused because the other party shirked her obligations, the transaction is not neutral from the standpoint of maximizing well-being, wealth, or anything else. What looks like an exchange that maximizes mutual benefits may not accomplish that end unless we know whether a party to the exchange is responsible when a party's legitimate expectations fail to materialize. The idea that we want to maximize the benefits of contracting does not reveal what obligations the parties voluntarily assumed.

4.2 THE PROBLEM OF MULTIPLE EQUILIBRIA

In a world of perfect information, we could identify the trade-offs the parties made (and thus identify their obligations) by identifying what burdens each party took on so that the other party would benefit. Moreover, if the parties had perfect information about the counterparty's private projects, alternatives, risks, and attitudes toward risk, the parties would negotiate a deal that minimized each party's costs and maximized each party's gains until there were no additional exchange gains possible. That deal would be surplus maximizing in two equivalent senses: no additional gains (or lowered cost) could be achieved by further negotiating, and the wealth (well-being) created in the exchange would be maximized. The parties could, in other words, identify the optimal bargain – the bargain that maximizes the joint gains of the parties – a point at which no party could be made better off without making the other party worse off.

Yet that ideal, which mirrors the ideal of perfect markets, requires that private project incentives are properly aligned with the interests of the collaboration. When incentives are not aligned to maximize joint gains, the ideal solution to the bargaining process cannot be reached. And because each party cares about the well-being of the other party only to the extent that bargaining allows the parties to enhance their private projects, there is no reason to assume that incentives will be aligned to maximize the interests of both parties. Indeed, economists have recognized for some time that in the face of information asymmetries and bargaining dynamics, the ideal exchange is unlikely to be reached through bargaining; many potential wealth-producing exchanges may be passed up because of information constraints.

In the bargaining process, each party enters a negotiation with a range of options that it is willing to consider, which we can understand to be a range of prices that they are willing to pay, or accept as payment, for various qualities of the subject matter of the exchange. For each party, the range of these options depends on each party's alternative means of achieving its private projects. Each party will substitute between price and quality; the buyer will pay more for higher quality goods and less for low quality goods, while the seller will demand more for high quality goods and less for low quality goods. The parties, in other words, are negotiating along a range of options that have dimensions (price and quality, including payment terms, termination rights, and many other quality determinants). Each party is willing to lower its demands along one dimension in order to get more along a different dimension. Moreover, the parties do not bargain with perfect information; numerous uncertainties create barriers to the perfect bargain, including uncertainty about the success of their own private projects, uncertainty about the counterparty's contribution to those projects, and uncertainty about the future environment.

We can visualize the range of trade-offs the parties anticipate in terms of the Edgeworth Box, which illustrates how much each party is willing to give up to advance its private projects.[1] Because each party will substitute price for various aspects of perceived quality, we can depict, by a convex curve, the kinds of substitutions one party might consider along the X (price/apple) and Y (quality/banana) axes. We can do the same for the other party. But we must recognize that to one party, higher quality means, to the other party, higher price. Accordingly, to capture the price quality substitution of the second party, we must invert the curve on the X and Y axes. We can then see the range of exchanges that each party will accept. J will not accept any terms that are below its substitution curve, (J1) (by definition, it would be better off with its alternatives) while K will not accept any term above its substitution curve (K1) (for the same reason). The parties are negotiating over the terms of the transaction that fall between the two curves.

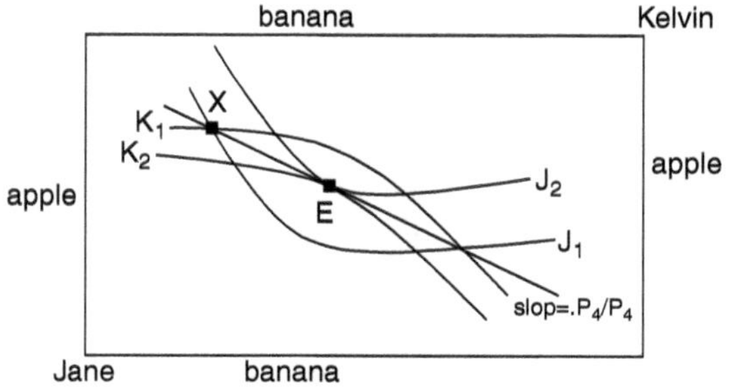

[1] Bolton & Dewatripont (2005) at 6 (depicting the contract curve of Edgeworth Box).

Within the space between J1 and K1, both parties are made better off, and they will be willing to make the exchange. If both parties had perfect information, and bargaining was costless, the parties would bargain until they reached point E, which would be the surplus maximizing exchange. But perfect information is not available and bargaining entails transaction costs. In the absence of perfect information, the exchange the parties actually make will depend on their options and their bargaining skills. Whatever point the parties choose will signify the equilibrium of the exchange (and will be efficient in one sense),[2] but the division of the gains from trade will be different at different points. More importantly, there will be many points between the two curves that could be described as equilibrium points – that is the condition of multiple equilibria – and it is impossible to predict which point the parties will choose.

Given the range of contractual options that each party will consider, and the trade-offs they might make, the final deal could be struck at any point within the range of potential trade-offs, each of which would be surplus maximizing in the sense (a different sense) that given the bargaining constraints, no deal that is better for one party could be reached without providing a detriment to the other party. But this shows the ambiguity of the term "surplus maximizing." Given the trade-offs each party is willing to make and each party's options for achieving its private projects, there are any number of surplus maximizing exchanges the parties could have made, and no one surplus maximizing deal is, on efficiency grounds, better than any other. The idea that the goal of contracting is to maximize surplus provides no basis for determining what final deal the parties actually choose when the terms of the contract do not settle disputes. If we believe, as we should, and as economists do, that contract law should determine and enforce the deal the parties actually made, economic analysis has met a dead end. It cannot tell which of the possible pairing of burdens and benefits the parties actually chose.[3]

2 The terms will be efficient in the sense that at that equilibrium point, no party can be made better off without making the other point worse off.

3 As to multiple equilibria in contract law, *see* Geis (2008),reviewing Goldberg (2006). Geis cites standard works on game theory such as Dixit & Skeath (2004) and Baird, Gertner, & Picker (1994) (pointing out that there may be more than one efficient contract design). Multiple equilibria reinforce the contextuality of promising and contracting because their existence means that negotiating parties are bargaining over a range of trade-offs, each of which is Pareto efficient, which makes the outcome of bargaining indeterminate. That, in turn, requires a method of knowing which equilibrium point the parties actually chose. These ideas came from an e-mail communication from Professor Emeritus Ron Coffey. *See* e-mail from Ronald Coffey, Professor Emeritus, Case Western Reserve University School of Law, to Juliet P. Kostritsky, Everett D. & Eugenia S. McCurdy Professor of Contract Law, Case Western Reserve University School of Law (Sept. 8, 2010, 19: 59 EST) (on file with authors). See *also* Binmore (2005) at 14 (noting the importance of fairness norms that can help the parties select from among multiple equilibria and stating that "fairness is evolution's solution to the equilibrium selection problem for our ancestral game of life."). The idea of multiple equilibria is applied in my study of property law in Gerhart (2014).

In other words, a large number of equally efficient arrangements will increase one person's well-being without decreasing another's well-being. If efficiency means that no person's well-being can be increased without decreasing another person's well-being, that constraint can be satisfied in a wide variety of ways. Bargaining parties choose between various efficient bargains that could be made; they bargain in the face of multiple equilibria and settle on one equilibrium point that represents the trade-offs they have made. Once the deal is agreed to, the alternative terms drop away and the parties have reached an equilibrium that characterizes their collaboration. Accordingly, a court that is asked to understand the exchange is asked to identify, from the set of trade-offs the parties could have chosen, the trade-offs that the parties actually chose.

The problem of multiple efficient equilibria reflects the contextuality of promising and contracting. It all depends on what persons A and B agreed to, and the obligations implied by their relationality. The problem of multiple equilibria creates, but does not resolve, the need to reason from what we know about the exchange so that we can determine each party's obligations given the assumptions the parties must have made. The law seeks to reflect the equilibrium chosen by the parties, for they would not have agreed, explicitly or by their conduct, to act interdependently had they not reached an equilibrium. And, I maintain, they have implicitly agreed to maintain that equilibrium as circumstances change. Legal analysis functions to determine what that equilibrium is – which efficient outcome the parties actually chose.

The problem of the economic approach, in other words, is that the obligations of promising and contracting do not reveal themselves without further analysis. Economists imagine that they can determine the obligations of contracting because they imagine a determinate surplus maximizing deal. But that puts them in a dilemma. If they imagine the ideal deal, that would take obligations out of the hands of the parties. If they endorse the autonomy of the parties to determine their own obligations, they must invoke a method of reasoning about obligations that is "economic" only in the sense that we must identify the balance of burdens and benefits as the parties identified them.

The search for obligations does not get easier by switching to an incentive perspective. The incentive approach assumes that if we design efficient incentives, we can correctly align actual behavior with required behavior. However, an incentive designed to force one party to bear a burden is efficient only if the benefit to the counterparty outweighs the burdens to the cost-bearer. Given the problem of multiple efficient equilibria, on what basis do we determine those burdens and benefits? A particular assignment of obligations (burdens and benefits) depends on a method of correctly discerning what the parties agreed to, and that method is not revealed by the efficiency criterion alone. Put another way, once we have a sound method for determining the appropriate assessment of burdens and benefits of various possible obligations the parties agreed to, we can call a particular set of obligations efficient. Legal decisionmakers would then be in a position to determine the correct incentives. But without that method of reasoning, the label of efficiency is an insufficient basis for identifying and evaluating the factors that led to that label. We must know the inputs (the determinants of obligations) in order to know the outputs (the efficient obligations).[4]

4.3 BARGAINING OVER RISKS

The problem of multiple equilibria reflects the dynamics of exchange. Bargaining involves a kind of joint problem solving. As transaction cost economics demonstrates, the barriers to bargaining are formidable because parties need to address the hidden costs of transacting. The selection of bargaining parties may attract parties to an exchange who present either unknown or unrecognizable risks to the exchange (the problem of adverse selection). And, once formed, a bargain gives each party discretionary power over the other party, which gives one party, or both parties, residual control and decision rights over the other. Moral hazard (which arises when the terms of exchange provide that one party is responsible for the risk another party faces, so that a party whose risk is covered has an incentive to take unreasonable risks) gives rise to the problem of opportunism and shirking, and these transaction cost problems increase the cost of design and specification, and thereby increase the costs of contracting.

Bargaining parties also know of the many risks they face as they attempt to achieve their private, self-directed aims; bargaining is about which party should bear those risks and how the risks might be reduced. Two of the risks are generally acknowledged. One is the risk of underperformance by the counterparty. A second is the risk of post-contracting changes in the circumstances of one or both parties. But it is helpful to highlight another aspect of risk, a risk that a party faces in completing its private projects. Each party must determine the risks of achieving its private projects that are not influenced by the terms of the transaction. After all, the value of the contract is in facilitating the collaboration that will make a party's private projects more successful, and it is the success of a party's private projects that induces the party to absorb the burdens of performance obligations. Accordingly, the parties come to the negotiation with a set of expectations about the risks they will face in completing their private projects that are independent of the performance of the counterparty. A farmer contracting to buy a pesticide to grow crops on her property will consider the factors that influence the profitability of her crop. A drought or excessive rain will impair her private projects but will also decrease the value of the

[4] The incentive perspective is further complicated by the existence of both carrots and sticks as incentives and the difficulty of knowing which set of incentives are at work in any particular relationship. Although economists have traditionally tended to think of external sanctions as the source of incentives, many economists now perceive that the internal incentive to know that one has done a good job or to keep one's commitments – the incentive of the carrot – can also have a powerful influence. See the discussion of internal versus external incentives in Chapter 8 ("Relationality Redux: Law on the Ground and Law on the Books").

contract for pesticides. The farmer bears that risk because the risk of drought or excess rain is a natural part of her private projects. A party can, of course, seek to shift that risk to a pesticide seller by making the obligation to purchase the pesticide contingent on actually needing the pesticide. But that requires the party that naturally bears the risk to make the contingency an explicit part of the negotiations. Parties often negotiate to shift the risks they face in completing their private projects to another party, and must pay for that risk-shifting.

4.4 THE EX ANTE/EX POST PROBLEM

The time dimension of promising and contracting also befuddles the search for obligations that we would call efficient. Promises and contracts are implemented over time, in the face of a changing world and a changing environment that affect each party's private projects. Even simultaneous exchanges have a time dimension, for they involve preparation for the exchange and satisfaction from the exchange, neither of which occurs at the time of the exchange. The item sold may not be adulterated, it must meet the buyer's legitimate expectations, and it must be paid for with legal (not counterfeit) tender.

Economists correctly claim the ex ante perspective as the appropriate perspective through which to view contractual obligations; the terms of the bargain form the basis for understanding contractual obligations. Because the legitimacy of third-party enforcement of contractual obligations depends on assent, the obligations that arise from promising and contracting (the ones we can call efficient) should be determined as of the time at which the obligations arise, based on the bargain the parties made, not at the point at which disputes arise or the obligations are sought to be enforced. Courts do not function to determine what a fair bargain would look like ex post (after the world has changed) because that would remove decisionmaking about obligations and risks from the parties and transfer it to the court. Courts are to enforce the obligations fairly implied by the exchange the parties made, given the circumstances that were known and existed, and expectations that were formed, at the time of the exchange.

Yet given contractual incompleteness, changing circumstances, and the problem of multiple equilibria, what does it mean to identify obligations that preserve the ex ante bargain? Because of multiple equilibria, we lack confidence that we can discern the ex ante obligations of the parties even if nothing changes. As things change, and disputes arise, it is even more difficult to determine what obligations are implied by the ex ante exchange. Change rearranges the burdens and benefits of the ex ante bargain. If a supplier's cost goes up more than the supplier anticipated ex ante, the ex post situation yields the supplier fewer net benefits. How does our search for contractual obligations accommodate that change?

Consider, first, the discretionary power that a contract gives the parties. Because each party confers power on the counterparty, the purpose of legal interpretation is to channel that power in a way that is consistent with the terms the parties agreed to. The power comes from terms that are insufficiently specific or do not cover contingencies that arise, what Oliver Hart calls "residual control or decision rights."[5] Under those circumstances, each party has the ability to make decisions that impose burdens on the other party. If a coal company agrees to supply coal to an electric utility, and the coal's purity that the utility needs for its private projects cannot be contractually specified or monitored, the coal company may produce less pure coal that is cheaper to mine while the power plant may want higher-quality coal that produces energy more cheaply.

This is the problem of underperformance, shirking, or opportunism. The discretion provided by the terms of the contract allows one party to get unearned benefits – benefits for which it did not offer an offsetting benefit to its counterparty. Notice also that the problem implicates both explicit and implied obligations; it implicates terms that under-specify obligations and obligations that must be implied from each party's private projects and the relationality of the collaboration. Because the contract gives the parties discretion over performance that is not fully specified, each party has ex post bargaining power over the other during performance. It all depends on each party's options to achieve its private projects outside of the contract. Accordingly, even if the parties settle their dispute and renegotiate the contract, one party will have ex post bargaining power in negotiating a modification. This is the hold-up problem.

Moreover, the bargaining power that determined ex ante terms shifts in response to changing circumstances as new opportunities arise for one or both parties. The discretion that was built into the contractual provisions becomes a potential weapon that can be used to extract unearned rewards from the other party (a different form of opportunism). A seller faced with new outlets for its product may exercise a right to terminate in order to receive a higher price. A buyer whose bargaining power is increased because other buyers have left the market may seek to use this new source of bargaining power to extract unearned benefits.

Such ex post risks might have been addressed by contract, of course, and the contract terms govern the relationship because they are the best evidence of the way the parties allocated the risks of changing circumstances. But sometimes courts excuse the performance of obligations when the environment has changed so much that the contractual division of risks no longer represents what the parties must have assumed about the future. More often, a changing environment gives rise to new risks that must be allocated, and that gives rise to the difficulty of determining from the way the parties allocated the ex ante risks what obligations are embedded or assumed or unallocated with respect to newly emerging, ex post risks. What contracting parties ought to do is then determined by a method of reasoning, from the risks the parties did allocate, what obligations the parties accepted with respect to unallocated risks.

5 Hart (2017) at 1732.

More broadly, a bargain represents a unique equilibrium point with a fixed ratio of burdens and benefits for each party, as adjusted by the risks taken by each party. To protect the ex ante exchange equilibrium, courts must, in theory, preserve the ratio of burdens to benefits represented in the equilibrium, after adjusting for the risks that each party accepted when determining the terms of the bargain. Changing circumstances may increase or decrease the surplus generated by the relationship, but each party is entitled to its private surplus, the share of the excess of benefits over burdens represented by the original equilibrium, given the risks each party accepted in the exchange.

That is why a theory grounded in how the parties ought to reason about their obligations is an important supplement to the economic approach to contracts. The parties know the nature and content of the negotiations leading to the exchange; they know the risks undertaken by each party; and they know the equilibrium point that was chosen as the risk-adjusted equilibrium point. They therefore know how much burden each party must accept in order to provide the benefits the other party bargained for. Values-driven reasoning provides a method of weighing and assigning burdens and benefits between the parties and therefore supplies what economic theory most needs.

4.5 CONCLUSION

Economic analysis successfully captures the relationality and contextuality of contracting. It successfully understands that legal remedies create incentives to conform human behavior to ideal, desired behavior.[6] Economic analysis can be understood to strive not for wealth maximization but for value maximization, and that can be understood to be the maximization of human well-being (allowing a person to determine what they find to be important for their life and private projects). Economic analysis therefore offers a great deal to those who seek to understand the obligations of contracting.

Economic analysis, however, does not itself embody a methodology for addressing the three barriers to discerning contractual obligations when the terms of the contract no longer unambiguously reveal those obligations: the problem of multiple ex ante equilibria, the allocation of risks to the private projects of each party, and the time dimension of obligations. If we had perfect information about the private projects of each party and the way the parties allocated the risk that their private projects could not be achieved, we could define a "surplus maximizing" allocation of risks. That surplus maximizing equilibrium would mean that no other arrangement of obligations would improve the well-being of either party without reducing the well-being of the other party. But given the incomplete information that each party has, and our

[6] Ideal behavior does not mean flawless or perfect behavior. It takes into account bounded rationality and behavioral traits. It allows humans to be human. But it does suggest that given what we know about the ways people process information, we expect them to reason in a way that allows them to minimize the costs of achieving sustainable relationships.

difficulty in determining the terms the parties rejected from the terms the parties agreed to, we need a method of reasoning that allows us to understand how the parties divided, explicitly and implicitly, the burdens and benefits of their exchange.

I offer values-balancing reasoning as a way of implementing the economic approach. Values-balancing reasoning allows the parties to determine what they value from among the options they have. It also facilitates a method of reasoning that allows legal decisionmakers to determine from among the comparative valuations the parties might have made the comparative valuations that the parties did make. Finally, given the ex ante exchange that parties made, values-balancing reasoning provides a method of reasoning about the parties' obligations to address ex post changes in their environment.

PART II

Values-Balancing Legal Reasoning

In Part I, I examined why the limitations of reasoning from authority give rise to the need for a form of moral reasoning that can successfully balance the values that determine the scope and content of promissory obligations. Unless one believes that promises reveal the content of their implied obligations, we need a method of reasoning to determine these obligations. In this part, I present a theory of values-balancing legal reasoning that addresses the gap between those reasoning from doctrinal, rule-based legal authority and the decisions courts make when they resolve disputes. Part II describes the method of reasoning that seems to best describe the foundations of appropriate contextual moral reasoning. This provides the framework for Part III, where I show how contract doctrine and its implementation in fact reflect how courts implement values-balanced legal reasoning.

Chapter 5 describes values-balancing legal reasoning and its relationship to the nature of law. It introduces the notion of other-regarding reasoning about ideal behavior – the reasoning against which promissory behavior is assessed. The chapter distinguishes the fact of obligations (the concept of duty to consider the well-being of others) from the scope of obligations (what that duty entails), allowing us to understand when obligations arise from promising and contracting and the reasoning that reveals the nature of those obligations. The chapter also discusses the normativity of other-regarding behavior and its relationship to the normativity of law.

Chapter 6 provides a more detailed description of how other-regarding reasoning can account for the scope of obligations that promising entails. If we assume, as we ought to, that a promise gives rise to obligations that generally are not revealed by the terms of the promise, reasoning from a values-balancing perspective will tell us what those obligations are. Here, I defend the thought process of the veil of ignorance as the core concept that other-regarding persons will undertake when they have made promises.

Chapter 7 elaborates on *when* obligations arise from promising and contracting. Here I show how the idea of obligations in contract law is related to the idea of obligations in tort law, and how that understanding helps us discern when a promise creates an obligation and when a promise may be retracted before an obligation to act on the promise arises. Taken together Chapters 6 and 7 account for both the existence of an obligation (Chapter 7) and its scope (Chapter 6).

Chapter 8 reviews the socio-legal literature that reveals how contracting parties treat each other in practice, the so-called law-on-the-ground literature. This analysis shows how that literature supports the view that other-regarding parties are able to form and sustain productive relationships by the way they reason about contractual disputes. Starting with the difference between law on the ground (how contracting parties normally treat each other) and law in the books (how the law expects people to treat each other), the chapter shows that the distinction reflects the difference between successful and unsuccessful other-regarding reasoning. This analysis illuminates ideas about trust and the "order without law" literature and further supports my claim that the normativity of practical reasoning and the normativity of legal obligations depends upon values-balancing reasoning.

5

The Foundations of Value-Balancing Legal Reasoning

Disputes arise from a clash of values; disputes are resolved by reconciling those values. At a superficial level, disputes appear to be about a clash of interests; each party is seeking to protect its private projects. But deciding between opposing interests is an inappropriate way to resolve disputes. Interests are inward looking and reflect only a person's self-centered, not other-centered, view of the world. Interests represent what the Holmesian bad person would like to achieve if the risk of serious punishment were low. Interests include the gains from opportunism or chiseling that can come from taking advantage of the gaps in contractual obligations. Settling disputes by picking between the private interests would mean settling disputes on the basis of personal or status characteristics. Certainly, equality before the law must mean that a person's well-being should be subjected only to neutral and universal values.

But a dispute that seeks to protect private interests can be understood as a dispute about how best to balance social values that those private interests put in play. Values are the means by which we evaluate the separate private projects in the context of a dispute. We do not seek to assign a value to private projects and decide the relative value of private projects. Rather, we seek to evaluate the social values that would be advanced by protecting one private project over another. Values, in this context, represent aspects of human endeavor that we find to be important for the institution of promising and contracting and that make private projects worth protecting when social values clash. Values are universal and neutral because they represent aspects of human flourishing that all respect.

The values that animate the obligations of promising and contracting are well known. The concept of autonomy is a handy shorthand for those values, although autonomy in fact is multifaceted – a mélange of values. Autonomy protects the private interest in being free from obligations – of not being forced into relationships without having exercised the choice to do so; freedom *from* contract is an important social value. Autonomy also protects the freedom to choose one's private projects and to choose the relational obligations that a person believes will advance her private projects. That is the social value of choice. Finally, autonomy also protects our ability to rely on others in order to advance our private projects. This is the social value of reliance.

These values are not absolute; they are, in fact, in tension with one another. The challenge for any theory of promising and contracting comes from the relationality of promising; because of relationality, the values of the two parties in a relationship often pull in different directions. One party values freedom from contract; another values reliance on the implicit commitments of a promise. The relationality of promising and contracting requires that we determine, in a particular context, which values take precedence over the diverging, competing set of values the counterparty represents. How is it possible to compare the autonomous decisions of two people when they are advocating for different values that are a part of the concept of autonomy?

I suggest that the contest over values can be reconciled by the method of reasoning that people who are advancing their private interests are required to use if they are reasoning morally, a method that we might call other-regarding or values-balancing reasoning. This is a method by which a person reasons about the relevant importance of the social values that are in conflict in a dispute; the dimensions of autonomy that, by virtue of a dispute, diverge. Other-regarding reasoning is a method by which a person can reconcile the values supporting her private interests with the values that support the private interests of another person, all without surrendering the value of values.

The other-regarding person does this by means of the thought process behind the veil of ignorance, a thought process that ensures that the appraisal of conflicting values is neutral in the sense that it is not dominated by achieving her own private projects. She reacts to the underlying clash of values as if she appreciated both parties' private projects but did not know which private project would be favored by the reconciliation of values.

The intuition underlying this conception of appropriate reasoning is straightforward. People cooperate. When they cooperate it is because they are able to find some common ground that allows them each to advance their private projects. Finding common ground, however, depends on a mutual appreciation of what each party values in terms of their private projects. That, in turn, suggests that people are often other-regarding in the sense that they understand their own private projects, and associated values, in the context of another person's private projects; they understand the values that validate their private projects in the context of the values that validate another's private projects. They determine how competing interests can be reconciled in the form of competing values. A person who promises to have lunch with a friend the following week knows that the friend will consider the promise to be revocable (freedom from contract) but that the friend will rightly expect that the cancellation was for good reason and with adequate notice (reliance).

The same is true if attempted cooperation fails. When relationships fail it is because one or both parties realize that the values that their private projects represent are not reconcilable with values associated with the other party's private projects. In those situations, one party's freedom from relationships will keep relationships from forming. This too is a form of other-regarding reasoning. Once a party realizes that the values represented by both parties' private projects cannot be reconciled on a mutually acceptable basis, the relationship does not continue. A person who invites a friend to lunch the following week and is told by the friend that she accepts, as long as her grandchildren do not come to town, can adjust her reliance interests and negotiate another date if she wants more certainty

Once we know which party's values take precedence in a particular context, we will know which party's well-being should be sacrificed in order to protect another's well-being. That allows us to translate a clash of values into a clash of well-being, for the interests of the parties are a measure of what the party will lose if its well-being is not sufficiently protected. A clash of interests is turned into a clash of values that those interests represent, and the clash of values decides which parties interests are to be vindicated. That, in turn, determines which party's well-being must be reduced in order to rectify the loss of another's well-being.

Two kinds of issues dominate the domain of other-regarding reasoning. First, we must decide whether any obligation to another person has arisen, the domain we normally associate with contract formation. That question addresses the issue of whether a person has the obligation to think about another's well-being; a promise contingent on a future event may not impose the obligation to think of another's well-being (and would not ordinarily lead to reliance by the other party). The second question concerns the scope of the obligation if an obligation have arisen. That question addresses how a person who has the obligation to think about the well-being of another should undertake that thought process. I will treat these two aspects of obligation separately. In Chapter 6, I explain how other-regarding reasoning can help determine the scope of the obligations that adhere in promising and contracting. In Chapter 7, I explore the sources of obligations and their relevance to contractual obligations.

Several prefatory words may help the reader evaluate the idea of other-regarding reasoning. The first relates to the issue of the existence of obligations and its relationship to contract doctrine. The second relates to determining the scope of obligations and relates to the normativity of law.

5.1 THE EXISTENCE AND SCOPE OF OBLIGATIONS

Concerning the existence of obligations, in legal parlance, the term "gratuitous promise" is used to denote a promise that is not enforceable, while a promise that is matched by consideration or justified detrimental reliance is enforceable. However, the notion of a "gratuitous promise" conflates the descriptive with the normative. As a descriptive term, we can recognize a gratuitous promise as one in which there is no apparent reciprocal promise, but this descriptive fact has no particular normative weight. The normative question is the enforceability of a promise made without a return commitment; to answer the normative question, we must determine whether and why the promise is unenforceable (and therefore gratuitous) or enforceable (and therefore not gratuitous). The descriptive term "gratuitous" is the term we apply once we determine, on normative grounds, that a promise is not enforceable.

In reality, there are no truly unilateral promises. A promise of the kind we are discussing is a promise to someone to do something. Promises therefore have the character of relationality, self-directedness, and contextuality that are characteristic of any potential contractual relationship. Even when promises are from a single source, without a return promise, promises must be treated as reciprocal, bilateral events. A promise's meaning depends on the credible commitment of the promisor (a choice to be bound) and the reaction of the promisee to the promise (justified reliance or a return promise or performance). The meaning also depends on the promisor's reasonable perception of the promisee's understanding of the promise, and the promisee's reasonable understanding of what the promisor intends by the promise. In Chapter 7, I show how the concepts of no-duty and duty, the bedrock of private law, explains what courts are doing when they determine which promises give rise to legal obligations and which do not.

Once it is determined that a promise creates a legally enforceable obligation to make decisions that reasonably account for the well-being of another, legal decisionmakers must determine the scope of obligations. The terms of the contract are determinative, of course. However, when disputes arise, the terms must be interpreted, and when the meaning of the terms runs out, disputes over obligations must be settled. This too requires a method of reasoning. Values-balancing legal reasoning allows legal decisionmakers to connect the disputed features of promises and contracts with generalized legal and moral authority. I present the general framework for understanding an appropriate method of reasoning in Chapter 6.

5.2 BEHAVIOR AND REASONING

The methodology I recommend requires that we focus briefly on the relationship between ideal reasoning and behavior. Conventionally, legal analysis is thought to focus on how actors behave, and moral and legal analysts take for granted that human behavior is the appropriate unit of analysis. We ask: Was the driver going unreasonably fast, or did the actor keep her promise or perform in good faith? Yet before there is behavior there is reasoning, however fleeting, unreasonable, or badly motivated. We do not have to doubt the centrality of behavior to understand the role that ideal reasoning plays in evaluating behavior. Reasoning is so ingrained in how we understand behavior that we take it for granted. As Justice Cardozo said nearly a century ago, driving at ninety miles an hour means one thing on a highway and something else on a racetrack.[1] Judge Cardozo was saying more than that context matters; he was alerting us to the idea that the meaning of the behavior, and its moral weight, is provided by the way the ideal person would reason about the contexts, and about the relationship between those contexts and our obligations. The behavior (driving at ninety miles an hour) is morally neutral; it takes its moral meaning from our ability to reason about the behavior in context.

Justice Cardozo is in good company. A theory that reasoning ought to be the determinant of behavior embodies the Kantian notion that thinking about how to act comes before acting, as well as the notion that the value of one action over another depends on whether that action is consistent with the action that would be taken by a morally thinking person. The point of the Categorical Imperative, I will argue, is not that reasoning gives rise to moral absolutes. The point, rather, is that our behavior should be judged, by ourselves and by others, on the basis of the behavior that would be deemed moral if we had behaved as if we had first reasoned in the required way about our behavior.

The idea is that behavior should be evaluated by determining whether it is a behavior that would be taken if one had reasoned in the ideal way. We know that promises give actors reasons to act.[2] But they do not, by themselves, give actors a reason to act in one way rather than another. Because context matters and promises are conceptually separate from obligations, a promise gives actors more than a reason to act; it also gives actors a reason to reason about how to act, including especially reasoning about the effect of their promise on the promisee. Accordingly, a values-balancing methodology focuses not on what people say (their promissory behavior); it focuses on how people reason (or ought to reason) about the meaning of what they say. We do not complete the relevant analysis by saying: "What did the actor promise?"; we go on to ask: "How should the actor have reasoned about the obligatory implications of what the actor promised?" We move from the empirical world of what was said or done to the moral, contextual world of the obligations that follow from reasoning about what was said or done.

In this way, the unit of analysis in law is not what the person did but whether what the person did comports with the behavior the person would have engaged in had their decisions given appropriate weight to the well-being of the decisionmaker and others. The unit of analysis in law is an actor's choice, and, in particular, the decision the actor would have made had the decisionmaker been reasoning as an ideal decisionmaker would reason. Decisions determine action, and action is wrongful or not as it stands in comparison to the action of an ideal decisionmaker. The ideal human decisionmaking is central to an evaluation of human behavior.

1 *Palsgraf* v. *Long Island Ry. Co.*, 162 N.E. 99, 100 (N.Y. 1928).
2 This notion is found especially in the work of Joseph Raz (2009) at 170.

Naturally, legal decisionmakers evaluate an actor's behavior against the required legal standard. But when the moral or legal standard is indeterminate, as it is for a practice as context-laden as promising, what is the moral or legal standard taken to mean? Under the approach I present, the behavioral norm against which an actor's behavior is evaluated is determined by asking how a reasonable person would have reasoned about how to behave under the relevant moral or legal standard. If an actor, taking into account the terms of a relevant promise or contract, behaves as if the actor had reasoned in the appropriate way about her obligations, then the actor has fulfilled her obligations (whether or not the actor was conscious of, or actually used, the required method of reasoning). If the actor does not behave as if she has reasoned in the appropriate way about how to act under the standard, then the actor has behaved wrongfully. Reasonable decisionmaking determines the implementation of the behavioral standard against which an actor's actual behavior is evaluated.

Moreover, because morality depends on a method of reasoning, one cannot understand the content of moral principles without understanding the reasoning that led to the principles, and it is that method of reasoning that ought to determine a principle's implementation The distinction between behavior and how one decides upon, or evaluates, one's behavior reflects the distinction between *what* and *why*. An actor's behavior tells us what the actor has done; to evaluate the behavior we need to understand why the actors has behaved in that way – not in the sense of what motivated the actor, but in the sense of what reasons the ideal actor must have had in mind when the actor decided what to do.

5.3 REASONING AND NORMATIVITY

Just as the authority of authority comes from either reason or coercion, the law's normativity – its ability to command obedience without sanctions – comes from either its coercive power or from its reasoning. When a legal dispute is settled by authority, it is accepted because legal authorities have the ability to force its acceptance, or it is accepted because the losing party understands the reasons the dispute was settled as it was. Even if a party does not accept the decision resolving the dispute, if the party accepts that the decision was reasoned in an acceptable way, the party is likely to act in accordance with the decision. Reasoning is a substitute for coercion.

Yet the relationship between legal reasoning and the reasoning people use to order their affairs when thinking about their obligations outside of legal authority is not well understood. A widespread belief is that legal reasoning is a distinctive form of reasoning, one that legal specialists use to resolve disputes. Under this view, the way people reason is one thing; the way people reason about legal authority is another. Legal reasoning is the realm of lawmakers and specialists, while the way people reason about their obligations is the realm of practical reasoning. Increasingly that view is contested, and the theory of other-regarding reasoning follows the view that the normativity of legal reasoning is closely related to the normativity of practical reasoning.

In *The End of Jurisprudence*, Scott Hershovitz explored the relationships between the normativity of law and the normativity of everyday understanding of our obligations in these terms:

> When we post rules or make promises, we are aiming to shape the norms that govern our lives. But we do not shape those norms by creating, out of whole cloth, new sorts of normativity or even quasi-normativity, unique to those activities. Rather, we shape those norms by shifting the social facts in ways that have moral or prudential consequences. If law is continuous with practices like posting rules and making promises, we might think that legal practices shape the norms that govern our lives in the same way.[3]

Although Hershovitz was contributing to jurisprudential debates about the nature of law, not to the difference between reason and doctrine, I interpret his view to support the view I develop in this book. If norms of promising shape social facts in ways that have moral or prudential consequences, as Hershovitz says, it is because people can reason about what social facts are relevant to the creation of obligations and why those social facts, and not others, are given the weight they are given. And if law's function is to settle disputes by authoritatively determining what social facts matter and how they matter, legal authority serves to endorse a method of reasoning that builds coherent guidance based on social facts that people put in play when determining their obligations. When people consider their obligations outside of legal authority, they identify the values (a form of social fact) that are relevant to their obligations; when legal authorities dispute their conclusions, legal authority is weighing those values in ways that persons do not always weigh them. As long as the normativity of a practice or of the law is based on reasoning, it is difficult to see why legal normativity should not "shape our lives in the same way."

That is the view that I implement in this book. The method of ideal reasoning that I portray here – the one that I believe the law implements – is a method of reasoning about one's obligations that people use in their relationships generally. It is a method that responds to the social construction of meaning in relation to particular contexts. Accordingly, it is a method that aligns legal normativity with the way people who would act morally would reason about what decisions they will make in response to the obligations of promising and contracting.

If that is correct, if legal normativity exists as an extension of general human reasoning about obligations, we can draw several tentative conclusions. That would explain why the way people act within contractual relationships, so-called law on the ground, appears to be different from the way they appear to act if we focus only on judicial opinions (law on the books). This is the topic discussed in Chapter 8 ("Relationality Redux"). It would also suggest that the Hartian good person and

[3] Hershovitz (2014–2015) at 1192.

the Holmesian bad person may present the wrong dichotomy. Perhaps the relevant distinction is between persons who can reason in the appropriate way about their obligations and those who are unable to. And, it suggests that the law's claim to obedience comes from the law's ability to successfully convey to those who act under the law the method of reasoning and values-balancing that it employs to determine obligations.

5.4 CONCLUSION

If, as I assert, reasoning *from* the authority, doctrine, or a contract's text and context hides too much of the reasoning that determines whether authority is interpreted one way or another, then we need a basis for reasoning *about* authority that allows us to reason by identifying, and reasoning from, the factors that determined the authority in the first place. This chapter has outlined a method of reasoning about the determinants of authority that I believe identifies the values that were balanced in order to arrive at the authority of doctrine and the contracts text. Although the details of this claim have yet to be discussed, it is important to recognize several claims that underlie the idea of values-balancing reasoning. First, the reasoning that I commend, what I have called ideal reasoning, is the kind of reasoning that determines how we want people to behave under the authority; we want people to behave as if they had reasoned in an ideal way. Second, reasoning about how to choose between two possibly ideal behaviors that implicate two sets of values is not different from ordinary reasoning about what we ought to do when faced with the authority of legal doctrine or contract text. The normative force of that reasoning comes from the reasoning itself, and not from any special form of legal reasoning that implicates a special kind of normativity. The ideal reasoning commanded by the law is the kind of reasoning that people do when they want to determine what is the right thing to do.

6

The Scope of Obligations

This chapter develops a methodology of reasoning that is both universal and contextual. Universality ensures that reasoning touches base with basic human values of the kind that are implied by reference to autonomy, consent, reliance, empowerment and efficiency, one that is capacious enough to encompass the wide variety of contexts in which promises matter. Contextuality accounts for the myriad of details that may influence, in particular situations, the implementation of any reasoning methodology.

The heart of the theory of values-balancing obligations is to provide a method of reasoning an actor ought to use to determine whether the actor should bear burdens in order to benefit another; that is what an other-regarding person does. The obligation to bear burdens arises only if an actor has an obligation to account for another's well-being. That is the obligation that I discuss in the next chapter; it is akin to the concept of duty in tort law. Such a duty, I claim, arises when a person makes a choice from which the obligation to be other-regarding can fairly be implied, including, of course, choices reflected in promissory and contractual commitments. In this chapter, I assume the existence of a duty to be other-regarding and elaborate on the requirements for other-regarding decisionmaking by examining the factors that ought to inform a person's decisions about her well-being in the context of the well-being of a person to whom she owes a duty.

6.1 OTHER-REGARDING BEHAVIOR

The common distinction between rational self-interest and altruism is inadequate, for it suggests a dichotomy between actors who think only of their own interests and actors who think only of other people's interest. This is a false dichotomy, for people are often simultaneously self-interested and other-regarding. It is often in an actor's self-interest to be other-regarding – that is, to take the interests of another into account when making decisions.[1] That is the underlying nature of cooperative

[1] Ronald Dworkin captured this thought by referring to the values of self-respect and other-respect. Dworkin (2011) at 306.

decisions. A good bargainer asks: How can I achieve my private projects by satisfying another person's private projects? That outlook requires and enhances a person's ability to understand her self-interest in terms of the interests of the other person, which means that people are often self-interested and other-regarding at the same time.

Such reasoning is a necessary part of promising because, under ordinary circumstances, the promisor is aware of the effect the promise will have on others. Because, as I argue in the next chapter, statements that might influence another's choices create a duty to others, that potential effect creates the obligation to reason about the effect in a way that takes into account the rational self-interest in being other-regarding. And that method of reasoning is what reveals the content of the promisor's obligations and the contextual details that determine the content.

Although the thought process of the other-regarding promisor can be complex (and disputed), the general idea is not difficult to understand; it pervades the law of contracts. Consider an old chestnut. [2]The defendant hired a contractor to paint her house; it is an enforceable contract with consideration. Sometime later, the defendant realizes that the painter is painting the house across the street, thinking that the house across the street is the one subject to the contract. She knows that he has made a mistake, and she has reason to believe that it is an excusable (reasonable) mistake. But she does not tell him of his mistake. Instead, she lets him paint the wrong house and, being under no obligation under her contract with the painter, refuses to pay him for his mistake. After all, he tried, but failed, to perform his contract to paint the defendant's house.

Under the conception of obligations presented here, she had a duty to the painter, one founded on her choice to hire him. Any other-regarding person in her position would know that she ought to tell him about his mistake because the burden he was taking on was far greater than the benefit to her (the benefit of not having to take the trouble to tell the painter of his mistake). In terms of value-balancing, once she formed the relationship with the painter, the value of her freedom not to get involved was far less than the value to him of not having wasted his time and resources. Any right-thinking person in her position would have recognized the unbalanced burdens and benefits of her action, and thus her duty to warn the painter of his mistake before he invested too many resources in it. That is the efficient result because the defendant, by investing few resources, can prevent a great deal of waste.

Looking at the case from the perspective of risk, one would ordinarily think that the painter bore the risk of painting the incorrect house; after all, painting the correct house determined the success of his private projects, and he controlled the risk by not making a mistake. Absent the contractual relationship, the defendant would have had no obligation to warn the painter of the mistake. But the contract changed the calculus; by committing to the relationship, the homeowner committed to the

[2] Scott & Leslie (1993) at 10.

painter and his private projects. Although the defendant's only obligation in the contract was to pay the painter for painting her house, the homeowner had an obligation to the relationship, which was to use the information she had for the painter's benefit. A contract signifies a level of commitment to the counterparty's private projects.

The obligation to account reasonably for the well-being of others does not imply any particular obligation. It implies only the obligation to reason appropriately about what obligations attach to their relationship. The promisor's obligation to consider the well-being of the promisee in light of the expectations she has created does not, by itself, mean that the promisor has a broad obligation to do any particular thing or to accept unbounded burdens. The promisor may reasonably conclude that the values that protect another's expectation are insufficiently strong to require anything of the promisor. Perhaps the promisor is entitled to think that any expectation of performance that the promisee has is unreasonable. When the promisee assesses her expectation in the same way as the promisor, both parties might understand that the expectation is easily defeasible and that it gives rise to no obligation. A statement of intent that is short of a promise often creates an expectation that both parties understand to be unenforceable. This conceptual separation between the obligation to think about the well-being of the counterparty, on the one hand, and the reasoning method one uses to determine the scope of obligations, on the other, is an important feature of a contextual account of promising. Because an obligation's existence is separate from the obligation's scope, a promisor's obligation can be fine-tuned to the circumstances of the promise and the parties' relationship. This separation preserves the idea that not all promises are alike and that the content of obligations may not be apparent from the face of a promise. As we will see in Chapter 14, the conceptual separation also allows appropriate remedies to be inferred from the circumstances of the promise. This allows the idea of promissory obligations to be multidimensional and to respond to contextual details. Naturally, a promise to have lunch next week creates the promisee's expectation, but it does not create the expectation that the promisor will perform under all circumstances. The expectation the promise creates may well be accompanied by the expectation that the plans can be revised under certain circumstances. Although this might excuse performance, the obligation of the promisor to think about the well-being of the promisee might still lead to the obligation to notify the promisee of the change in plans and to give the promisee the reasons for the change. What the other-regarding promisor promises is not a particular outcome but a way of reasoning morally about the content of the promise, and it is to that method of reasoning that we turn.

6.2 REASONING ABOUT ANOTHER'S WELL-BEING

Reasoning about obligations must apply general notions of fairness and right treatment to contextual details in a way that generates determinate answers, by which

I mean answers that either draw wide approval or that narrow the range of disagreements about how people ought to reason about their behavior. The method of reasoning must therefore enable a decisionmaker to identify the circumstances that she ought to account for under the appropriate moral principles and to determine what weight those circumstances ought to be given when making a decision. Further, in order to provide the neutrality that is the foundation of any system of fairness, the method of reasoning requires the decisionmaker to integrate the interests of the promisor and promisee in a way that each would find to be acceptable if they did not know which role they played in the relationship. This is no easy task, for the contextuality of promises reveals the plethora of relevant circumstances, while the generality of moral principles of fairness and justice makes it difficult to evaluate the moral relevance of the many contextual details. In this section I describe a method of moral reasoning that can bridge the gap between moral ways of acting and the contextual details of a promissory situation.

Immanuel Kant has shown us a way forward.[3] In the interpretation I advance, the Categorical Imperative suggests a method of reasoning that allows (and requires) a decisionmaker to move between the general and the particular under principles of moral interpersonal behavior. "Act only on that maxim whereby thou canst at the same time will that it should become a universal law" says Kant in the first manifestation of the Categorical Imperative.[4] Although it is sometimes thought that the Categorical Imperative requires a decisionmaker to reason in a way that results in a maxim that can be applied in all times and places, that view is, to me, inaccurate. When Kant writes about the need to adopt a maxim that one could will to be universal, he is referring to a maxim that one would accept no matter what position the person is in. Kant makes two demands on moral reasoning: first, that an actor behaves as if the actor had used a method of reasoning of a particular type to determine and evaluate the actor's behavior; and, second, that the method of reasoning that one adopts leads to a maxim that one would have others adopt under the same circumstances.

The first requirement – the requirement of reasoning – is the summation of Kant's theory of the will. Because humans have the unique ability to reason, the exercise of their will demands that reason be the basis of action and behavior. Kant does not specify the method of reasoning that is required; he specifies only the end of the reasoning – the development of the required maxim by which to guide behavior. Accordingly, Kant's interest is not in how people actually reason, only the fact that a person has acted as if the person had reasoned in the required way. The imperative in the Categorical Imperative is the imperative of behaving as if one had reasoned in the appropriate way. Whether one's actions are instinctual, habitual, or well thought-out, the requirement is to act as if one has first reasoned about what to do.

3 Gerhart (2014).
4 Immanuel Kant (1785).

Kant's objective was to provide the discipline of reason to human instincts, for human instincts may well reflect the evolutionary and biological needs for self-preservation that favor self over others.

Kant's second requirement reflects that anti-selfishness principle. Although Kant does not specify a method of reasoning, he does specify the ends of reasoning, which are to develop a maxim that one would wish to be universal. What he is looking for is a maxim that contains enough neutrality that one would accept to live under the maxim no matter what position the person was in.[5] That method of reasoning requires that the decisionmaker construe her own interests in the context of the interests of others, so that one acts only after determining that her interests are not given undue weight when deciding how to act. The actor must make difficult, other-regarding choices about whether to temper her interests in her own well-being in order to advance the well-being of another. This kind of interpersonal comparison requires an actor to determine, for example, whether her obligation to keep her promise outweighs the detrimental effect that breaking the promise would have on the promisee. Interestingly, the kind of neutrality of reasoning that Kant searched for was captured at almost the same time by Adam Smith in the person of the "impartial spectator."[6]

Daniel Markovits has expressed the same idea in more rigorous philosophical terms.[7] Kant's later iteration of the Categorical Imperative, known as the Formula of the End in Itself, or the Formula of Humanity, posits this requirement: "Act in such a way that you always treat humanity, whether in your own person or in the person of any other, never simply as a means but always at the same time as an end."[8] As Markovits explains, Kant had two distinct commands in mind:

> first, that one should never use persons merely as means; and, second, that one should always treat them as ends in themselves . . . . The principle that one should never use persons merely as means prohibits actions that follow principles or rules (Kant called them maxims) that could not possibly be accepted by the person whom the actions affect. The principle that one should always treat other persons as ends in themselves prohibits actions in pursuit of ends that the person whom they affect cannot share.[9]

5 The idea of a universal maxim has led some analysts to assume that a maxim derived under the Categorical Imperative must be broad and a-contextual – a maxim such as "always tell the truth no matter what." But a maxim can be universal and also contextual. The maxim could be "always tell the truth except when not telling the truth is necessary to save another person's life justly." Or a universal maxim could be even more contextual: "always tell the truth unless doing so would imperil a Jewish family that is being unjustly sought by the Gestapo."

6 Adam Smith (1758) at 16. For discussions of the implementation of moral sentiments to promising, *see, e.g.*, Note, (1999). Smith used the theory of moral sentiments to justify the enforcement of gratuitous promises between family members in LECTURES ON JURISPRUDENCE, Smith (1762–1763).

7 Markovits (2004) at 1423–1428.

8 Citing O'Neill (1989) at 112–113.

9 Markovits (2004) at 1424–1425. Here Markovits cites Korsgaard (1996) at 137–138.

These two principles, as Markovits explains, form the terms of engagement for the other-regarding method of reasoning. Using another person merely as an end is important because the other-regarding person, while understanding that promising is self-interested behavior, will also, and simultaneously, understand that promising must meet the ends of the promises recipient, treating that person as "not merely available" but also as persons with "independent intellects and wills."[10] The second principle signals that people ought not "act against others in pursuit of ends they cannot share"[11] because doing so acts against the very shared goals that promising seeks to achieve. One should make no commitments that do not take another's ends (private projects) into account and once one has made the commitment the other's ends restrain one's freedom of action.

These two principles of the Formula of Humanity provide constraints on reasoning about one's obligations; they describe what I call other-regarding reasoning. Although the principles do not, by themselves, provide a method of reasoning that responds to those constraints, two methods of reasoning about one's obligations serve to implement moral reasoning in a way that respects the Kantian constraints: the Rawlsian Veil of Ignorance and a modified Golden rule. Let us first understand each method of reasoning and then show how a person can implement them as a method of reasoning about the obligations of contracts.

The Veil of Ignorance is the method of reasoning adopted by John Rawls to develop a rule governing the distribution of resources and opportunities in society. I appropriate it here as a method of reasoning about one's obligations to others in an interpersonal setting. Veil of Ignorance reasoning requires an actor to reason about an appropriate rule of behavior for a particular context as if the actor did not know his status as either promisor or promisee. It forces the actor to determine what weight to give to various contextual factors when reasoning behind the Veil of Ignorance. The decisionmaker is required to rule out contextual factors that relate to the decisionmaker's status or private projects. A promisor is permitted to know the losses from keeping her promise and the circumstances of those losses, but not whether she will, in fact, suffer those losses. She knows the value of promise-keeping and the situation of the promisee but must develop a maxim governing her behavior without knowing whether she is the promisor or the promisee.

Alternatively, Kant's goals can be understood and implemented as a modified form of the Golden Rule, a precept that social scientists understand to be a foundation principle for virtually all cultures and religions. That precept is: do unto others as you would have them do unto you if you were in their position.[12] That is, adopt a method of reasoning that reflects how you would want to be treated if you were in the other person's position. This familiar idea of understanding another person's position by walking in their shoes helps ensure the kind of neutral

10 Markovits (2004) at 1425.
11 *Id.*
12 This formulation was suggested by Binmore (2005).

evaluation of relevant circumstances that defines the concept of fair treatment and results in action that would universally be understood to be acceptable.

Several characteristics of these methods of reasoning make the general idea tractable in the context of promising and contracting. First, neither method of reasoning necessarily quells debate about how an actor ought to act. Although many applications of these methodologies will draw wide approval, the methods of reasoning function to focus the terms of reasoning on discrete aspects of a relationship that give rise to obligations to act in one way rather than another. By allowing reasoning to focus on particular aspects of a relationship, these methodologies identify assumptions and worldviews that account for different positions on a disputed question. By allowing disagreements to be particularized, and by moving reasoning to a contextual level, they invite further thought about underlying assertions and assumptions. In that way, reasoning focuses on the precise issue that needs to be resolved. The general search for fairness or efficiency is changed into a particular question about what circumstances and values matter.

In essence, both the Veil of Ignorance and the Modified Golden Rulecall for a dialogical mental conversation between promisor and promisee about each person's perceptions of relevant contextual criteria that would lead to an outcome a neutral party would consider to be fair, a kind of internal Socratic process that can be carried out by an individual deciding how to act in light of a promise.[13] Interestingly, this same kind of dialogical process forms the basis of the adversarial system. The content of this dialogue focuses on the circumstances and values each person finds relevant and how they understand and evaluate the behavior of the other person in light of various ways in which a fairness norm could be implemented. Each would invoke concepts of fairness – a change of position, shared understandings of communicative norms, values revealed by social practices, the amount of harm, and the weight to be given to various kinds of harm – to argue about the fair way to treat others. This dialogical debate would result in a concept of fair dealing that would be both contextual and values-balancing, reflecting either shared values or a method of reasoning about how values ought to be structured and balanced.

Admittedly, interpersonal comparisons of well-being are difficult. But they are useful and inevitable; we make them every time we decide how to act in a relationship. If one actor wants to go to a hockey game and her partner, at the same time, wants to go to an opera, each partner ignores the well-being of the other partner at the risk of impairing the relationship. The actor and her partner can each do what they want, but if they find the relationship to be important they will consider

[13] Under this approach, fairness is not a concept that provides its own content. We cannot, in others words, start with a concept of fairness and reason about what fairness requires. Instead, the method of reasoning defines what we mean by fairness in particular contexts. The content of the idea of fairness is not the input into determining how people ought to act. The method of reasoning is the input into determined what we mean when we say that one person has treated another fairly.

the well-being of the partner (in order to support the well-being of the relationship). Reasoning about their obligations to the relationship by reasoning about the well-being of another makes interpersonal comparisons possible because it focuses reasoning on the weight that one ought to give to the well-being that is at stake in a relationship. And because a method of value-balancing reasoning focuses on values rather than interests, it facilitates impersonal comparisons. It focuses not on whether A's interests should be subordinated to B's interest, but on whether the values that A is advancing should be subordinated to the values that B is advancing.

Importantly, the well-being that is important to a theory of promises is the well-being that an exchange implicates. An exchange, when voluntary, enhances the well-being of both parties. That well-being is protected by values of autonomy in the form of freedom from obligations, freedom to rely on others, and freedom to choose relationships. And those values are what is being balanced when a person thinks about her obligations or when a legal decisionmaker makes a decision about her obligations. This is not a free-wheeling inquiry into how contract law can pick a party that deserves to be made better off. It is, instead, an inquiry into the terms of an exchange that imply how the parties must have ordered their individual claims to freedom from obligations, the freedom to rely, and freedom to choose relationships. Exchanges give the parties a reason to reason about their relationship in a neutral way that takes into account aspects of their individual autonomy.

Consider, also, how this method of reasoning understands the obligations of promising and contracting in light of bargaining power and information disparities. A methodology of reasoning from behind the Veil of Ignorance reacts to concerns about the imbalance of power between promisor and promisee. Exchange occurs even between people with disproportionate bargaining power. Because an actor's leverage reflects the actor's options prior to and outside of an exchange, a voluntary exchange of promises can occur whenever the promise makes a person better off than that person's next best option. Accordingly, the exchange is unlikely to distribute its contractual benefits equally, and the greater options of the party with options is likely to give that party disproportionate leverage over the counterparty. When one party exercises disproportionate leverage over the other, the actual or threatened breach of a promise can actually exacerbate the imbalance of power between the parties by making credible the demand for even more concessions Because the veil of ignorance requires a person with bargaining advantage to reason about how she would want to be treated if she were in the position of the promisee, the methodology constrains the use of bargaining power. The methodology takes the preexisting power imbalance into account and makes it easier to disables the promisor with bargaining power from threatening to walk away from an obligation in a way that amounts to the bad faith use of that bargaining power.

Veil of ignorance reasoning also provides insights concerning shared understandings and information that ought to be revealed as part of the exchange. Where both parties share social norms, the parties may assume that the promisee will define her well-being in a way that is congruent with how her counterparty would define his well-being. If the promisor and promisee have homogeneous worldviews, the parties will understand that Party A will define her loss of well-being from the absence of a promissory obligation in the same way as Party B would define it; the parties act as if they stood in the shoes of the other party. However, when Party A knows that Party B may not share the same worldview, the requirement that Party A stand in the shoes of Party B may require Party A to identify and deal with disparate assumptions that are shaping the exchange.

Because this method of reasoning requires an actor to put himself in the shoes of another, it requires an actor to consider the other's information base. Does the other share the actor's cultural norms and understandings, which makes it easier to predict how another will understand the exchange of promises? An actor is generally not required to take responsibility for the unknown and idiosyncratic understandings of another; in the absence of information to the contrary, an actor is permitted to assume that a person from the same cultural and social background and experience will have habits of thought that are similar to the actors. Under those circumstances, a person with unrecognizable idiosyncratic beliefs has the burden of making those beliefs known. But an actor who is obliged to look out for the well-being of another does have an obligation to reasonably observe signals that the other has idiosyncratic or mistaken beliefs. The other's different social or cultural background, unfamiliarity with the context, or the other's own communications, may provide the actor with enough information of possible discrepant understandings so that the actor ought to bear the burden of clarifying their understandings.

In other words, discrepant worldviews that might lead the parties to misunderstand each other puts pressure on each to consider whether a discrepancy might exist and to take steps to clear up the discrepancy. Whether the burden falls on the promisor or the promisee depends on the information base that each has and the ease with which that discrepancy can be identified and addressed. In instances in which the discrepancy is the fault of neither the promisor nor the promisee, the risk of the discrepancy must be allocated to the person who had the best chance of recognizing and addressing the discrepancy.

6.3 CONCLUSION

The many instances in which courts say that parties to a promise or contract must take an objective view of their obligations suggests a method of reasoning that allows the parties to escape the boundaries of their own self-interest and to see the situation as an objective, neutral observer would see it. This chapter has sought to describe such a method of reasoning. That method of reasoning depends on a view of the underlying obligation to consider the values that the other person represents, which I call the other-regarding perspective – a perspective that affirms that it is within rational self-interest to be interested in the well-being of others. Such a perspective is, I claim, the embodiment of the Kantian theory of the will, and the search for a method of thinking about others as ends, and not just as means. I then offer several perspectives on how such a method of reasoning can be undertaken, the Veil of Ignorance and a Modified Golden Rule, and describe the significant attributes of those methods of reasoning.

Key to this understanding of the determinants of obligations is the issue of whether a person owes any duty to take into account the well-being of the others. It is to that understanding that I turn now.

7

The Source of Obligations

The last chapter discussed the scope of one person's obligations to another by developing a methodology of reasoning when a person is under a duty to another. In this chapter, we explore the logically prior question of what circumstances give rise to obligations to others in the first place. The idea of duty or obligation serves as a kind of on/off switch that determines the existence of the obligation to care in the appropriate way about the well-being of another. The existence of the obligation (discussed here) serves to mark the boundary between duty and no-duty – identifying the point at which an actor is responsible for the well-being of another and distinguishing that point from the situation in which an actor is entitled to consider her interests only.

The source of moral and legal obligations is disputed. The conventional understanding is that contractual obligations come from assent (consent) to be bound, whereas in tort law obligations are imposed by law. That distinction has surface plausibility. Assent, the choice to be bound, occurs in many contract cases, which often involve hard bargaining, whereas in classical tort law, victims often had no relationship with the injurer, and thus no choice or opportunity to bargain. Yet the elegance of that distinction immediately calls to mind counterexamples. Many tort cases arise from the relationship between a seller and a buyer (or a seller and a distribution chain of buyers); retailers, hotel operators, doctors, landlords, and product sellers carry obligations imposed in the name of tort law, even though each relationship is, at its core, contractual, with the same opportunities to bargain that occur of contract law. On the other hand, many contractual obligations arise outside the terms of completed bargains and thus outside of traditional concepts of assent, including obligations arising in contractual negotiations, under the doctrine of promissory estoppel, and obligations in non-bargaining contexts, such as those formed through exchanges with standard terms. Perhaps it is time to challenge conventional distinctions between the source of obligations in contracts and torts by rethinking the idea of a legal obligation.

This chapter develops the idea that obligations, in both tort and contract, arise from identical sources – namely, from the natural implications of the choices people make. In tort law, people assent to obligations when their activity choices, including the choice to engage in relationships (which tort law calls special relationships) impose risks on others; in contract law, people make choices in the context of bargaining, but many obligations are implied by the assumptions people make that inform their choices rather than by the terms of the contract.

7.1 WHERE DO OBLIGATIONS COME FROM?

The idea that obligations in tort are imposed by law has a rich, but confused, pedigree. The idea begs the question of the grounds on which the law acts to "impose" an obligation. Justice Cardozo, for one, could not have been clearer. When a manufacturer markets an article that, if unreasonably made, imposes a risk on others, the manufacturer has an obligation to reasonably address the risk.[1] What Cardozo saw, but did not quite articulate, is that the source of the obligations is implied from the company's choice to put a product on the market; that choice, which is one of many the company could make, has natural implications for the care the manufacturer is obliged to take. Private, common law does not pluck an obligation out of the air and impose it; rather, private, common law understands obligations to be self-imposed, as a natural implication of the risks that arise from choices. The law says: when you made the choice to market an automobile, you also made the implied choice to take reasonable measures to ensure that people are not hurt by that choice. This concept is also deeply embedded in contract law: when you decide to be a baker you decide to take reasonable steps to make sure there is no pin in the bread you sell. This is not an obligation scooped out of the air, from skyhooks. It is an obligation that flows naturally from the way we interpret the burdens an actor has impliedly assumed in making the choice to sell automobiles or bread, and it is implied because of our construction of what it means to be an automobile manufacturer or baker. If you want no obligations to others, join a monastery.

Legal analysts need not mistake the functional for the formal, or resort to semantic distinctions.[2] If courts really were imposing duties, as opposed to determining the duties that are implied from choices that people make, there would be no limit to what they could ask actors to do to protect others. Private law would be set free to solve the problems of the world. But courts do not create duties out of whole cloth, nor do they decide, the way a legislature might, which duties would promote the common good. Common law courts decide disputes and their decisions about the existence of duties are grounded in choices that people make. We can trace the concept of duty back to the choices that a party to the dispute made, which

[1] *MacPherson* v. *Buick Motor Co.*, 217 N.Y. 382 (1916).
[2] Dworkin (1986).

makes the choice people act on the unit of analysis in the law. Autonomy provides a person with the right to make self-defining choices; it also gives the person responsibility for accepting the natural consequences of those choices.

The common law recognizes choices as the source of obligations by recognizing the distinction between no-duty and duty. An actor has no duty to rescue another from a risk the actor did not create unless the actor has chosen a special relationship with the victim.[3] This no-duty concept embodies the notion that unless an actor makes a choice that implicates the well-being of another, the actor has no obligation to the other. It would be unjust, or so it is thought, to give the person who needs to be rescued a legal claim against a putative rescuer simply because the putative rescue could prevent harm. As one court colorfully put it, a person is allowed to sit on a bench, smoke a cigar, and watch another person drown as long as the cigar smoker was not implicated in the drowning person's predicament. The actor, having made no decision from which an obligation to rescue can fairly be implied, is under no duty to reasonably attempt a rescue. On the other hand, once an actor decides to start a rescue, and does start the rescue, that actor is under an obligation to take reasonable steps to complete the rescue. No obligation exists until a person has acted on a choice that fairly implies the obligation to take into account the well-being of others. This no-duty principle forms the bedrock of tort law, finding expression in the idea that tort law imposes no duty of easy rescue, which itself is the expression of the idea that in the absence of a special relationship a person has no duty to confer a benefit on another. In contract law, the no-duty principle reinforces the freedom *from* contract, the idea that promissory obligations are freely consented to by the decisions that a person has acted upon. Obligations to others do not arise unless a person makes a decision that naturally implies the assent of the person to be bound.[4]

Although the no-duty concept is most prominent in tort law, we can see the principle at work in contract law. In fact, the no-duty principle illuminates one of the most perplexing cases in the contract canon, *Mills* v. *Wyman*.[5] When a young man,

3 As to tort law, *see* Gerhart (2010) at 105–125.

4 Some, perhaps most, tort scholars believe that the duty to act reasonably, is imposed by the law, not chosen by the person to be bound. They would give legal decisionmakers free range to create duties and to move the boundary between duty and no-duty based on some vague notions of public policy. It is true, of course, that courts recognize duties and determine the circumstances under which duties arise; that is not the issue. The issue is the grounds on which courts recognize duties. When courts recognize obligations based on choices an actor has made, their recognition is grounded in matters an actor can control. This is a far cry from the image of decisionmakers who determine independently the choices an actor should have made, The Restatement (Third) of Torts is quite explicit. Duties to others exist for a person who has created a risk or one who stands in a special relationship with a person facing a risk. Under this conception of duty, actors assent to the duty to others when they create a risk, which is a voluntary, not a mandatory or law-created decision, as well as when they have a special relationship with another person, which is also an act of assent rather than freestanding legal compulsion.

5 20 Mass. 207 (1825).

aged twenty-five, returned from a sea voyage he became ill and was cared for by the plaintiff until he died. When the plaintiff wrote to the young man's father to inform him of the death, the father wrote back promising to compensate the plaintiff for his expenses. Later, the father changed his mind, and the plaintiff sued on the promise. The Supreme Court of Massachusetts framed the question of the adequacy of consideration for the promise: the plaintiff's aid had been gratuitous, the father had not asked for the aid, and the father's promise to compensate the plaintiff came after plaintiff paid the expenses. The court found that because no consideration had been given for the promise, the promise was unenforceable.

The court framed its discussion in terms of consideration; but its opinion is resonant with the common law conception of duty as something voluntarily assumed from the decisions a person makes. The son, aged twenty-five had "long since left his father's family,"[6] and "was in no respect under the care of the" father, which meant that the father had no duty to the young man.[7] There must, according to the court, be "some preexisting obligation, which has become operative by reason of positive law, to form the basis of an effective promise."[8]

In other words, the finding of no consideration reflected the no-duty principle. It would have been easy enough for the court to hold that the father had a duty to care for his son, but the idea that private law imposed only a restricted set of obligations kept the court from finding consideration. Moreover, the no-duty principle that underlies *Wyman* was in keeping with the temper of the times. It was accepted that a stranger who saw a baby lying on railroad tracks had no obligation to rescue the baby, even if a train was speeding toward the baby. The value of freedom from the claims of other people – what the court in *Wyman* referred to as the "[g]eneral rules of law established for the protection and security of honest and fair-minded [people]" – kept the court from finding consideration.

The line between no-duty and duty has shifted over time and that shift helps explain shifts in both tort and contract doctrine. In tort law the "special relationships" that give rise to duties to others are, in the main, contractual relationships in which one party depends on the other party to be reasonable: landlord–tenant, common carrier–passenger, and so on. The decision to enter into such a relationship is the decision that courts recognize as the source of the duty to take into account the well-being of others. In contract terms the duty is an implied term of the implicit contract involved in what tort law calls the "special relationship." Similarly, the obligations of sellers of products implies a duty to others, a duty that is expressed in tort law through doctrines of product liability and in a warranty action.

6 The court was aware of cases in which such a promise had been enforced because the child, being underage, was still under the care of the father. Plaintiff's counsel cited *Andover & Turnpike Corp.* v. *Gould*, 6 Mass. 40; *Andover* v. *Salem*, 3 Mass 438 and *Davenport* v. *Mason* 15 Mass. 94 for the proposition that a promise to pay for a minor child's expenses is enforceable.

7 *Id.* at 209.

8 *Id.*

The perception that obligations to others can be implied from decisions to enter into relationships sheds new light on another otherwise-puzzling case: *Webb v. McGowin*.[9] There, an employee, while at work, suffered injuries when he risked his own safety to protect his employer from injury. The employer, in his gratitude, promised to pay the employee a pension for life. At first glance, the promise would appear to be gratuitous and without consideration. The employee's act of rescue was complete at the time the employer made his promise. And the employment contract was silent on the obligation of the employee to rescue the employer. Yet, the court enforced the contract, saying that the moral obligation to prevent injury to the employer was sufficient to establish duty that supported consideration to make the promise to pay the pension enforceable. In the context of the employee/employer relationship, the implied reciprocal obligations of the employer and employee were sufficient to make the promise enforceable. If the employment contract had read: "if you, the employee, exert extra effort on my behalf I, the employer, will pay you a pension for life" the agreement would have been enforceable. Although no express term created that obligation in *McGowin*, it is not hard to see how the obligations stemming from employer/employee relationship contained the implied term that the employer would fulfill a promise to compensate the employee for extra effort.

Let me summarize the role that the no-duty principle plays in contract law. Once a contract is formed, the concept of obligation to attend to the well-being of another is clearly operational and legal decisionmakers move on to consider the scope of the obligations. As a result, when there is a traditional exchange of promises, the idea of one person's obligation to look out for the well-being of another is not prominent in contract law. But under the no-duty concept, a person cannot be bound by a promise unless the promise reflects a decision from which the obligation to be other-regarding can fairly be implied. The duty arises from the promisor's decision to make a commitment that implies the obligation to look out for the well-being of the person to whom the promise was made.

7.2 DUTY IN CONTRACT

The no-duty role finds expression, of course, in the idea that no person can claim that another must negotiate or bargain with her, and in the idea that no person can claim that the failure of negotiations is the source of responsibility (even if the promises implied during the negotiations can be the source of obligations). Until reasonable actors would understand that bargaining is going on, no actor has acted on a decision that would fairly imply the obligation to look out for the well-being of another. Yet once bargaining has begun and has been acknowledged by the parties' words or conduct, each party, by its conduct, takes on the obligations that adhere during contract formation. Duty attaches to bargaining as soon as bargaining has

[9] 232 Ala. 374 (1935).

been acknowledged by both parties through word or conduct. It attaches at the point where communications between the parties indicate that each is relying on the other to look out for one another's well-being.

During negotiations, before a bargain is made, the scope of one party's obligation to another is implied by, and flows from, the decision to negotiate. The duty is to avoid action that others would find to be misleading or deceptive, and to avoid action that would materially burden another party if a contract is not formed. But once the negotiations ripen into a promise, the situation changes. Because a promise, if it exists, is a promise to someone to do something, promises have the character of relationality, self-directedness, and contextuality that are characteristic of any potential contractual relationship.

The reciprocal bilateral nature of promises means that traditional approaches to the obligations created by promising are inadequate. The decision to make a promise to someone is the decision to undertake an obligation to attend to the well-being of the promisee as a way of honoring the relationship. The obligations of promising depends on the promisee's reaction. Yet, the reliance must be justified, which implicates the nature of the promise and the social construction of the promise's meaning.[10] The promisee's expectations do not create a duty, for expectations do not create obligations for the promisor, or, equivalently, entitlements for the promisee. People frequently create expectations in others that create neither promisor obligations nor promisee entitlements.[11] The promise may be contingent. Or, it may be the kind of promise that is understood to be subject to revision, and is therefore subject to implied contingencies. A promise between social friends is not enforceable because it is known, as a matter of social practices, to be subject to revision for acceptable reasons. Under some circumstances a promisee's expectations are known by the promisee to be subject to revision by the promisor for reasons the promisee will understand.

The mystery of promising, then, is to determine what turns an expectation, even a contingent one, into the promisee's moral or legal entitlement that the promisor will take the promisee's well-being into account when acting on that promise.[12] The reciprocal, bilateral nature of promising suggests that obligations from promising arise from the perception of two people to two variables: the promisor's credible commitment and the promisee's change in her position. Without the credible promisor's commitment, the promisee's reliance cannot be justifiable, but without the change in position of the promisee, the credible commitment can be revised. The promisor must take into account the meaning attributed to her promise by the

10 Fuller & Perdue (1936) at 46.

11 Moreover, not every promise-like expression or action creates an expectation in the promisee. Some expressions are understood to be mere statements of present intention that can be revised; these are not statements from which expectations can be formed. Such statements create no expectations because both the promisor and the promisee know that the expressions will have no impact on the listener.

12 *See* John Finnis, (1980) at 304 ("For the making of a promise creates a new criterion of impartiality, relative to the person concerned and the subject matter of the promise.")

promisee, and the promisee must take into account the meaning attributed to the promise by the promisor. Whenthe promisor and the promisee understand the meaning and implications of a promise in the same way, no dispute arises about the existence of an obligation. That is why a promise to have lunch with a social friend the following week can be understood to be revocable as long as the promisor gives timely notice for a good reason. With such notice (and a common understanding of the social meaning of the promise), the promisee will accept the revocation without feeling slighted.

When the promisor and promisee have no shared understanding of the meaning and implications of a promise, the obligations that flow from promising must be determined by which party has the more reasonable understanding of the meaning and implications of the promise. The reasonableness criterion captures the bilateral, reciprocal nature of promising because it suggests that objective meaning – the meaning that one would attribute to words if one were thinking about the meaning from the perspective of the impartial observer – would be the meaning that an actor ought to attribute to the promise. The reasonableness criterion is contextual. It is ascertainable by reference to social practices, and it is values-balancing because if social practice does not reflect the correct balance of values between a promisor and a promisee, the practice can evolve toward a new equilibrium through law or social interaction.

No obligation obtains if the parties ought to understand that the promise is revocable without notice. But obligations do obtain if both parties understand that a revocation is contingent on the promisee's reaction to the promise. Because the theory of values-balancing legal reasoning takes an actor's decision as the unit of analysis, it makes sense to consider the effect of a promise on the offeree's decision-making process. After all, there is value in protecting the promisee's decisionmaking autonomy and if the promise rearranges the factors that influence the exercise of that autonomy, protecting the promisee's autonomy is value-producing.

In the view I offer, reliance takes the form of the harm that can flow when the promisor alters the promisee's decision space.[13] An actor's decision space encompasses the factors an actor is likely to take into account when deciding what to do with her life. It is made up of the decisionmaker's options and the factors that the decisionmaker is likely to use to decide between options. The promisee must make decisions about how to conduct her life, and the information conveyed by the promise may narrow the space within which she makes those decisions. A promise to have lunch next week alters the promisee's decision space by inducing her to leave

[13] Ronald Dworkin has captured the same thought by referring to the promisee's changed "information base." Dworkin (2011), at 306. Because of the promise, the promisee is working with new information about what the future will hold. I extend this idea to emphasize the impact that the revised information base has on the promisee's decisions, an extension that reinforces the idea that the unit of analysis in law is the decisions people make. The major point is not only that the values-balancing promisee has a revised information base; what matters is that the promisee uses that information to make decisions, which is why the emphasis on decision space is important.

open the time for the planned luncheon and to restrict voluntarily her decisions about how she uses that time. A promise to sell a house alters the promisee's decision space by allowing the promisee to begin to plan where the furniture in the new house will go, to plan improvements, and to think about getting to know her neighbors. The promisee's patterns of life are altered, as is the way she thinks about her world.

Protecting the promisee's decision space is important because the decision space defines the scope of the promisee's autonomy. A person with many options has a great deal of autonomy. As the options are reduced (even if reduced voluntarily), the decision space is narrowed. Protecting that decision space when another intentionally intervenes to influence the decision space is an important protection of autonomy. The point, of course, is not that the protection is always given, or even that affecting another decision space implies the nature of the resulting obligations; questions of the scope of the obligation come after we know that an obligation exists. But the alteration of the promisee's decision space is the aspect of the promisee's well-being that the promisor must account for when the promisor decides how to reason about her obligations. The argument is this: the promisor's appraisal of how the promisee's decision space is altered allows the promisor to reason about her obligations under the promise. Sometimes that means that the promise must be kept, of course; this occurs when the promisee's decision space is especially and irretrievably restricted. But at other times it may mean that the promisor must notify the promisee if the promise cannot be kept. The implications of the promise depend on the reasoning that a promisor ought to use to determine her behavior in light of the reduced decision space that she has created and the relative weight of the well-being of the promisor and promisee.

Naturally, the extent to which a commitment alters the promisee's decision space, and the promisor's perception of that alteration, depend on the commitment conveyed by the promise. A promisee, if reasonable, would not change her decision space on the basis of a promise that was not a credible basis for reducing her decision space. Under this reading of promissory obligations, a promise gives rise to obligations if it materially changes the decision space of the promisor and the promisee, but not otherwise.

7.3 CONCLUSION

The source of legal obligations is disputed. Legal obligations are recognized by law, of course, but we need to know the basis on which the law recognizes obligations. Under the view presented here, obligations are implied by the decisions a person has made and are therefore self-imposed in the sense that obligations flow from a person's will. Promises can be the source of obligations to others because the decision to make a promise implies the obligation to think about the well-being of the person to whom the promise is directed. Yet obligations to someone imply a connection between promisor and promisee over the shared meaning implied by the promise, for without a shared meaning no obligations can arise. In order to determine whether the meaning of a promise is shared, it is helpful to consider whether the promise affects the decision space of both the promisor and the promisee. When a promise changes the decision space of the promisor and promisee, the promise has affected the future fortunes of the two parties in a way that is significant enough to trigger the bilateral obligation to attend to the well-being of the other party in a reasonable way.

8

Relationality Redux

Law on the Ground and Law on the Books

When, in 1963, Stewart Macaulay published his study of contract relations between business people in Wisconsin, he identified a fissure between law on the books and law on the ground. Law on the books specifies an authoritative set of rules and methodologies for determining the obligations that are grounded in promising. But law on the ground, the study of how contracting parties interact, made it appear that business people were using a different set of normative understandings, one that was far more flexible and far less rule-bound. That led to the possibility that contracting parties viewed their obligations to be different than contract law would view them. That, in turn, cast doubt on the normative role that contract law plays. But any normative divergence is an illusion. As I will argue in this chapter, we can understand the distinction between law on the books and law on the ground to reflect the success or failure of understanding relationships through other-regarding, values-balancing reasoning.

In his study, Professor Macaulay determined that contracting parties acted as if neither the contract nor contract law determined their obligations or their behavior. He documented what business people thought they ought to do when things do not go as the parties anticipated ex ante. Contracting parties acted as if what matters is the relationship, not the contractual or legal authority governing the relationship. Hence, contracting parties routinely overlooked contractual breaches, modified their obligations, and took on burdens not allocated to them under the contract.

These findings were not meant to, and did not, diminish the importance of the contract or of legal authority; the private resolution of disputes, although an alternative to formal dispute resolution, is done in the shadow of formal dispute resolution. But Macaulay's findings did seem to create a distinction between the normativity of promising and the normativity of legal obligations. Because I claim that the normativity of law reflects the normativity of how people reason about authority, it is worth exploring the relationship between law on the ground and law on the books to see if that relationship supports my claim about the identity of social and legal norms.

8.1 SUCCESSFUL AND UNSUCCESSFUL RELATIONSHIPS

The seemingly disparate accounts of promissory normativity Macaulay uncovered can be reconciled by recognizing that Professor Macaulay's study involved successful relationships, while the law addresses failed relationships, ones that arise because the parties could not successfully address their disagreements without a neutral, third-party decisionmaker. Given the relationality of bargaining and contracting, it does not surprise us that the private self-directed goals of one party sometimes diverge from the other party's view of contractual obligations. After the parties have signed a contract, the world is likely to change from what the parties anticipated. Those changes require, as Professor Macaulay documented, accommodation and flexibility if the relationship is to be maintained.[1] Such accommodation and flexibility signal an other-regarding, successful relationship.

Nor should it surprise us that potential disputes will increase over time as each party faces new options; any relationship will is likely to encounter potential disputes as circumstances change (and Professor Macaulay's research suggested that things rarely go as planned ex ante). Nor should it surprise us that sometimes the potential disputes are so great that the relationship formed by the contract is so imperiled that the parties will seek an independent assessment of the obligations required to wind down the relationship.

Accordingly, it would not surprise us that the dynamics of successful relationships (ones in which parties work out potential disagreements) seem to display a form of reasoning about obligations that is not present when the parties are unable to reconcile divergent private projects. Nor should it surprise us that when parties cannot reason about flexible accommodations, contracting parties will seek a neutral specification of their rights and obligations. This is but a ramification of the observation that legal systems operate to account for both the Holmesian bad man and the Hartian good man.[2] As Holmes said, if we want to know what law is, simply ask a person who does not want to be bound by the law; that person would ask about the probability of being punished and the amount of the punishment.[3] That view – the view that law is about sanctions – is different from the Hartian image, which is that law tells people who want to be law-abiding what to do because of the normative guidance it gives (without regard to the punishment for disobeying legal norms).[4] The law serves both those who would be good and those who would not, making both good and bad internal motivations a basis for understanding what law is.

But the facile difference between relationships that we can call successful and those that we call unsuccessful begs the question of why some relationships succeed while others fail. The importance of Professor Macaulay's study was to recognize

[1] Braucher (2012) at 667 (advocating a morality of adjustment, release, and forgiveness).

[2] Stone (2016) (explaining different economic perspectives on contract from the external (Holmesian) and internal (Hartian) point of view).

[3] Holmes (1897) at 461.

[4] Hart (1994) at 57, 88–91, 102.

that relationships are a social institution that can continue or end, and that we ought, therefore, to study both the relationships that are successfully completed and ones that unravel. When we evaluate relationships through the lens of success or failure, we see that both relational categories depend on the way individuals in the relationship respond to the well-being of the other party. Other-regarding reasoning explains relationships as an institution, whether they are successful (as accounted for by law on the ground) or unsuccessful (as accounted for by law on the books).

This is not to say that unsuccessful relationships necessarily reflect the faulty reasoning of one of the parties. Perhaps the parties should never have formed a relationship; perhaps ex post circumstances make the relationship unworkable, or perhaps further bargaining becomes fruitless in the face of self-directed aims. The parties must determine how to unwind the relationship (even if only at the bargaining stages), and settle accounts (as it were), which means that each party must consider its other-regarding obligations, given the relationships terms and context. The parties can adjust the relationship by settling accounts in a way that accommodates the legitimate values that both parties advance (and therefore settles disagreements) or the parties can advance claims lead to disagreement over the distribution of the costs of ending the relationship. That too depends on a method of reasoning about obligations in light of the terms of the contract and the changing external environment that affects the relationality.

Professor Macaulay's study also suggests that we ought to think of contracts and relationships as related but distinct institutional frameworks. A contract with well-specified terms is one way by which the parties can attempt to lock-in the burdens and benefits of the relationship. The legal enforceability of the contract terms assure the parties that those terms will be respected as circumstances change. But legal enforcement, and the threat of legal enforcement, are not the only way (or even the best way) of addressing relational tensions.[5] Relational burdens and benefits are not static, and they are often not ascertainable until the parties work together to build trust. While some scholars view the process of contracting to function to protect against opportunism and shading, others see the process of contracting to be to build cooperative systems that reinforce joint goals and commitments and build the trust and flexibility that enhances continuing relationships. For some, contracting is designed to preclude bad behavior; for others contracting is designed to encourage cooperative behavior.[6]

5 Schilke & Lumineau (2018) (alliance contracts that seek to control counterparty performance are less successful than alliance contracts that require continuing coordination between the parties); Gil & Marion (2013) (unspecified obligations can allow for self-enforcing obligations held together by the "continuation value" of the relationship).

6 Consider the implications of this insight for how parties structure negotiations. Scholars now recognize that "companies have traditionally used contracts as protection against the possibility that one party will abuse its power to extract benefits at the expense of the other." but that these "protections may foster negative behaviors that undermine the relationship and the contract itself." Those scholars

By viewing relationship as an institution of cooperation in joint objectives, Professor Macaulay recognized that relationships generate a framework for accommodating the interest of the other party and that the underlying reasons for the collaboration induce one or both parties to sacrifice their private projects to accommodate the private projects of the other party, even beyond what the contract requires. The parties accommodate the relationship, not the contract. As Professor Macaulay wrote two decades after his study:

> Even discrete transactions take place within a setting of continuing relationships and interdependence. The value of these relationships means that all involved must work to satisfy each other. Potential disputes are suppressed, ignored, or compromised in the service of keeping the relationship alive. That is possible only if both parties are able to integrate the needs of the other party in with their own private projects.[7]

Private dispute resolution, in other words, is a central characteristic of a successful relationship. When Professor Macaulay says that "all must work to satisfy the needs of the other" he signifies, as he says, that each party must continually balance its private projects with the needs of the collaboration. Private dispute resolution depends on a way of thinking about the relationship as an institution that pulls people together by reasoning about the reasons for the collaboration, without standing on the ceremony of contractual or doctrinal authority.

One impact of this insight is to realize that contract doctrine is organized around the circumstances that give rise to unsuccessful relationships. We have doctrine to address many contingencies: bargaining that begins but breaks down (offer and acceptance); when one party had made relationship specific investments but the bargaining does not result in a contract (one application of promissory estoppel), relationships that fail because of mutual mistakes (the mistake doctrine); contractual relationships where the breakdown comes because the words used in the contract mean different things to the two parties (contract interpretation), or where the interpretation appears to amount to cutting corners and failing to deliver promised benefits in order to minimize costs (shirking, opportunism, and lack of good faith); or instances in which the implicit assumptions of the contract turn out to be wrong (impossibility, frustration, and impracticality); and relationships in which one party finds a more beneficial alternative and wants to terminate the relationship.

The inference from Macaulay's study is that parties whose relationship is threatened for one of these reasons find ways to accommodate, through values-balancing reasoning, the other's interest in ways that settle disputes about the rights and obligations of two parties in an unsuccessful relationship. This is not to say that Macaulay showed that all potential disputes are settled in a way that legal sources

believe that negotiations may be better structured so that each company has a vested interest in each other's success." *See* Frydlinger, Hart, & Vitasek (2019) at 5–7.

7 Macaulay (1985) at 468.

would settle them. The decisions to settle potential disputes may reflect the preoccupation of the parties in the potential dispute with avoiding third party dispute resolution because of expense, uncertainty, and the desire to get problems behind them. But it does mean that people in a relationship often think about their options through other-regarding reasoning about how to accommodate the reasonable needs of others in the relationship.

Moreover, it suggests, as I have argued, that legal normativity – the normativity of contract law – may not be distinct from the normativity of how people reason about their obligations when they address relational disputes. Each of the contract doctrines that help parties address unsuccessful relationships provides a set of doctrines and methodologies by which a neutral arbiter can, if the rules are correctly implemented, authoritatively resolve disputes by determining the rights and obligations of the parties based on how the parties should have reasoned about their differences. If I am right that satisfactory implementation of the rules requires a method of reasoning about the determinants of the rules, then contract doctrine reflects the failure to reason appropriately in the context of a relationship.

In other words, we might surmise that disputes that are not addressed by private dispute resolution end up with a neutral decisionmaker precisely because one of the parties has not thought about its obligations to the relationship in a way that will satisfy the relationship. If a party who finds herself in circumstances that induce her to withdraw from a relationship, and the party inquires about burdens their withdrawal puts on the other party, they are thinking about the burdens and benefits of the bargaining relationship in an other-regarding way. Can they rely on any other method for resolving the dispute?

That is why this book starts by saying that at its core contract law requires the parties to act as they would if they thought reasonably about their obligations to the relationship. That is the method of reasoning that adjusts rights and obligations of a relationship in the context of a dispute over what obligations promising and contracting imply.

8.2 MOTIVATIONS, INCENTIVES, AND TRUST

The post-Macaulay literature reveals a great deal about what motivates other-regarding behavior and the role of trust in determining relationships. Not surprisingly, the literature is divided about whether the law serves the Hartian good man (tell me the norm you want me to follow) or the Holmesian bad man (tell me the punishment and the chance of getting caught). For some, the motivation for other-regarding reasoning is an inner compunction to do the normatively correct behavior; that motivation for other-regarding reasoning corresponds to the Hartian good man.[8]

[8] Indeed, the 2019 Nobel Prize in Economics was awarded to two economists who have explored nonfinancial incentives as the motivation for behavior. Duflo & Banerjee (2019).

For others, corresponding to the Holmesian bad man, the motivation for other-regarding behavior is the threat of social or legal sanctions. Upon analysis, these two forms of cooperative motivation both seem to be grounded in other-regarding reasoning.

Macaulay himself thought that the motivation for being other-regarding was an internal compulsion for doing the right thing. He reported two norms that seem to be followed by contracting parties that would explain why law on the ground exhibits flexibilities and adjustments to contextual realities and relational dynamics. As he wrote, contracting parties acted is if two norms mattered:

> (1) Commitments are to be honored in almost all situations; one does not welch on a deal; and (2) one ought to produce a good product and stand behind it.[9]

These norms are explicitly other-regarding. They are norms which allow a person to feel good about herself because her self-interest is identified by the effects of her decisions on others. This motivation can be understood in noninstrumental terms; it is the desire to think well of oneself by knowing that one has done well by another person in the relationship. Notice that when a contracting party inquires about local customs and practices, the inquiry need not be because the person is concerned about external reputational sanctions. It could be because that person has an inner compunction to do the right thing, and looks to social norms to determine what that is. Sanctions for violating norms can be internally, not externally imposed. For others, the motivation for cooperation is to avoid social sanctions that might be exerted through shunning or reputational damages. The loss of potential future business provides a powerful incentive for thinking about how other people are going to react to certain behavior. A reputation for chiseling can impose great harm on bargaining and raise the cost of contracting. Even a person who is a one-time player in the market, and therefore immune from social sanctions – a chiseler who will leave for a new market – needs to know how to chisel in a way that minimizes and risks of being apprehended and punished. That too requires other-regarding reasoning. The idea behind reputational sanctions is that reputations rise or fall on the strength of social perceptions about the values that a party follows when making decisions. Accordingly, social sanctions are driven by social perceptions about whether a promisor is sufficiently other-regarding, and that, in turn, implies that people outside the relationship are themselves other-regarding enough to recognize the shortcomings in another's behavior.[10]

[9] Macaulay (1963) at 63. Professor Macaulay also referred to these norms as the source of "non-legal social sanctions." *Id.* It is important to recognize, as the text does, that these norms are self-generated, not socially generated. They reflect an internal, not an external, compulsion. They may be the source of regret that social sanctions play upon, but they are not generated by external social sanctions.

[10] Experimental economists explore the motivations for keeping promises in Mischkowsky, Stone, & Stremitzer (2019).

A person who would obey the law has motivations for cooperation that reflect the ability to act as if they were other-regarding because that makes the person feel good, and that person knows how other people will reward that behavior and punish other behavior. The person who needs to know the social sanction for violating social norms needs to know the basis on which the social sanction is imposed, which occurs only if others think that the person was not sufficiently other-regarding. And for the intentional shirker who is immune from social sanctions, that person needs to know the chance of getting caught and prosecuted, which also requires an assessment of how far the person can deviate from the socially accepted form of other-regarding reasoning.

Not surprisingly, trust plays a large role in understanding the relationality of promising and contracting. Trust allows parties to take risks they would otherwise not take, which reduces the cost of relationships and allows the parties to design relationships in which the parties address contingencies as they arise. Yet trust implies the ability to predict what someone else will do, which implicates the ability to reason about how a counterparty will reason. The literature on trust focuses on the determinants of trust, suggesting that trust can be nurtured by repeat dealings, by shared expectations, and by routinized operations.[11] Trust can also be advanced by private governance structures that facilitate open-ended relationships through transparency and mutual oversight. The determinants of trust seem not to be in dispute.

What is of interest, however, is to identify the reasoning that underlies those trust determinants. We accept the conclusion that repeat dealings lead to trust, but what characteristics of repeat dealings have a positive impact on trust? We accept that shared expectations help to create trust, but how are shared expectations created and what happens to trust when expectations change? And we accept that routinized operations increase trust, but what characteristics make routinized operations a source of trust, and how can those be maintained, especially when relationships move beyond routinized operations? When one examines these kinds of questions, it is difficult to escape the conclusion that trust is a reflection of other-regarding reasoning.

Repeat dealings allow a person to predict how their counterparty will react in certain situations, which is to understand how that person makes choices. A party trusts a counterparty when the party can accurately understand its private projects in the context of how the counterparty will view *its* private projects. I trust you if I have a basis for predicting how you will view your private projects in the context of a relationship, including my private projects. Such predictability is created by understanding, through repeated interaction, how you implement (and thus display) your value system in various contexts. If I have experience about how you view your obligations in the context of potential differences in our private objectives, I know a great deal about what to expect in the future.

[11] Bernstein (2016); Connelly, Crook, Combs, Ketchen, & Aguinis (2018).

That does not guarantee, of course, that a counterparty will act on the basis of values that determined the person's behavior in the past, but it does help a person predict a counterparty's future action in similar situations and also to identify situations in which past dealings are not a good predictor of future behavior. A person who monitors another's behavior in light of the value system that influences a counterparty's decisions can identify situations in which trust may not be enough to guarantee that the relationship will be successful without a costly monitoring mechanism.

Similarly, shared expectations reflect a common way of understanding one's obligations in the context of another person's private projects. Shared expectations arise because both parties approach their common project with a set of values that allow them to be confident in how the parties are going to address the needs of the relationship and make some sacrifice of their private projects. When a contract term is specific, it expresses a shared expectation about what will happen at the time of a specific contingency. But shared expectations also govern contingencies that the contract does not address. Shared expectations go beyond those expressed by the terms of the contract and also address contingencies that arise during the performance of the contract that are not addressed by the contract. In those circumstances, shared expectations may not be about what the parties will do in a certain situation; if the shared expectations were known they would have been written down. Instead, the shared expectations are about how the parties will reason about their obligations when unaddressed contingencies arise.

Routinized operations create a basis for determining how the contracting parties should view their obligations if one party deviates from the routine. But even aside from the legal enforcement of obligations based on course of dealings, routinized obligations are derived from a basis for reasoning about one's obligations, and therefore display a form of reasoning that ought to govern future relationships. The fact that routines are developed implies that the method of reasoning each party used to establish the routine is the method of reasoning that ought to govern the obligations that are sufficiently like the obligations displayed in the routine.

Each of these mechanisms for developing trust point to the importance of expectations about what a partner will do by learning from and anticipating how a partner is going to reason about what to do. Consider the definition of trust as: "the expectation that both actors will behave in a mutually acceptable manner, including an expectation that neither party will exploit the other's vulnerabilities."[12] That too implies that trust depends on a way of reasoning about what another person is likely to do, which depends on a method of reasoning about what another person is going to reason about what they ought to do.

In other words, it seems as if people in successful, trust-building relationships develop a method of cooperative reasoning that allows each person to predict what

[12] Schilke & Cook (2005) at 277.

the other will do and to identify instances where "trust me" may not be enough. Each party must be able to rationally expect what the other party will do by developing a method of reasoning that is reciprocal and other-regarding. Behavior builds trust because behavior reveals the way in which the other party reasons about her behavior. This predictive ability allows each party to address divergent points of view before they become a source of friction. Reasoning with someone about how they reason before frictions arise is the best way of developing the kind of mutual view of the world, and one's relationship to it, that builds trust.

8.3 ORDER WITHOUT LAW

Macaulay's work has been followed by a bouquet of literature that explores successful relationships, some in the domain of property law[13] and some in the context of contact law.[14] Although we will not explore that literature in depth here, the literature is noteworthy for several of this book's themes. It should not surprise us that the literature on private norm development ignores the boundary between property and contract; property and contract norms both create entitlements, which makes norm development a unifying outcome of social interaction. Further, the literature on private norm development is grounded on the ability of people to be other-regarding. Cooperation depends on people accepting norms of accommodation (fairness) that take seriously the values that express a person's self-regarding projects, while balancing those values in a way that creates acceptable norms. The normativity of private ordering supports the idea that normativity of private reasoning need not be separated from the normativity of legal decisionmakers.

8.4 CONCLUSION

Relationships must be managed in the face of unanticipated changes in the relational environment. It should therefore not surprise us that people "on the ground" form relationships that are characterized by fidelity to the relationship, adjustment, and accommodation. Nor should it surprise us that many relationships leave the precise obligations unspecified; parties know that over-specification may increase the fragility of the relationship by precluding the kinds of adjustments that will make the relationship successful. Yet relational adjustments and accommodation are possible only if parties are able to reason about achieving their private projects through their relationship with another, which requires a way of thinking about one's obligations in the context of the needs of the other party. That requires a form of other-regarding reasoning that allows one party to make sacrifices to its own projects in order to take advantage of the benefits the counterparty provides.

13 Ellickson (1994).
14 Bernstein (1992).

Even relationships that are unsustainable – those for which private projects are not complementary – need a method of reasoning that allows the relationship to unwind without unresolved differences. And when parties have different views of their obligations and cannot resolve their different views, they need a method of reasoning that allows them to reach a mutually acceptable accommodation.

If people have developed a method of reasoning that they use to continue, or to wind down, relationships, then it would make sense for courts to use that method of reasoning to determine how parties ought to view their obligations when unresolvable disputes arise. That, I believe, is what courts do when they apply contract doctrine in specific contexts; it is time to provide support for that belief, which I do in Part III by examining the application to values-balancing reasoning to contract doctrine.

PART III

Applications

Thus far I have claimed that when private parties settle their relational disputes they resort to a method of reasoning about their own well-being in the context of the well-being of their counterparty. That allows the parties to be faithful to the relationality of their collaboration. I have also sketched what the method of reasoning entails and how the method of reasoning can help us understand relational obligations. And I have claimed that this method of reasoning helpfully supplements, and illuminates, contract doctrine and theory.

Because none of this is intuitive for scholars steeped in, and teaching, contract doctrine, I turn now, in this Part III, to illustrate the ways in which the core ideas of values-balancing reasoning work themselves out in the creation and implementation of contract law. My thinking leads me to raise other nonintuitive possibilities, so that the analysis in each chapter leads to hypotheses that are suggested by the method of reasoning I champion. Although I do not pretend to prove the hypotheses, I find support for them in legal doctrine, and offer them as alternative understandings of the source and scope of obligations of promising and contracting.

Here, I highlight the conclusions I reach in these application chapters:

- Chapter 9 ("Legal Enforceability: Formation"): concludes that formation doctrines are designed to answer this question: when may a promise be revoked or revised? This account makes legal doctrine the output of reasoning about the circumstances that preclude a person from revoking or revising their promise, rather than as the input into the question of whether a promise is legally enforceable.
- Chapter 10 ("Performance Obligations: Methodological Issues"): suggests shortcomings in existing methods of reasoning about obligations.
- Chapter 11 ("Performance Obligations: The Values-Balancing Method"): shows how tort law determines obligations in contractual relationships by identifying unreasonable relational risks. It also shows how other-regarding reasoning provides analytical traction to the concept of good faith and describes

the decision-tree methodology that allows contract interpretation to efficiently account for both text and context.

- Chapter 12 ("Consumer Contracts and Standard Terms"): suggests, consistent with the Draft Restatement of Law: Consumer Contracts, that values-balancing reasoning allows courts to freely invalidate seller-supplied terms that do not adequately account for the buyer's well-being.
- Chapter 13 ("Excused Performance and Risk Allocation"): makes the point that the excuse or modification of an obligation depends on how the parties allocated the risks their private projects face, and not on whether an event was unexpected.
- Chapter 14 ("Remedies"): argues that contract remedies serve to protect the private surplus of the aggrieved party, and that the appropriate remedy is determined by the parties as an implicit obligation of the exchange they have undertaken.

9

Legal Enforceability

Formation

Determining the legal enforceability of promises has proven to be elusive. Before discussing the values-balancing, other-regarding approach to enforceability, it may be helpful to consider why this is so.

9.1 THE DOCTRINAL DIFFICULTIES

9.1.1 *The Domain Problem*

Consider first a domain problem. The enforceability issue can be resolved in various ways: determining which promises give rise to legal obligations (the domain of contract formation, consideration, and promissory estoppel), determining what a legal obligation entails (the domain of interpretation), and determining whether an otherwise enforceable promise will be excused or deemed unenforceable (excuse and illegality domains). These domains are, in a sense, substitutes for each other; a court can fit a predetermined result into one of those domains, finding no legally enforceable contract through formation doctrines, interpretation doctrines, or excuse doctrines. Although contract doctrine appears to follow a straight line (from formation to interpretation to excuse), the boundaries between the domains may be more malleable and overlapping than it first appears. Not surprisingly, in each of these domains contract law reflects the parties' disputed autonomous decisions.

Because the various enforceability domains are so well-ingrained, they are followed here. However, overlapping domains present doctrinal problems. Take, for example, the issue of a bilateral choice to be bound. Under standard contract doctrine, both parties must assent to be bound, either by promising performance (accepting an offer and promising something in return) or by doing the thing requested. Each party must use the objective standard of the reasonable, other-regarding, negotiator when interpreting a negotiating communication; each party must interpret the communication as the other party, being reasonable, must have meant it, given customary standards of interpretative meaning. Moreover, each party must act on their subjective knowledge of the other's intention. If the offeror knows that an offeree's communication was not meant as an acceptance, the communication does not bind the offeree, even if a reasonable person would think that the communication signaled acceptance. The offeror's knowledge of the intention of the offeree in responding to an offer is tantamount to being in the shoes of the offeree; an other-regarding offeror would not seek to bind the recipient. Actual knowledge of another's meaning trumps what a reasonable person ought to know.[1]

On the other hand, assent is not a straightforward concept, for assenting to a legally binding relationship does not necessarily determine the terms that govern the relationship. When one party presents the other with standard terms, or when the parties exchange standard terms with different content (initiating the battle of the forms), assenting to a relationship need not also determine the terms that were assented to. Moreover, because obligations, such as warranty obligations, can be implied from the nature of the exchange, sometimes assent to a transaction can mean assent to obligations embedded, but not named, in the transactions. And assent to a transaction may include assent to obligations that the party specifically knows about which become a basis for the exchange because the person to be bound goes forward with the exchange with that knowledge. Assenting to an exchange is separate from the question of what terms govern the exchange.

That is why consumer contracts get their own chapter in this book.[2] Consumer contracts cross doctrinal domains, which requires us to examine several dimensions of consumer choice: does the enforceability of particular terms depend on issues of formation (assenting to the exchange relationship), of interpretation (assenting to a particular term or interpretation), or of invalidity (assenting to an impermissible term). Doctrine might be taken to imply that assent to a relationship implies assent to a particular set of obligations that are attached to that relationship, but that is not a necessary conclusion. Assent in the formation sense does not address the question of what obligations a party has assented to, and assent is irrelevant if a term is unenforceable.

The theory developed here suggests that the domain problem can be addressed by identifying the substructure of reasoning from which each domain springs. It asks: What form of non-doctrinal reasoning supports a determination that a contract has not been formed, or that certain terms do not become a part of the obligations of an exchange, or that certain terms are unenforceable? I explore that substructure by suggesting that values-balancing, other-regarding reasoning provides a method of reasoning that is common to each domain, one that identifies the common source of the various domains that together determine a contract's content. That common

[1] Eisenberg (2001) at 212.

[2] Chapter 12 ("Consumer Contracts and Standard Terms").

source may allow us to analyze contractual disputes without getting trapped by doctrinal categories.

9.1.2 *The Formation Problem*

The central enforceability issue is whether promises and other means of raising expectations create legally enforceable obligations. Admittedly, distinguishing between legal and extra-legal obligations,[3] or between gratuitous and legally enforceable promises, is not easy; legal doctrine does not make it easier. Rather than confronting the formation issue directly, contract doctrine substitutes doctrinal proxies, such as consideration and promissory estoppel, as ways of determining legal enforceability. Under these proxy doctrines, the law seems to suggest that a thing called *consideration* exists in nature, and that, if we could identify and justify it, we could address the issue of legal enforceability. We are then drawn into debates about the form and justification for the consideration doctrine and deflected from the underlying issue, which is to identify the factors that make a promise legally enforceable. If, as Patrick Atiyah has argued, early judges used the term *consideration* to recognize that they found a good reason to enforce the promise,[4] the original function of *consideration*, which was to describe a conclusion, has been transformed into doctrinal form without a clear function.

The problem is that proxy doctrines do not implement themselves and do not easily reveal their own determinants. Courts find consideration or they do not, but the reasons on which they make their findings are not determined by the concept of bargain or the related concept of exchange. The determinants of enforceability, are, I claim, defined by a method of reasoning legal decisionmakers use to determine whether a promise ought to be legally enforceable. The proxy doctrines, and their cognates (bargain and exchange) state a conclusion rather than a basis for reasoning about the factors that determine whether a legal decisionmaker will find consideration or promissory estoppel. Once we understand the determinants of these proxy doctrines we have a different view of their function and meaning.

Seeking to identify the determinants of consideration and promissory estoppel distinguishes the approach here from many other ways of understanding the proxy doctrines. Unlike Daniel Markovits, I am not trying to show why the idea of a bargain is valuable in itself; nor am I examining its distinctive connection to the values of contracting.[5] I am assuming that a valuable connection exists but am asking what circumstances determine whether it exists. Nor am I exploring the functional markers that support a determination of non-enforceability, such as the evidentiary,

3 Obligations that are not legally enforceable may give rise to moral obligations. As I discuss below, promises that may be revised give rise to social negotiation; the scope of moral obligations subject to social negotiation are not discussed in this book.

4 Atiyah (1986) at 179 to 243. The analysis was foreshadowed in Corbin (1917–1918).

5 Markovits (2004).

cautionary, or channeling function, that Lon Fuller has suggested as reasons to have the proxy doctrines.[6] Those are important functions, but one does not need the doctrine of consideration to promote them; courts ought to protect those values transparently. And I am not, unlike Robin Kar,[7] trying to determine what the doctrine of consideration does when consideration is found to exist. To be sure, when consideration is found, both parties are empowered, but empowerment does not define the boundary between legally enforceable and legally unenforceable bargains. Empowerment is the effect of locating the boundary, not its determinant.

Confusion about consideration doctrine manifests itself in several ways. To an impressive list of scholars, the doctrine of consideration is incoherent, elusive and lacking in moral force.[8] Even those who advance a theory of consideration admit that the doctrine does not reveal its own determinants.[9] And I am not the first to point out that if a promise can be made legally enforceable with the reciprocal promise to pay a peppercorn, it is hard to see what function the idea of accepting a burden in return for a benefit can perform.[10] How are we to believe that the finding of consideration is more than a fig leaf that is covering something important?

Moreover, consideration is not a necessary condition for a promise to be enforced. A plaintiff can also invoke the proxy of promissory estoppel. Neither proxy is well defined, nor is the relationship between the two clear, for they appear in some sense to be at war with each other.[11] One wonders whether courts first determine whether a promise should be enforced and then, if they believe it should be, slap on it a label called consideration or promissory estoppel. Perhaps doctrine is an unexplained conclusion about the question of legal enforceability.

Not only is consideration unnecessary; it is not always a sufficient condition of legal enforceability. Contract law has found it necessary to append to proxy doctrines other doctrines about implied-in-fact and implied-in-law contracts, adding a doctrinal wrinkle to understanding legal enforceability. Such doctrinal additions to proxy doctrines give the court discretion to choose a label to fit the outcome they feel is right. They also suggest that an unidentified substructure of reasoning may be supporting these doctrines. The doctrine of consideration also breeds confusion and doctrinal misdirection; Lucy Duff Gordon's attempt to avoid scrutiny of her

6 The functional view of consideration is derived from Fuller (1941). The most recent rebuttal of the functional approach is in Lewinsohn (2020).

7 Kar (2016).

8 Fried (1981) at 33 ("the bargain theory of consideration not only fails to explain why [the] pattern of decisions is just; it does not offer *any* consistent set of principles from which all of these decisions would flow:) (emphasis in the original). Baird (2013) at 26 (defining exactly what constituted consideration proved elusive); at 31–32 ("consideration is itself a convention that falls far short of being an independent and immutable law that definitely established" its reasons). Scanlon (2001) at 107 (doctrine "provide[s] no moral basis for the idea that [consideration] is always required").

9 Lewinsohn (2020) at 690.

10 Fried (1981) at 30.

11 This idea prominently figured in Grant Gilmore's death certificate for contract. Gilmore (1974) at 68 (calling promissory estoppel the anti-contract). *See also* Hillman (1997).

contractual obligations is the most infamous example.[12] And the doctrine of consideration has intruded into the issue of contract modification in unhelpful ways.[13]

Most importantly, the focus on proxies for determining legal enforceability is unnecessary in light of our ability to reason directly about the grounds of legal enforceability. If the parties did not intend their relationship to create legally enforceable bargains, then, given the value of autonomy, the relationship should not be legally enforceable. Further, if an offer (a conditional promise) does not meet an objective standard of promise, it is not a promise that can lead to an enforceable contract. And reasoning about why the law would leave some promises in the realm of social, rather than legal, obligations directly addresses the question of legal enforceability. Why employ proxies as a basis of reasoning about something (legal enforceability) that can be the subject of direct reasoning?

This chapter builds on the concept of duty outlined in Chapter 7 ("The Source of Obligations") to argue that values-balancing, other-regarding reasoning provides a direct method for determining when a promise may be revoked or revised, and that such a determination makes unnecessary the proxy doctrines for determining legal enforceability. In Section 9.2, I review the scholarly literature to understand the question that proxy doctrines seem to be answering. That literature shows that legal enforceability seems to depend on whether the promisor may revoke or revise the promise, and that leads me to suggest that legal analysis should focus on the circumstances that determine when a promise may *not* be revoked or revised. Section 9.3 then presents the values-balancing method of determining when promises may no longer be revoked or revised, thus providing a direct method of reasoning about the determinants of legal enforceability. Section 9.4 further elaborates on the determinants of revocability to explain why some promises do not result in legal enforcement, making this point: when the parties want the norms of promising to be

[12] *Wood* v. *Lucy, Lady Duff-Gordon*, 222 N.Y. 88 (1917). For the definitive background of the case, *see* Goldberg (2006) at 43. Lucy appointed Wood as the exclusive marketing agent for her fashions, and Wood promised "to pay the defendant one-half of the profits and revenues resulting from the exclusive agency and to render accounts monthly." After operating under this agreement for a time, Lucy entered into an agreement to market her fashions directly to Sears Roebuck. Wood objected that this was a violation of the exclusive rights she had promised him, and she attempted to void the deal by alleging that the original contract was unenforceable for lack of consideration (even though she had accepted payments under it). Judge Cardozo, who was not one to allow legal doctrine to be used opportunistically, construed the contract to include an implied obligation to use reasonable efforts and thus found consideration for the contract. Whether it would have been better to rule that the course of dealing showed an enforceable agreement is a matter of debate. Cardozo's point was to deny Lucy's attempt to misuse the doctrine of consideration as a way of avoiding question about whether her sales directly to Sear violated the contract.

[13] When a contract is modified, the modification is either valid or invalid, which, as I argue in Chapter 12 ("Excuse and Risk Allocation") depends on which party assumed the risk that the modification addresses. The concept of consideration, and the preexisting duty rules in which it is encapsulated, is unhelpful in that analysis; it serves as a conclusory label, not a basis for the analysis. In Chapter 12, I explain how the doctrinal mistake occurred and why it should be abandoned in favor of a risk-based approach.

subject to renegotiation as part of an ongoing relationship, the parties will not want their relationship frozen into a legal obligation and the promises should not be legally enforceable. This conclusion applies to both social and commercial relationships.

9.2 THE PROXY DOCTRINES

Two conceptions of legally enforceable exchanges seek to identify the determinants of consideration: exchange as reciprocal conventional inducement (the motivation theory) and exchange as indebtedness and discharge (the remuneration theory). The idea of reciprocal conventional inducement, building on a noteworthy pedigree,[14] posits that an enforceable exchange occurs when one party takes on a burden to induce another party to accept a reciprocal burden, one that will benefit the first party. This conception captures the idea of exchange as an institution characterized by reciprocal burdens that each party induces the other to accept.

The other conception, the debt and discharge (remuneration) conception, posits that an enforceable exchange occurs when one party owes a debt (an obligation) to the other, which, when extinguished, ends the exchange (and any further obligation).[15] This conception not only captures the idea of obligation (debt), it also embodies the important notion that once the debt is paid, any obligation is discharged, which restores the parties to the status of strangers who are free of any (non-tort) obligation to each other. That conception is framed around the no-duty principle of private law discussed in Chapter 7; naturally, I find this feature of the debt and discharge (remuneration) theory to be attractive.

But are these two conceptions of consideration really competing? I have cast both conceptions in terms of burdens and benefits reciprocally exchanged. That sounds, of course, like a version of the reciprocal conventional inducement (motivation), but it is also a version of the debt and discharge (remuneration) view of consideration. As a paraphrase of the reciprocal inducement theory, it emphasizes that a promisor may not revise his promise if it induced another to change *their* position in an important way. The reciprocal inducement precludes the promisor from changing their plans and commitments. As a paraphrase of the theory of debt and discharge (remuneration), the focus on burdens and benefits emphasizes that by accepting the burden of an exchange, one creates and accepts a debt to another. But accepting a burden in a way that creates a debt also involves an act of reciprocity because only certain kinds of burdens create a debt. I may impose on myself the burden of training for

14 Famously, Oliver Wendell Holmes generated the idea of consideration that turns a promise into a legally enforceable contract as "reciprocal conventional inducement." Holmes (1881) at 293–294. We can understand the idea by understanding, as we do below, the nature of reciprocity, the role of convention, and the idea of inducement.

15 Lewinsohn (2020).

a marathon, but that burden creates no debt to another.[16] I may revise the promises I make to myself as circumstances change. Hence, the concept of debt that lies behind the debt and discharge (remuneration) conception also flows from the concept of reciprocity. Because the debt is to another and induced the other to restrict their decision space, the debt is enforceable because it precludes the debtor from changing their mind without the other's permission. But the debt and discharge view begs the question of what kind of debts (or obligations) have the requisite quality that I may not revise my debt without my counterparty's permission?

In the end, we are left with the feeling that the reciprocal conventional inducement (motivation) approach (I incurred a debt to accomplish something) and the debt and discharge (remuneration) approach (I incurred a debt that I may not extinguish without performance or discharge) are looking at different manifestations of the exchange concept. The reciprocal inducement (motivational) approach emphasizes the instrumental function of the promise (getting something in return) as the means to advance one's private projects. The debt and discharge (remuneration) theory emphasizes the effect of the promise (to be indebted to someone), the end reached by the means. Means and end are both reciprocal.

More importantly, both approaches address the same underlying question: When may a promisor unilaterally change their mind and revise their plans, and when must they seek another's permission before revising their plans? Each theory is other-directed and each begs the question of the circumstances under which a person is bound by the expression of the choices they have made.

Interestingly, promissory estoppel doctrine confirms the notion that legal enforceability is determined by circumstances that would preclude a person from revoking or revising a promise. To be sure, the language of promissory estoppel differs from the language of consideration. Instead of referring to debt, discharge, and reciprocal inducements, promissory estoppel uses the language of justified reliance. But the different vocabulary simply emphasizes the idea that a promisor must be other-regarding in terms of understanding when the recipient of the promise is likely to change their position to their detriment in a way that makes the promise or conduct non-revocable. In fact, promissory estoppel, like consideration, recognizes the bilateral interdependence of relationality that makes it legally impermissible for a promisor to revoke or revise a promise.

Consider the academic debate about promissory estoppel – namely whether the doctrine should be understood to be benefit-based (because the promisor was likely to benefit from the promisee's burdens) or reliance-based (because the promisee's burdens are justified).[17] According to the reliance interpretation, the obligation

[16] Compare *Bosea* v. *Lent*, 44 Misc 437 (N.Y. 1904) (refusing to enforce a promise to stop drinking in which the husband agreed to forfeit certain property to his wife if he started drinking again; this debt was not enforceable).

[17] *See* Knapp (1998) (reliance-based), Farber & Matheson (1985) (nature of commitment determines enforceability); Kostritsky (1987) (benefits-based), Barnett & Becker (1986) (consent-based).

arises from the promisee's justified reliance on the promisor's statement of future intentions.[18] According to the benefits interpretation, the obligation arises from the idea that the promisor, sensing the justified reliance, stands to benefit from the promisee's changed position.[19] But benefit theories and reliance perspectives together demonstrate the reciprocity that is at the heart of promissory estoppel doctrine. The promisor's benefit makes the promisee's reliance justifiable, and the promisor's awareness of the promisees's justifiable reliance justifies assigning the promisor the burden of non-revocability. Assent to be bound comes from a promisor's acquiescence under circumstances in which a reasonable person would think more about the well-being of the recipient and prevent the recipient from reducing their decision space to their detriment.

This analysis suggests that our two proxy doctrines – consideration and promissory estoppel – are determined by the circumstances that restrict a promisor's freedom to change their plans. Consideration signifies that the promisor is prohibited from changing their plans because the promisee has incurred a debt or induced a reciprocal burden. Promissory estoppel signifies that a promisor has forfeited the right to change their plans because another has taken on burdens for the promisor's benefit. Either way, legal doctrine functions to identify the circumstances that preclude a person from changing their plans and revoking or revising their promises. The contract's literature seems to assume that if the requirements of an exchange are satisfied, a promise will be binding on the promisor (and therefore legally enforceable). But could the causal arrow run the other way? Could it be that we should first determine when promises are revocable and use the answer to that question to define when an exchange or bargain has occurred? After all, autonomy includes both the right to bind oneself and the right to change one's mind.[20] If a promise can be revoked or revised, it cannot burden the promisor; only an irrevocable commitment imposes a burden on the promisor and it is the irrevocability that turns an extra-legal obligation into a legally enforceable obligation.

Thus characterized, the question of legal enforceability suggests this hypothesis: the function of formation doctrines is to identify the circumstance under which a promisor is no longer legally free to revoke or revise a promise, circumstances that turn the exercise of autonomous choice into a legally enforceable obligation. The theory of values-balancing, other-regarding reasoning provides a way of reasoning about those circumstances.

Support for this hypothesis comes from many quarters and presents a unifying picture of contract formation. Personal autonomy includes freedom from contract

[18] Fuller & Purdue (1936) (asserting the predominance of reliance as the goal of contract law); Knapp (1998).

[19] Farber & Matheson (1985).

[20] Kimel (2014) at 97 (self-authorship must include some capacity to commit and some capacity to change one's mind) and Bagchi (2018).

(the right not to be bound without assent), which reinforces the no-duty principle. Persons have no free-standing duty to benefit another, which means that a promisor cannot be bound by a promise unless a relationship suggests that the promisor ought to be legally restricted from revoking or revising the promise. Gift promises, which legal doctrine generally considers to be revocable, follow the logic of the no-duty principle. The idea of a gift implies that the affinities that moved a person to make a gift continue to influence the promisor. Gift promises do not signal an intent to be bound precisely because the social construction of a gift would lose its meaning if the gift is not given by a motivation for altruism rather than a motivation for exchange. One has no duty to benefit another in part because the moral valence of voluntary benefits would be blunted if those benefits were to be made mandatory.

The idea that the right to revise a promise demarks legally enforceable promises reinforces the foundational contract principle that values the intent to be legal bound.[21] Revocability, for example, is at the heart of doctrines surrounding offer and acceptance. An offer is a contingent promise (contingent on acceptance) to be legally bound, but the promise can be withdrawn until the promisee objectively manifests acceptance with at least a reciprocal promise. Manifestation of assent "is not a mere appearance of assent; the party [to be bound] must in some way be responsible for the appearance. There must be conduct and a conscious will to engage in that conduct."[22] Moreover, a promise to keep an offer open (a firm offer) does not by itself normally prevent revocation of the offer unless another has paid the promisor to keep the offer open. If the promisee does not know of the promise, the promise is not binding on the promisor and can be revoked;[23] communication to the promisee is a necessary condition of making the promise irrevocable. Our understanding of legal approaches to contracting might be better off, then, if we addressed the issue of legal enforceability by asking this question: under what circumstance should a person have the right to revoke or revise a promise?[24]

[21] Restatement (Second) of Contracts, §21 ("the manifestation of intention that a promise shall not affect legal relations may prevent the formation of a contract"). Smith (1758) at 87 ("If I should say that I intend to give you voluntarily 100 {pounds) next new years day, but make this declaration in such a manner as plainly shews I don't intend you should depend upon it, and expressly say, 'you need not depend upon it, but this is my present design,' the spectator could not here imagine that he to whom I made the promise would have any reasonable expectation . . . ." Adam Smith's impartial spectator is a spectator who can determine which person in a relationship is acting appropriately.

[22] Restatement (Second) of Contracts, §19 (2) c.

[23] *Shall* v. *Miller*, 287 F. 502 (1922) (son executed a document transferring his interest in the family firm to father upon certain conditions; however, it was not communicated to the father and is not enforceable).

[24] Limiting the question of formation to the question of a promise's revocability, preserves other, separate grounds of unenforceability, including duress, unconsionability, and illegality. Under this view, a promise's revocability becomes a distinct reason for denying legal enforcement.

9.3 ENFORCEABILITY: THE VALUES-BALANCING APPROACH

Under the view developed here, the foundational moral obligation of promising is the obligation to make decisions that take into account the well-being of the promisee. Although one is generally free to revise a promise, a moral obligation attaches when the promisor conveys to the promisee that the promisor is irrevocably changing their decision space to account for the well-being of the promisee. It is a legally enforceable obligation when the change in the promisor's decision space implies the obligation not to revise the promise if the promisee materially changes their decision space. Such a promise creates a reciprocal obligation on the part of the promisee if the promisee understands that the promise is intended (or, to a reasonable person, would be understood) to change the promisee's decision space in a way that makes the reciprocal promise irrevocable (and therefore legally enforceable). The reciprocal irrevocable change in the decision space of promisor and promisee creates the bond between persons that provides the bilateral obligations that characterize legal enforceability.

Under this conception, it is not the exchange that makes promises legally enforceable; it is the relationality embedded in the exchange – namely, the fact that the promisor and promisee, if they are sufficiently other-regarding, will recognize the reciprocal restrictions the parties have placed on each other's decision space. It is not, in other words, bargaining that leads to the enforceability of promises; it is the relationality of justifiable understandings about the decision space of the other party that a court looks to in order to limit a promisor's right to revoke or revise a promise. Both promisor and promisee form expectations, and each has expectations about the expectations of the other party. When disputes arise, a legal decisionmaker must determine which party's expectations about the expectations of the other party are unreasonable. A legally enforceable promise limits the promisor's decision space and induces another to limit the other's decision space. In order to turn a promise into a legal obligation, the promisor must make a promise of the kind that limits their decision space in a significant way, while having reason to know that the recipient will limit their decision space in an equally significant way.

A legal decisionmaker's task, therefore, is to determine the social construction of revocability as the speaker and recipient should understand it. When both parties have the same assessment of revocability, there is likely to be no dispute over legal enforceability. Enforceability disputes arise when the speaker and the recipient have different views of the promisor's freedom to revoke the promise and the court must choose between them; this occurs when the recipient has changed their decision space but the speaker has not changed theirs. When this occurs, a court must consider which party is wrong in their interpretation of the social facts because their interpretation was, given all the facts, less reasonable than the interpretation of the other party.

As a selective review will confirm, the cases are consistent with the idea that legal enforceability depends on the reasons a promise may not be revoked or revised. The answer to that question depends on an assessment of what counts as a burden or benefit that so changes the decision space of a party as to remove the option of revoking or revising the promise without the promisee's permission. In addressing this question, we do well to remember that Holmes understood consideration to implicate not just reciprocal inducement by itself but reciprocal *conventional* inducement. Under this conception, the relevant convention determines what is identified as a significant enough burden or benefit to make a promise irrevocable. Consider some familiar categories of promises as they relate to conventions that control the conditions under which a promise may be revoked or revised.

9.3.1 *Familial Promises*

The convention that made the promise in *Hammer* v. *Sidway* [25]enforceable was the convention that conceived of youthful experimentation as conventional behavior, which made the agreement to forego that behavior a burden on the promisee. Had it been taken for granted that young men did not experiment with alcohol, the promise to do what was conventional (that is to forgo alcohol) would have produced no burden and therefore no irrevocable promise by the uncle.

9.3.2 *Indefinite Promises*

A promise given by a father to assure his son of support by saying "I will give you $5,000 as soon as I have the money"[26] would not justify a court in holding that the promise could not be revoked or revised. The promise's contingency ("as soon as I have the money") makes it the kind of promise that should not induce the son's reliance or a change in the son's decision space. Nor does the promise display an intent to be bound. And because convention would not consider such a promise to be one that dad's conventionally make to change another's behavior, it would be understood to be revocable.

9.3.3 *Unilateral Promises*

An aunt who promises to give $1000 to a favorite nephew if he will spend it only on books is making a contingent promise whose very contingency suggests that it would not change the nephew's decision space. Buying books is identified as the very burden that the nephew would have to take on in order to get the benefit of the payment. The promise creates no obligation until the nephew starts buying

[25] 124 N.Y. 538 (1891).
[26] The illustration is from Restatement (Second) §79.

books.[27] A contingent promise would, conventionally, be interpreted to be revocable until the performance of the contingency is started, provided that the promisor give adequate notice of revocation.

9.3.4 *Moral Obligation Promises*

Consider again *Mills* v. *Wyman*,[28] in which the father promised, after the fact, to pay for the costs a stranger incurred in coming to his son's aid. The convention at play there was the convention that would impose no duty to help a stranger, nor a duty to an adult son when no familial duty to benefit the son existed. If the father felt that he had no duty either to his son or to the plaintiff who aided his son, it would not surprise us to find that he assumed that his promise was revocable. The legal embodiment of that sense of duty reflected the belief, common at the time (and therefore customary) that one person cannot compel another to bestow a benefit on the person.

9.3.5 *Charitable Gift Promises*

In the *Allegheny College* case, Judge Cardozo knew that when a person promises a future gift to a charitable institution with sufficient definiteness and publicity, the promisor will not only know, but will intend, the consequences that make the charitable institution revise its decision space, even before it has the money. The institution will use the promise of the gift to attract students, borrow money, and make investments, often in the name of the promisor, because of the promise. Moreover, the promisor will get the benefit of the promise as soon as it is announced, for the reputation for charity is one of the benefits the promisor seeks.

9.3.6 *Promissory Estoppel*

The revocability of promises depends on the interplay between the benefits to the promisor and the burdens to the person who relies on the promise. From the promisee's side, the question is whether the recipient is justified in thinking that a promisor's commitment is irrevocable, for it is the perceived irrevocability of the promise that justifies the promisee's reliance. That too is a question of how language is customarily understood. If the recipient's reasonable belief is that the promisor will benefit from the promisee's investments, the promisee is likely to believe that the promisor will not change course or revoke the promise. That belief, if reasonable and correct, make reliance reasonable and thus justifies holding the promisor to obligations to compensate the promisee for the burdens undertaken.

27 This illustration is from Lewinsohn (2020) at 690. Of course, once the son starts buying books, the promise is no longer revocable.

28 20 Mass. 207 (1825), discussed earlier on in Chapter 7, Section 7.1.

Whether a promisor is reasonable in their belief that their promise can be revoked depends, of course, on the directness and seriousness of the promisor's representation and its tendency to induce a change in the recipient's decision space. The more serious the representation and the more likely it is to change the recipients decision space, the more a reasonable person ought to understand that the promise is not contingent but, instead, is intended not to be revoked. If the promisor has facts that would lead a reasonable person to believe that the promisee is changing their decision space based on the representation, the promisor, if reasonable, ought to realize that the other views the promise to be binding if contingencies are met. The length of time the promise is extant is also relevant. The longer a promise exists without revocation the greater opportunity the promisor has to learn about the recipient's change of position in reliance on the promise. Under this conception, a promise that the promisor should know will alter the promisee's decision space and induce the promisee to incur burdens is a promise that may not be revoked.

9.4 INTENT TO BE LEGALLY BOUND: EXTRA-LEGAL ENFORCEABILITY

People sometimes make reciprocal promises with the joint understanding that either party may revise the promise. When the parties feel justifiably free to revise their promises, the burden on their decision space is not significant enough to amount to the kind of burden or benefit that calls for legal enforceability. Promises made in the context of a relationship in which both parties expect to be free to revise their promises are the product of expectations that we should not make legally enforceable. Accordingly, the moral principle that all promises must be kept cannot be implemented until one evaluates the nature of the promise that a person has made and determines which promises were intended to be revocable and which were intended, and known to be, irrevocable. Revising a promise that both parties understood to be revocable is not immoral.

The idea that people sometimes make promises that they understand to be revocable supports the distinction between extra-legal and legal obligations. Promises are often made in relational settings that support an inference that people would prefer to rely on social (rather than legal) dispute settlement to determine the implicit obligations of promising. It would surprise us if a promise to have lunch with a friend the following week would require that the promise be kept at all costs. And even if the promise to have lunch next week would impose an obligation on one person to notify the other if their plans changed, it would surprise us if the obligation to inform that other party would lead to legal sanctions. That is because neither party to the relationship would want or expect legal intervention to determine the terms of their relationship.

Legal decisionmakers recognize that some obligations should not be subject legal sanction because legal intervention would disrupt the evolution of relational norms in situations in which the evolution of the terms of the relationship is the very point of having the relationship.[29] When human interactions are being negotiated through fluid promises and expectations, the point of human interactions is to define the relationship and to allow expectations to form or evaporate in response to the dynamics of the relationship. The meaning of the relationship depends on that evolution. Promising, as we recognized earlier,[30] is a social practice, which means that promising comes with its own set of social expectations, and with expectations about those expectations. The definition of the social obligations that arise from promising are subject to renegotiation that defines both the social norms and the relationships to which those norms attach. Some promises are made in contexts where the meaning of a change in plans must be interpreted by the people in the relationship and not by courts.

Social interactions are akin to courting between people in a potential intimate relationship. The process of courtship depends on finding the meaning of the relationship to both parties. That depends on both parties having the freedom to walk away from the relationship or the promises that define it; that freedom from legal obligations is the means by which the relationship fosters trust and defines expectations. The relationship may evolve into a pair of legally enforceable promises, say through marriage, but until the point of irrevocability is reached, the obligations and meaning of the interactions rightly remain fluid and up to the parties to interpret.

Imagine the consequences if the promise to have lunch with a friend were legally enforceable. Fewer lunches would be planned, the terms of the luncheon promise would have to be carefully negotiated, and the obligations of the promise would be frozen in a legal "default rule" that would halt the development of the social implications of promising.[31] When social understandings of the meaning of promises need to develop organically, legal decisionmakers rightly stay their hand lest the implication of the common understanding be frozen and made immune from the evolving relationship. If one party to the "agreement" to have lunch feels that he has been mistreated, that feeling

[29] The scholar coming closest to the spirit in which I write is Mindy Chen-Wishart, who suggests that "[g]ratuitous promises are normally embedded in a framework of ongoing [personal] relationships with normative implications, which provide the code for interpreting the significance of acts and omissions." Chen-Wishart 2013). Daniel Markovits hinted at this point in Markovits (2004) at note 179 (promises among benevolently motivated intimates "may be destroyed when their terms are enforced" legally). Others posit that some promises are self-enforcing and for that reason are called gratuitous; Charles Goetz and Robert Scott suggest that "[e]xtralegal sanctions are likely to be effective in the donative context because promisors generally care about the welfare of promisees. In contemplating a promise, the promisor may regard costs suffered by the promisee as equivalent to costs suffered by himself." Goetz & Scott (1980).

[30] *See* Chapter 3 ("Promises and Obligations").

[31] This may explain why Judge Posner posited that enforcing promises in many social settings would impose more harm than benefits. Posner (1977) at 417 ("the real reason for the law's generally not enforcing gratuitous promises is . . . an empirical hunch that gratuitous promises tend . . . to be made in family settings where there are economically superior alternatives to legal enforcement.").

implicates a social disagreement not a legal disagreement. It is, in fact, a disagreement about what the relationship is about, and that disagreement can be settled only through the relationship.

In short, the law is rightly limited in its willingness to intervene in relationships that are evolving and that reflect obligations that are continually negotiated from various social and cultural perspectives. The parties would not wish to be bound because legal intervention would turn practices and conduct that ought to be fluid and revisable into prescriptions that seem to be doctrinally fixed and immutable.[32]

But the special status given to promises in a developing relationship are not limited to social and interpersonal relationships; there is no reason to believe that legal enforceability draws a line between personal, interfamilial relationships, on the one hand, and commercial relationships, on the other. Some personal, interfamilial relationships do result in enforceable promises, as *Hammer* v. *Sidway*[33] demonstrated. At the same time, some commercial arrangements are designed so that norms governing the relationship evolve through iterative interactions that, in fact, define the contents of the relationship's evolving obligations.[34] A relationship between two companies to explore a new product or to experiment in new supply chain arrangements may take on the characteristics of a romantic relationship in which building trust, and breaking down barriers to trust, are part of a process of developing a mutual understanding of obligations that become enforceable when their content is breached. The parties incur obligations during those "courting periods" but they are not the kind of obligations that lend themselves to concrete specification. The large literature on contract design makes it clear that agreements to explore the possibility of a more detailed and contract-rich commercial agreement may well signal the parties' shared intention to be bound only by the obligation of good faith cooperation. In both interpersonal and commercial relationships, context matters.

32 In addition, the very contextuality of promising that is subject to the social construction of obligations suggests that some disputes over promissory obligations are of too little moment to invite legal intervention. The stakes are too small and the cost of legal intervention too great when compared to the benefits of social norm creation; on these grounds, legal intervention may be unwarranted. Gerhart (2014) at 179. Private law sometimes avoids relational controversies because the stakes involved and the nature of the dispute ought to be subject to private, social negotiation. Baird (2013) at 32 ("Given the extralegal pressures that are at work, the limited competence of courts, and the costs that come with making promises legally enforceable" we cannot say that because keeping promises is a good thing that promising ought to be legally enforceable).

33 124 N.Y. 538 (1891) (promise to pay nephew if nephew refrained from certain behavior is enforceable).

34 *See generally* Gilson, Sabel, & Scott (2013) at 95 (where the outcome of the relationship is uncertain, a promise to cooperate in jointly addressing an opportunity "depends centrally on courts enforcing the chosen methods of mutual cooperation on terms consistent with the underlying arrangement . . . . [t]he court's role [is] limited to policing the relationship not enforcing the outcome"). The article notes that courts are avoiding the dichotomous choice of either binding or refusing to bind the parties, finding a middle ground of obligations that account for the relationality of the arrangements. *See also* Kostritsky (2018–2019).

9.5 CONCLUSION

Under a theory of other-regarding obligations, the idea of exchange that animates contract law comes from the reciprocity of obligations that arise from promise-like conduct. The theory of other-regarding obligations therefore depends on a basis for finding that both parties in a relationship have taken on obligations in order to get the benefits of the reciprocal burdens on the other party. Doctrines of consideration and promissory estoppel both serve that idea. The concept of consideration captures this idea by understanding that conventions govern the meaning ascribed to words by both parties. The doctrine of promissory estoppel captures this idea by determining when a person should know that another is relying on their words or actions, and that reliance reflects the benefits the person is getting from the reliance. A person can say: I will confer a benefit on you if you confer one on me (consideration); or one can say: I am accepting burdens that I believe will benefit you because I believe, based on what you have said or done, that you will confer benefits on me (at least in the form of compensation).

Yet, under the reading presented here, doctrines of consideration and promissory estoppel function as ways of determining when promises move from mere statements of future intentions to statements of future intentions that the promisor may not revoke or revise. The doctrines serve as conclusions about the circumstances under which a relationship reaches the point that disallows revisions. Reliance and reciprocal conventional inducement have in common a change in the promisee's decision space. The change in the decision space is the cost that the promisee takes on in order to get the benefits of the promisor's changed decision space. This can occur by giving up something or by taking on a burden. The justification for legal enforcement comes from the promisor's obligation to think about the well-being of the promisee when the context is such that the promisor knows of the reduced decision space of the promisee. That is the point at which statements of future intentions become irrevocable.

10

Performance Obligations

Methodological Issues

Performance obligations are governed by the terms of the agreement and the method of reasoning the parties or courts use to determine unaddressed obligations. As we saw in Chapter 8, contract parties often successfully work through potential disagreements about performance obligations; the parties display flexibility and other-regarding reasoning as they seek to accommodate each other's private projects and preserve the relationship.[1] When the parties are unable to resolve contractual disputes, they can call on governance mechanisms or courts to allocate costs or wind up the relationship. In either setting, the goal of determining performance obligations is to preserve the ex ante balance of burdens and benefits that each party bargained for in the exchange, the ex ante exchange equilibrium.

Performance disputes arise from contractual gaps and from post-contracting circumstances that upset the tacit assumptions on which the parties based their exchange. Contractual gaps arise from ambiguous terms and unaddressed circumstances. Post-contracting circumstances challenge the distribution of the burdens and benefits of the original bargain; they may suggest that the relationship is no longer viable, in which event losses from post-contracting circumstances must be allocated. Both gaps and unanticipated circumstances raise overlapping questions of contract performance and excused obligations, for they implicate the question of how the parties divided the risks the relationship faces. The parties and courts have the option of allocating a performance obligation to one party or, instead, to excuse a performance obligation as it has been allocated. The determination of performance obligations is discussed in this chapter. Excused performance obligations are discussed in Chapter 12.

This, and the next, chapter advance the idea that the best method of preserving the ex ante exchange in the face of gaps and unaddressed circumstances is to require each party, and then a legal decisionmaker, to use other-regarding, values-balancing legal reasoning to determine obligations. Under this approach, the traditional trappings of interpretation – good faith, appeal to text or context, gap fillers, default

[1] Chapter 8 ("Relationality Redux").

rules, and the allocation of relational risks – require each party to use values-balancing reasoning to determine their performance obligations. Performance obligations can be implied from the parties' agreement and its context, including private projects, shared assumptions and conventions, exchange context, and risk allocation. The formalist notion that obligations are limited to those specified in the contract has melted away under the searing view that contractual obligations are determined by the choices each party has made.

This chapter raises questions about current methodologies for determining obligations, all in an effort to shift our focus from rules to reasoning. The next chapter puts values-balancing reasoning on display as a supplemental method of determining performance obligations. In this chapter, I critically examine several ways by which performance obligations are currently discussed that seem to me to short-change the requisite reasoning about obligations. Section 10.1 challenges several popular methodologies: resort to the intent of the parties, the hypothetical bargain, and party autonomy. Those gap-filling methods fail to recognize the self-directed aims of each party. Section 10.2 then closely examines the idea of gap filling, arguing that values-balancing reasoning profitably supplements these methods. Section 10.3 concludes.

10.1 INTENT, AUTONOMY, AND HYPOTHETICAL BARGAINS

The institution of contracting is appropriately considered to be an institution of collaboration. The parties enter the collaboration with a joint intent to accomplish shared goals. But when disputes arise, it is, I believe, a mistake to think that contracting or collaboration tell us anything meaningful about obligations, except under the clearest circumstances. Because each party is using the contract to pursue private projects, a contract, and the relationship that it embodies, includes competing, not necessarily cooperating, interests. The tension from those self-directed interests give rise to potential disagreements, The contractual relationship is held together by the promise of a continuing relationship, by reputational sanctions, and by a third-party mechanism for dispute settlement, but it is subject to the stresses of diverging interests as circumstances change. As a result, it is difficult to determine performance obligations by appealing to the intent of the contracting parties, the idea of party autonomy, or what hypothetical reasonable parties might have done in similar circumstances.

It is not at all clear, for example, what it means to search for the intent of the parties when the parties dispute their obligations.[2] Although contract terms express the intent of the parties, the contract does not express the intent of the parties when the parties dispute the meaning or implementation of the contract's terms. The

[2] Geis (2008) at 599 (contractual intent invokes epistemological concerns and competing objectives that are difficult to reconcile, even under an economic frame).

parties bargain to advance their private projects, over the allocation of the risks their joint projects face, and over the terms that will govern their relationship. But they do not bargain over the implementation of the decisions they express in their text. The fact that a dispute exists means that the parties disagree on what their intent was, which means that determining performance obligations requires determining which claim about party intent provides its better expression. Intent does not determine performance obligations; it cannot be declared by an outsider. Performance obligations are determined by which expression of individual intent is the best understanding of the obligations that flow from the contract's text and context, which depends on a method of reasoning that accurately determines which of two versions of intent is accurate. To be sure, both parties want certainty, but they want certainty over different aspects of their relationship; the certainty each party wants is the certainty that the collaboration and the counterparty's performance will advance its private projects.

Consider one prominent portrayal of the way scholars use intent as a gap-filling methodology.

> The judicial goal in contract cases is to recover and then enforce the parties' apparent intentions as they existed at the time of the contract. This goal implies that courts are reluctant to fill gaps with rules that are inconsistent with the ex ante intentions of the contracting parties, insofar as a court can recover those intentions from the issues the contract did resolve. Hence, the contracting parties' prospective intentions function as a constraint on, and sometimes as a guide to, the courts' rule-creating function.[3]

This depiction of the dispute settlement process depends on something called the "ex ante intentions" of the parties, but it does not specify how those ex ante intentions are to be determined. It is hard to imagine how a gap can be filled by an ex ante intention, because the existence of the gap demonstrates that the parties are disputing any ex ante intention with respect to the matter at hand. If there is a dispute, it is because the parties have different views of their ex ante intentions or even different ex ante intentions. The idea of dispute resolution is to determine which view of ex ante intentions is most appropriate to the exchange at issue; ex ante intentions form the question and not the answer.

Similarly, unhelpful as an interpretive method are appeals to respect the autonomy of the parties; because the autonomy of at least two parties is at stake, interpretation depends on a method of choosing which party's autonomy matters and why. Because the parties have independent goals in contracting, a contract represents the autonomy of the parties only to the extent that the performance obligations are not in dispute. When disputes arise, the existence of the dispute means that the parties and third-party enforcers must find a method of prioritizing autonomy. Appeals to preserving autonomy of the parties therefore require a method of reasoning about

[3] Schwartz & Scott (2016) at 1546–1547.

which performance obligations best preserve the autonomous decisions of each party.

It is also common to say that gap filling is a process of determining what hypothetical parties would have agreed to had they thought about the issue that must be resolved.[4] That is, however, an unpromising method of describing gap filling because it substitutes a counterfactual generalization (what reasonable people might have decided) for the actual question (what bargainers did decide). Because any bargaining involves bargaining over multiple equilibria, the exchange could take a large number of forms, none of which is more reasonable than another. Reasonable people could have filled the gap of uncertainty in a variety of ways, and that gap filling would not necessarily coincide with the equilibrium that two negotiators settled on. One set of reasonable bargainers will not necessarily arrive at the same terms of exchange as another set of reasonable bargainers.

10.2 GAP FILLERS AND DEFAULT RULES

Gap filling is an apt term to describe what parties and courts do to determine performance obligations that are not clear from the contract's undisputed terms. Gaps create the uncertainty that allows disputes to bloom. When one of the parties presses a dispute about performance obligations, the dispute must be resolved, and the resolution fills the gap, at least for that contract.

Gaps are defined by disputes; if the parties can fill the gap by reasoning about their obligations, or by adjusting their obligations to preserve a relationship, there are no gaps. The existence of a gap, like the existence of a dispute, tells us little about how to determine the obligations that fill the gap; we must know the source of a gap to know how to fill it.[5] In that respect, consider how gaps and disputes relate to the parties' reasoning. If both parties reason in the same way about their obligations, they will fill the gap through reasoning, thus extinguishing the gap. Gaps exist because one or both parties use deficient reasoning, and courts must determine how reasoning contractual parties would determine their obligations.

Courts and commentators sometimes talk about gap fillers as "law supplied terms" of "default terms." This is also an apt description insofar as the idea of contractual gaps signifies that a third party or court must determine the inadequately addressed obligations. And third-party dispute resolution resolves disputes authoritatively and thereby determines the law that binds the parties. But the idea of a "law supplied term" or "default term" is inapt if it is taken to mean, as it sometimes seems to be, that the law has a set of terms that it takes off the shelf and applies to a contract if the parties do not make their contrary intentions clear. That understanding of gap fillers

4 Schwartz & Scott (2016) at note 114 (claiming that the search for hypothetical bargains is misleading); Kraus (1993).

5 Eggleston, Posner, & Zeckhauser (2000) (suggesting eight reasons that parties leave gaps in their contract and showing how the cause of the gap is related to the reasoning that will fill it).

and default terms would be inconsistent with the notion that contracting parties choose the burdens they accept.

Gap fillers are better viewed as the output of a reasoning process the parties use when the parties leave obligations for later negotiation. Under this view, "law supplied terms" reflect the bargain the parties made (as reflected by the contract terms and exchange dynamics). Under this view, however, gap fillers are not rules around which the parties negotiate. They are, instead, decisions about implied obligations that fit the bargain the parties made. As such, they are not off-the-shelf terms that can be plugged into other contracts to bind the parties; they are, at best, presumptions that require the analyst to first determine that the gap fillers fit the contractual context. They are the obligations implied by the requirement of behaving as the other-regarding, values-driven person would reason.

The appropriate method of filling gaps is to ask what obligations *these* parties (not hypothetical reasonable parties) would have settled on, given the exchange they actually made, if using values-balancing reasoning they had reasoned from the terms and context of the exchange to addressed the gap that led to the dispute. It is not the reasonableness of the parties that fills the gap; it is the method of reasoning that takes into account the known terms of the exchange and the private projects of the parties that determine the implied terms these parties would have settled on to fill the gap. The parties, knowing of the deal they did make, also know of the deal they would have made if they had used values-balancing reasoning to fill the gap of uncertainty. Gap filling, under this view, is a process of determining from the terms and contextual details we know, the obligations that must have been implied by those terms.[6] Any other method of gap filling fails to respect the terms of the exchange the parties made.

Default rules are gap fillers,[7] of course, but they too fail to identify the nature of the reasoning that must be employed to govern a default rule's application. The appropriate view of default rules is that they provide a shorthand way of thinking about obligations once an analyst identifies the background features that determine the default rule's applicability; they are presumptions about the obligations implied by the terms and context of the contract. Once we identify a number of cases that have similar features and identical results, we can identify a rule-like presumption that applies unless the background features indicate that a different presumption better fits the exchange the parties made.[8]

6 *See, e.g.*, Eggleston, Posner, & Zeckhauser (2000) at 92. ("the relative complexity of a contract can tell a court something about the contractual goals of the parties, the process of negotiations, and the environment that the parties faced when they negotiated the contract.")

7 *See, e.g.*, Kraus & Walt, (2000) 193, Scott (1990) at 598 ("The principal task of the law of commercial contracts is to set default rules for commercial actors and other repeat players who, presumably, are quite capable of bargaining for customized alternatives").

8 This understanding of default rules is especially important with respect to contract remedies and is further developed in Chapter 14 ("Remedies").

Unfortunately, default rules sometimes appear to conceived as rule-like; that is, as strict rules that bind the parties unless the parties negotiate around them. Under this strict-rule view, a default rule will determine the parties' obligations unless the parties provide otherwise. But a strict default rule cannot determine the domain to which it applies and therefore does not determine its own implementation. For example, one default rule requires the breaching party to pay expectation damages; yet if that remedy is deemed to be "inadequate" the remedial default rule is specific performance. Neither default rule determines which rule the parties are to apply. Neither default rule is strictly rule-like in the sense that they apply unless the parties negotiate around them; their application depends on the circumstances that govern their application, circumstances not given by the rule. If the exchange has certain features it will be governed by one default rule; if the exchange has a different set of features, it will be governed by a different default rule. The default rules govern their own application only if we can reason about the features that determine their application.

Consider the role that strict default rules would play in an exchange.[9] A strict default rule puts one of the parties at a bargaining disadvantage if the default rule does not adequately express the choices the party would otherwise make. Requiring a party to negotiate out of a default rule requires the party to bear a burden and expense even before bargaining starts. Strict default rules are not costless. A party who wants to buy a painting they find uniquely valuable should not be required to bargain out of a default rule that says the "usual" remedy for a breach is damages rather than specific performance. It does no good to argue that because the parties can either accept strict default rules or craft their own rules, party autonomy is preserved; what matters is the individual autonomy of the bargainers, not their collective autonomy. If a party must bargain around a strict-default rule, that party's autonomy is decreased.

Moreover, for me, any debate about whether rules or standards best determine performance obligations shows the futility of choosing any interpretive methodology that does not reflect non-doctrinal reasoning about the obligations determined by a particular set of bargainers. Consider the terms of the debate. Strict default rules are rule-like when they specify obligations with a fair degree of ease of application.[10] A buyer who must notify the seller within ninety days that delivered goods are defective is barred from objecting to the seller's performance on the ninety-first day. This, it is thought, does not hinder contractual autonomy because the parties can specify a different rule. It provides certainty and advance notice of obligations; it also tells a party what to do before the party decides what to do, reducing decision costs.

9 *See generally* Ayres & Gertner (1989).

10 These paragraphs summarize a large and sophisticated set of articles by Alan Schwartz and Robert Scott, principal protagonists in the debate about the function of default rules. *See* Schwartz & Scott (2003); Schwartz & Scott (2016) Schwartz (1993), Scott (1990).

A default standard, on the other hand, is thought to provide only vague guidance and, accordingly, could be retrospectively applied; it would tell a party what the party should have done, but only after the party has already made a decision. A default standard would provide, as an example, that the buyer must notify the seller of a defect in a delivered product within a reasonable time. This would leave it to the parties to determine when a notice of a defective product was timely under the circumstances, subject to a judicial determination if the parties disagree on the circumstances that should determine the reasonable notice period.

Champions of default rules point out several of their benefits: they are generated by the process of dispute resolution; by virtue of their "ruleness" they provide parties with bargaining certainty; they restrict judicial "intervention" in private disputes, and they preserve party autonomy by allowing parties to bargain for a different rule. By contrast, standards increase uncertainty and transfer power from the parties to courts, which are said to decrease contractual autonomy and efficiency.

Champions of standards, on the other hand, point out that standards avoid the procrustean effect of rules. Because they provide, for example, that buyers must give notice within a reasonable time, they allow the parties to adjust their obligations to meet new contingencies. If a buyer fails to give notice within ninety days because of an event beyond the buyer's control, notice may still be reasonable (even if it is beyond the time a rule might have provided) if it imposed no undue cost on the seller. They also argue that standards unify contract theory by providing an approach to determining contractual obligations that is "trans-contextual"[11] and "super-contextual" because it can be applied in many contexts to determine obligations based on contextual circumstances.

Debates over the rules/standards dichotomy reflect historical debates about the role of law and equity and have generated a large literature.[12] I wonder, however, whether the debate sets up a false dichotomy that overplays rule's advantages and underplays standard's advantages. Perhaps values-balancing reasoning elides the rules/standards debate by providing rule-like certainty with standards-like contextuality; it avoids the procrustean, acontextual nature of rules, while avoiding the amorphous, open-ended quality of standards. Moreover, values-balancing legal reasoning does the least damage to contractual autonomy by increasing fidelity to the choices the parties made.

Under this view, rules are determined by reasons and ought to be known by those reasons. It is not the rules that provide certainty and support party autonomy. The method of reasoning that led to the rules supports the autonomy of both parties, and

[11] The term was used in Schwartz & Scott (2016) at 1528 (using the term trans-contextual as a reason to avoid standards).

[12] Readers interested in understanding the historic origins of the rules/standards debate should become familiar with Schwartz & Scott (2016), 1533 to 1544, who trace the debate to the division between law courts and equity courts, and to the different perspectives on contract law provided by Professors Willison and Corbin.

courts ought to adopt that method of reasoning to provide certainty and support party autonomy. Those reasons ought to be the basis for determining how the rules can best be implemented. Imagine a seller who has agreed to deliver widgets to a buyer who is recovering from hurricane damage. Assume also that the seller has nonconforming goods the seller cannot otherwise market. What would prevent the seller from shipping the goods to the distracted buyer, hoping that the buyer would not inspect the goods in the time called for by strict default rule? The hurricane would provide the perfect opportunity for opportunism. The strict application of a strict default rule (even if it is in the contract) either supports such opportunism or requires the buyer to spend valuable resources trying to anticipate and bargain for a common-sense exception to the rule. Reasoning in an other-regarding way supports the institution of contracting by allowing the implementation of a strict default rule to be guided by the reasons for the rule. The rule devised for normal circumstances would be implemented to prevent opportunism under unaddressed circumstances.[13]

The idea of default rules also provides far less certainty than strict rule- advocates imagine. Consider again the relationship between dispute settlement and rule creation. Courts decide disputes; in my view they decide disputes by reasoning about which party has the better argument. Under this view, courts do not make rules when they decide disputes; they make reasons for an outcome they feel is correct. The first step of rule-skepticism is to ask how the settlement of a dispute can lead to a rule governing other disputes. What general rule can be decided by a particular decision? Admittedly, the reasons for one decision can be combined with the reasons for other, similar decisions, and the reasons for the various decisions can be the basis for a rule that incorporates those reasons. But the rule is dependent on, and derived from, those reasons; the rule cannot be understood independently of those reasons. The rule has a domain of application and the application depends on, and is limited by, those reasons.

Return to our rule about the time period within which a buyer may give the seller notification that the seller delivered a defective part. Assume that the "rule" is that the buyer must notify the seller within ninety days but that the buyer takes ninety-one days before notifying the buyer of the nonconforming goods. Assume also that the buyer claims that there was a good reason, beyond its control, for not meeting the ninety-day rule. Can we resolve that dispute by reference to the ninety-day rule or by divining the ex ante intentions of the parties? The gap requires more than just rule and application. Undoubtedly, the parties (or a court) can take refuge in another rule (even if not in the intention of the parties or the rule itself). We might turn to the "rule" about impossible performance to excuse the failure to abide by the ninety-day rule, but we would undoubtedly be making a decision about whether to apply the ninety-day rule, and that decision is not given by the rule itself.

[13] As Chapter 13 ("Excused Performance and Risk Allocation") makes clear, obligations are often modified and excused because of unaddressed ex post circumstances.

In short, rules provide certainty only if disputes about the rule's domain are not raised. But when disputes about domain arise, the rule's domain is the very thing that must be determined. In that event, the rule functions as a standard because the rule's domain is not given by the rule itself. If application of a rule imposes costs on one party without decreasing benefits for the other party, one would not want to apply the rule, but that turns the rule into a standard (the rule is to be applied unless there is a good reason not to apply it). On the other hand, standards are less troublesome than some people seem to imagine. This book's central theme is that values-balancing reasoning can efficiently fill the uncertainty created by the contextual gaps, while respecting the parties' bargain. If the buyer has a good reason for failing to comply with the rule, and the failure imposes no costs on the seller, other regarding parties would ignore the rule.

The UCC, recognizing the failure of the concept of default rules, has, by and large, replaced default rules with default standards, which are trans-contextual but require additional reasoning to be applied.[14] Some commentators dislike default standards, such as "good faith," "reasonableness," or perform "seasonably" and the like because they cede too much power to courts.[15] But these commentators unduly discount the extent to which default standards put control of the obligations of contracting in the hands of the parties precisely because they are neutral and do not require a party to bargain out of the default.[16]

10.3 CONCLUSION

The methods that are normally used to interpret performance obligations seem to leave gaps that fail to reveal the full set of reasons the interpreter is using to make the interpretation. Although contracting parties have a shared intention about what they seek to accomplish, determining how that shared intention works out the allocation of risks and obligations facing the two sets of private projects requires a method of reasoning that is not revealed by the fact that they parties share joint intentions. Moreover, I question whether gap fillers and default rules can be treated as rules; before they are implemented, the interpreter must determine whether the circumstances that led to the gap filler or default rule are also relevant to the interpretive dispute before the interpreter. Even when gap fillers and default rules serve only as presumptions, an interpreter needs to employ a method of reasoning that evaluates the basis on which the presumption was determined, and the relationship between that basis and appropriate reasoning about the obligations implied by the contract under scrutiny. Let me turn then to values-balancing reasoning as an appropriate supplement to existing interpretive techniques.

14 Schwartz & Scott (2016) at 1528.
15 *Id.* at 1529–1530.
16 The literature is summarized in footnote 19 of Schwartz & Scott (2016) and in part IV of that article.

11

Performance Obligations

The Values-Balancing Approach

In Chapter 10, I sought to show the ways in which resort to existing methods of interpretation might helpfully be supplemented by identifying and evaluating the values that determine performance obligations. Here, I illustrate how values-balancing reasoning can be implemented.

I first challenge the idea that tort law and contract law reside in separate domains. Because gap filling is a process of determining, from the party's choices, what they should do, it calls for a process of balancing burdens and benefits, which is the task of both tort law and contract law. Part of tort law *is* contract law, or so I argue in Section 11.1. Section 11.2 shows the way in which good faith embodies the requirement that contracting parties ought to reason reasonably about their implied obligations, defending the claim that good faith reasoning imposes no obligations external to a relationship. Section 11.3 addresses the related question of contractual interpretation. It dismisses the debate over whether text or context is the best source of contractual meaning, characterizing the debate as one between two inadequate methodologies. It recommends replacing those methodologies with a decision-tree methodology that allows the court to determine which of two interpretations is most likely to be an accurate expression of the obligations embedded in the exchange.

11.1 OBLIGATIONS IMPLIED BY TORT LAW

Tort law, like contract law, determines when a person is responsible for the well-being of another;[1] it thus determines when a person is responsible for the risks to another person's private projects. Tort law and contract law both reflect ways of understanding risk allocation. Often, tort law assigns risks when the injurer and the victim are strangers and had no opportunity to bargain over the allocation of the risks. But just as often, as this section demonstrates, the injurer and the victim have a relationship that would allow them to allocate risk and responsibility if they wanted to. They often do not. People in a promissory, contractual relationship often leave

[1] Gerhart (2010).

the allocation of risk unaddressed, making their allocation an unaddressed (but tacitly assumed) source of obligations. When the allocation of risk is unaddressed, tort law assigns responsibility for risks to the party whose private projects would be most directly impacted by the risk. This assignment is the source of the relationship's implied obligations.

Accordingly, to appreciate the role of tort law in contract law, we would do well to abandon the conventional wisdom that tort and contract inhabit separate domains based on the parties' opportunity to bargain over risks. Although it is sometimes thought that tort (and property) law "largely operate independently of, or prior to, transactions,"[2] and that tort applies "when the parties first contact is the accident,"[3] in fact, tort law is deeply embedded in determining the obligations of parties in a relationship; tort law has always worked alongside contract law (often pushing contract law) to determine the obligations that arise from relationships.

Seller obligations have been the subject of tort law ever since tort law emerged as a mechanism for assigning responsibility that was implied by a relationship but remained unassigned in a contract. This function has been most obvious when a seller is providing services (for then selling through a distribution network, which invokes the barrier of privity, does not obscure obligations). For sellers of products, the tort/contract interface was hidden from view because of privity, the idea that contractual obligations attach to those in privity with the promisor. Nonetheless, the idea of privity did not restrain the development of gap filling through tort law. Indeed, it was tort law that broke down the idea that obligations from sales transactions depended on contractual privity. When, in *MacPherson* v. *Buick Motor Co.*,[4] Judge Cardozo identified the source of a product seller's obligation as the seller's decision to market a product that could potentially cause harm, he made it clear that obligations followed relational choices that arise only from the nature of the relationship. The fact that it took contract law six decades to absorb this wisdom,[5] is no credit to contract law.

Ever since tort law emerged as a legal means of recognizing responsibility for risks, tort law has recognized risks that arise in relationships. As early as 1808 passengers on a stagecoach were able to recover damage from the stagecoach company that drove through a low gateway without adequately warning passengers sitting atop the coach that the passengers would have to duck.[6] The responsibility for that accident was laid at the feet of the stagecoach company, which knew of the low clearance and failed to warn the passengers. And this occurred even though the parties had an opportunity

[2] Schwartz & Scott (2016) at 1529.
[3] *Id.*
[4] 217 N.Y. 382 (1916).
[5] In contract law, the chains of privity were not finally broken until *Henningsen* v. *Bloomfield Motors, Inc.*, 32 NJ. 368 (1960).
[6] *Dudley* v. *Smith*, 170 Eng. Rep. 915 (K.B. 1808). The common law background is summarized in Gerhart (2010) at 202 and in Kaczorowski (1990).

to bargain over responsibility for that risk and probably had a contract of carriage that left the allocation of that risk unaddressed.

To see the role of tort law in determining gap-filling risk-assignment, consider a shipper of coal who hires a tugboat to transport barges of coal from Norfolk Virginia to New York City, a contractual transaction.[7] When the shipment was lost at sea, the shipper did not rely on the contract documents, but sued in tort, claiming that the tugboat operator was negligent for not having a radio on board that would have allowed the operator to avoid a sudden and unexpected Atlantic storm. It was, according to Judge Hand, negligent for the tugboat operator not to have the inexpensive and effective radio on board. This, of course, embodies an implied obligation that reflected the nature of the exchange relationship between the shipper and the tugboat operator.

It is not clear why the shipper did not sue in contract. The shipper might have wanted to avoid the defense of impossibility, although that defense would not have been available if the tug boat owner could have avoided the circumstances of the sudden and unexpected storm that led to the loss of cargo. It could also be that in 1938 contract law was allergic to the idea of implied obligations to look out for the well-being of a contractual partner. After all, this was well before contract law realized the unspoken warranties that sellers make about what they sell or provide. That was precisely the issue decided by Judge Hand's determination of negligence. More likely, it was accepted that obligations from transactions had to be implied if the contract did not address them and that the mechanism for implying obligations was to determine whether the party that bore the risk of loss had reasonably addressed the risk.

In this sense, tort law served to pull contract law out of its formalism, a formalism that seemed to say that if the parties did not bargain for an obligation the obligation did not exist. Under this view, if obligations were not clear from the terms of the contract, there was no gap to fill. But tort law disrupted that formalism. In tort law, the absence of an express term governing a future contingency was a gap that tort law could fill by identifying which party should bear that risk and asking that party to reasonably address the risk.

At the same time that tort law pulled contract law out of its formalistic allergy to implied terms, tort law respected the division of risks that lie at the heart of contractual relationships. Tort law understood that unless the contract specified otherwise, the risk of loss would be borne by the party whose private projects would be most directly affected by the loss. Because the tugboat operator's private project involved carrying the goods from one point to another, their private projects would bear the risk of loss and that allocation of risk determined their gap-filling obligation to use reasonable care to control the risks.[8]

7 *T. J. Hooper*, 60 F.2d 737 (2d Cir.), cert denied 287 U.S. 662 (1932).

8 Of course, the parties might have shifted the risk, and the obligation, during negotiations but this is a case in which that was highly unlikely. The risk was controlled by the tug boat company, not the

Tort law determines the obligations that doctors have to their patients, that common carriers have to their customers and that landlords have to their tenants. In *Georgetown* v. *Wheeler*,[9] a patient claimed that her negligence on the part of her doctors resulted in the worsening of her condition. Although the doctors did not cause her maladies (which resulted from a cyst behind her left eye), a jury found that the doctors had breached their duty of care to the plaintiff, and that this breach caused her injuries. Acting non-negligently was an implied term of the contract. In *Trimarco* v. *Klein*,[10] a case involving a different kind of special relationship, a landlord's failure to install shatterproof glass in a tenant's shower or warn the tenant of the unknown danger breached his duty to safely maintain the premises. Indeed, tort law has moved beyond just imposing an implied obligation to take care to avoid creating unreasonable risks; it also imposes an obligation to take due care to protect against risks that others pose. This is the heart of the "affirmative duty" that sellers have. Automobiles and apartments must be crashworthy. As an example, in *Larsen* v. *General Motors Corp.*,[11] the Eighth Circuit expanded the obligation of manufacturers to reasonably prevent harm. There, the driver of an automobile manufactured by the defendant was in an accident, but the driver did not allege that a negligent design caused the crash. Rather, the driver alleged that the negligent design of the automobile caused his injury to be more serious that it would have been in a reasonably designed automobile. The court found that where harm is readily foreseeable as an incident to the normal use of a product, a manufacturer's liability should not be limited to only design defects that cause accidents. In *Larsen*, a manufacturer's expanded obligation to a buyer reflects the requirement that it consider the consumer's expectations and the product's normal function. The court reflected that an automobile's sole function was not merely transportation, but "safe transportation."[12]

Tort law recognizes that the absence of an express term does not mean the absence of an obligation; the failure to name an obligation did not obliterate the obligations. Obligations could be, indeed had to be, implied from the nature of the transaction and the relationship between the parties; they exist even if not expressed. The implied division of risks, and implied obligations, were tacit, background assumptions of the transaction, one that the parties did not express because they were understood to be the basis of the bargain. Risks fall naturally on one party or the other, depending on whose private projects, and choices about those projects, are implicated in the transaction.

shipping company, and we can assume that the parties negotiated with the shared assumption that the tug boat company would bear the risk. In view of that shared assumption, if the tug boat company had wanted to shift the risk to the shipper, the company would have had to make that risk a part of the bargaining and discount the price considerably to get rid of the risk.

9 75 A.3d 280 (D.C. 2013).

10 56 N.Y.2d 98, 436 N.E.2d 502 (1982).

11 391 F.2d 495 (8th Cir. 1968).

12 *See also Mills* v. *Ford Motor Co*142 F.R.D. 271 (M.D. Pa. 1990).

Of course, through an exchange the private parties can shift risks that threaten the private projects of one of the parties. One party will accept a lower benefit if the other party absorbs the burden of the otherwise unassigned risk. Identifying those occasions is often not difficult. The party whose private projects would otherwise bear the risk will make the obligation to address the risk an explicit subject of the exchange, in which even the contract will make that obligation explicit. Such an explicit term naturally binds the parties. Other unassigned risks will be impliedly allocated by the parties from the information the parties have about each other's private projects at the time of the exchange. Contract law is adept at determining those implied allocations of risks, as we will see Chapter 12 ("Excuses") and Chapter 14 ("Remedies"). Under the circumstances that define an implied allocation of risks that would otherwise be allocated to the private projects of one of the parties, tort law may not be in a position to find an implied obligation because the exchange, properly interpreted, will determine which risk each party bears. Tort law will either adopt the contract notion that it will reason as reasonable parties would have about the implied allocation of risks and responsibilities the parties bargained for, or tort law will avoid providing a tort remedy in the domain where dynamics of the parties exchange make the allocation of risks unclear (the economic loss concept).

In short, tort law, like contract law, addresses harms that arise in relationship. Tort law operates when the allocation of risks is uncontroversial; it affirms the ability of courts to evaluate and fill contractual gaps through other-regarding reasoning.

11.2 GOOD FAITH

Critics of the good faith concept, when applied to performance obligations, raise two related objections.[13] One is that the concept lies outside of the idea of bargaining that is the foundation of contract law and thereby provides an unwarranted "intervention" that reduces the parties' autonomous decisions. This objection is sometimes expressed as the fear that the good faith requirement relocates contract interpretation from the parties to the courts, which by virtue of their institutional characteristics cannot handle the burden of determining whether a party has acted in good faith. Neither objection appears to be sound.[14] As I will argue here, values

[13] The obligation to act in good faith applies not only to performance obligations, discussed here, but to obligations during bargaining and obligations with respect to remedies. Under the view I express, the good faith obligation in any setting is the obligation to act as if one had reasoned in a values-balancing way about one's behavior. In this book, I focus only on good faith performance obligations.

[14] Scholarly debate about good faith contains many ironies. Often, those who recognize that contracting parties my shade or shirk on their obligations are the least likely to endorse the good faith obligation, even though a function of the good faith obligation is to identify shaders and shirkers. One gets the impression that the real debate is about who should decide who the shirkers and shaders are, the court or an outside commentator.

balancing reasoning is the way be which courts ascertain whether the parties have reasoned in a values-balancing way about their obligations.

Both expressions of the objections to the good faith requirement assume that the good faith obligation takes the terms of the bargain out of the hands of the parties, but that is true only if the good faith obligation becomes untethered from the parties exchange. In fact, the parties control the good faith obligation by the way they write their contract; the more precise they state performance obligations, the more the good faith obligation is defined by the terms of the contract itself. Even when a dispute is not addressed by the terms of a contract, the good faith obligation does not serve to alter, but to reflect, the obligations the parties agreed to (even if only by the implication). It does so, as this section argues, by requiring that each party reason about its obligations in a values-balancing, other-regarding way. This does not allow courts to determine what the obligations ought to be; it allows courts to determine the party's performance obligations by determining the exchanges implicit obligations.[15] This section describes what it means to require a party to reasonably reason about its obligations.

It is hard to imagine the institution of contracting without a concept like good faith. When applied to performance obligations, the basic concept is straightforward: because contracts leave so many performance questions unaddressed, each party must interpret its performance obligations using a method of reasoning that appreciates the best way of maintaining the ex ante equilibrium position of the parties; when each party implements the required method of reasoning in the same way, there is no dispute about their performance obligations. Both parties agree on, and thus maintain, the performance obligations that ex ante equilibrium bargain maintained. The concept of good faith interpretation, as implemented here, tells the parties what they must do to align their interpretations with the equilibrium the parties achieved through bargaining.[16] Without the good faith requirement, the difficulty of specifying in advance, in the face of changing circumstances, the party's precise obligations, each party would have power over the other party's well-being. The good faith requirement obligates each party to exercise that power only after evaluating the comparative burdens and benefits of various courses of action. When the terms of the agreement do not settle disputes about the parties' obligations, the parties (or courts) must address disputes in light of the agreed-upon terms and the obligation of good faith.

Imagine a contract in which the parties agree to make the good faith requirement invalid. How are the parties to know what they are to do when one or the other must make a decision not governed by the contract's terms? Whose "say so" is to prevail and how are we to know which party is to prevail? The good faith requirement

[15] The idea that each party must state its reasons for its action so that the judge can determine which set of reasons is strongest is foreshadowed by Listwa (2019).

[16] The good faith requirement in contracts also governs issues that arise in contract formation and enforcement, but those matters are not discussed in this book.

accommodates the need for certainty and flexibility that are the hallmarks of successful relationships. An inherent part of any relationship is a reciprocal obligation to favor the relationship rather than the private projects of either party.

In short, when the good faith requirement is understood to be the basis for other-regarding, values-balancing reasoning, the good faith requirement honors the parties exchange, cabins judicial discretion, reduces judicial mistakes, and enables courts to better explain and justify their outcomes. It provides a structured way of reasoning about performance obligations by reasoning about how a reasonable person in the position of a party to that contract would identify what burdens she must assume to protect that legitimate benefits due to the counterparty, accounting for both honesty and subjective motivation.

As Part II outlined, values-balancing legal reasoning requires an actor who is considering her obligations under a contract to consider whether, given the bargain the parties struck, she must accept burdens so that her counterparty can avoid a burden not fairly contemplated by the parties in the exchange. She must, in short, be reasonably other-regarding when considering how to behave under the contract. This can be determined by asking one of two questions, approaching the issue from the standpoint of either a party's burdens or a party's benefits. From the standpoint of benefits, one might ask: Has the promising party, when making decisions under the contract, adequately evaluated whether the private, personal benefits of her decision impose an unequal and therefore impermissible burden on the counterparty, given the benefits she has promised to deliver in the exchange? Or, from the standpoint of burdens, one might ask: When seeking to minimize costs under the contract, has the party making the decision adequately considered the burdens that a decision would place on the counterparty's reliance or expectation interests? Either way, a contracting party making a decision must compare interpersonal welfare in a values-balancing, morally reasonable way.

This method of reasoning is not information intensive; nor is it beyond the normal reasoning capacity of participants in a relationship. A reasonable person knows when gathering additional information is not worth the cost; economizing on information costs is built into the model of the reasonable person. Indeed, the reasoning of a reasonable person is the kind of reasoning that people use daily when making decisions about their activities; whether people are making decisions that affect only themselves or decisions that also affect others, they are continually evaluating how to make trade-offs between different goals. It is no objection to this methodology that people often make mistakes, that they make intuitional decisions, or that they exhibit behavioral biases. The ideal of the reasonable person fuels legal analysis because it adjusts to reasonable behavioral biases and seeks to reform unreasonable biases.

Often, the good faith requirement is a way of testing a party's interpretation of the contract. Each party must interpret the terms of the contract in good faith and not use the terms of the contract to try to exact a benefit that is not due them under the exchange. But sometimes good faith is not about interpretation, strictly speaking, but about what obligations a contracting party should voluntarily take on so that her counterparty avoids a loss. This embodies the idea that reasonable contracting parties will accept some burdens on behalf of the counterparty in order to provide that counterparty with the rewards that the counterparty bargained for. In these kinds of cases, a contracting party will act like any other reasonable person and sacrifice some advantage and absorb some costs on behalf of the counterparty. In essence, the good faith requirement insures fealty to the institution of contracting, and that insures that one party will make some sacrifices for the good of the contract. This is the ideal of the other-regarding contracting party, and it is part of the obligation that maintains the ex ante equilibrium that protects a contractual relationship.

Illustratively, consider two cases, one that requires a party to interpret the provisions of a contract and another that requires a party to consider implicit obligations.

In *Fred Feld* v. *Henry S Levy & Sons, Inc.*,[17] the defendant, a bread baker, agreed to sell all of its output of bread crumbs to a buyer. Although the bread crumbs were a by-product of the defendant's baking business, the defendant had to subject stale or waste bread to additional processing (and expense) to make them useful to the buyer. The baker was able to benefit from a by-product of its main business and the buyer had a steady supply of bread crumbs at an acceptable price. The contract contained a six-month termination provision, but when the buyer refused to modify the contract to pay an additional penny per pound for the bread crumbs, the defendant shut down its bread crumb operation, cut its processing costs, and sold the raw material to an animal feed producer. Did the seller act in good faith? Because a lower court denied the seller's motion to dismiss (suggesting that context matters) we can ask what method of reasoning would properly address this dispute.

The notice of termination provision, like a force majeure clause, could benefit either, or both, parties. Hence, the scope and meaning of the notice provision cannot be determined without taking a close look at the exchange dynamics. The seller would benefit from the notice provision because the seller would want to protect his investment in the processing equipment. The buyer would benefit from the notice provision in order to give him stability of price and to address the burdens of finding a different supplier. We might assume, along with Victor Goldberg, that because the contract was not an exclusive buying arrangement, the buyer may have had other suppliers, in which case the termination provision was not for the buyer's protection. This, however, is pure speculation, for we do not know whether other suppliers with similar terms were available, nor why the contract would not be interpreted to require the buyer to take the seller's entire output. As the court recognized this is not the kind of case that can be settled by conjecture or assumption; it must be decided on the basis of empirical information about the ex ante relationship. .

The seller's cost of continuing the relationship seemed to be significant; the seller was losing money on the deal and selling to a buyer who wanted unprocessed

17 37 N.Y. 2d. 466 1975.

crumbs allowed the seller to avoid the processing costs. That, of course, is not a reason to avoid performance. We must ask instead whether this is a cost that the seller should, under the contract, be expected to incur for the benefit of the plaintiff buyer. We do not know what costs the termination without notice imposed on the bread crumb buyer, although we know that the buyer would have to find an alternative supplier (perhaps at a higher price) or a substitute ingredient. If finding a new supplier of bread crumbs was frictionless, the buyer would not need the protection against termination, but the higher the buyer's cost of finding an alternative (and thus the greater the buyer's benefits from the notice provision), the higher the costs the seller would be expected to bear for the benefit of the buyer (including the seller's cost of delaying termination for six months). Thus, from the standpoint of values-balancing reasoning, the relevant determinants of the implicit obligations would be the seller's ex ante anticipated costs of continuing the arrangements for six months, compared to the buyer's ex ante anticipated benefits of having that protection. If the seller's ex ante costs of providing the protection were less than the buyer's ex ante benefits of the protection, the most reasonable interpretation would be that the seller had to give notice before ceasing bread crumb production. We could then say with confidence that the six-month notice provision was for the benefit of the buyer (unless, as we now discuss, the buyer was compensated for assuming the risk of the seller's termination.)[18]

Because the buyer might have bargained for a lower contract price in return for a no-notice interpretation, to preserve the equilibrium of benefits and burdens we must ask whether that is likely, given the bargaining history. Sometimes a legal decisionmaker can compare the contract price with the market price of a similar transaction; a contract price that is lower than the market price would support an inference that the buyer was compensated for accepting the risk of termination without notice. But the market for bread crumbs is not likely to be thick enough to allow this comparison. However, testimony about the negotiating history, and seller's perception about why the buyer wanted the protection, would allow a legal

[18] Victor Goldberg, in *Protecting* Reliance (2014) argues that the buyer did not need the protection of the termination notice because the buyer was not under an obligation to buy from this seller; the buyer could, under the contract, buy from a different supplier. He seems to think that the buyer did not rely on the contract to provide his sole source of supply. The buyer's discretion being unlimited, Professor Goldberg believes that the buyer had no reason to rely on the contract and therefore that the buyer had not paid for the continued supply of breadcrumbs during the six-month termination period. But that is the very question that the good faith requirement addresses, and, in my view, the question should not be elided by the assumption that the buyer had no reason to rely on the contract. We do not know whether the buyer could have easily gotten substitute bread crumbs at the same price. Moreover, the seller's investment had been protected by a "faithful performance" bond, so it looks off-hand as if the six-month notice provision was not for the benefit of the seller. That the seller found its performance to be onerous, or found a more lucrative outlet for its bread waste, is irrelevant to the seller's obligations to offer breadcrumbs at the contract price for at least six months. As the courts said, the seller could get out of its obligation to give notice only if its losses "were more than trivial" – which would signal in inquiry into whether the seller was excused from performance.

decisionmaker to determine the plausibility of any assertion that the seller lowered the price of the bread crumbs in order to buy the freedom to terminate the contract without notice. Importantly, if the seller lowered the price of the bread crumbs to buy the narrower termination clause, the seller is likely to have evidence to that effect available.

This illustration demonstrates that whether the seller acted in good faith depends on whether the seller used the appropriate method of reasoning to interpret the termination provisions of the contract. But often the requirement of good faith is not a matter of interpretation, strictly speaking, but a matter of the obligations taken on to show fealty to the relationship that is important to the institution of contracting.

An example of this is *Market Street Associates, Ltd. Partnership* v. *Frey.*[19] A developer leased property to be developed from a finance company, promising to give the finance company the right to finance additional development on the property. To restrict the finance company's discretion, which would otherwise give the finance company power over the developer,[20] the contract also provided that if the finance company did not negotiate in good faith, the developer could buy the property from the finance company at a price established in a contractual formula. The development company first rejected the finance company's offer to finance new development (after seeking financing from other companies), and later returned to the finance company, which apparently had not remembered its obligation to bargain over financing of new development in good faith, or the consequences of not bargaining.

The developer knew that if the finance company did not bargain in good faith, the developer had the option to acquire the property at below market rates. When the finance company turned down the request to again discuss financing (thus failing to negotiate in good faith), the developer waited a month and then wrote to claim ownership of the property because the finance company had refused to bargain in good faith. Thus, the court was presented with the question of whether the developer acted in bad faith by its second request for financing when it had reason to believe that the finance company did not know of the high cost of its failure to bargain in good faith?[21] Put another way, the developer failed to remind the finance company of the penalty for the finance company's choice, was the penalty clause inoperative?

19 941 F 2d 588 (7th Cir. 1991).

20 The developer faced the problem that as a lessee it had trouble putting up collateral to secure additional financing, which made it dependent on the continued good will of the finance company. By providing that the developer could buy the property if the finance company did not offer development financing in good faith, the developed was protected from this use of leverage.

21 Todd Rakoff has provided a methodology of reasoning about the case that is complimentary to, and foreshadows, the methodology I provide. Rakoff (2006). His methodology would have us construct the types of provisions that the parties might have drafted if they had wanted to provide for the resolution of the circumstances that latter occurred. Once the range of possible provisions is identified, a legal decision maker can evaluate the burdens and benefits of the options as the parties would have seen them *ex ante*, choosing the one that seems most reasonable under the circumstances (given the nature of the exchange).

Following a lengthy doctrinal discussion, Judge Posner described the good faith standard, at least in this case, as one of avoiding "trickery," a standard that connotes the intent to deceive or to take advantage of another's lack of knowledge. He provided two narratives to help guide the trial court upon remand, both of which focused on the developer's motivation. The first narrative, one that would support a finding of trickery, was built around the idea that the development company knew that the lessor did not know about the forced sale clause. The other narrative – the narrative of benign behavior – was built around the idea that the developer reasonably thought that the finance company knew of the penalty clause and thus could have protected itself but chose not to.

Judge Posner evidently articulated the "trickery" standard because he believed that good faith signaled an interest in the developer's subjective intent. But this is unwieldy. He seems to have lost sight of the fact that an actor's intent is already a part of the reasonableness notion. When an actor knows, with a substantial degree of certainty, of the likely consequences of the actor's behavior, the actor is deemed to intend those consequences. As a result, because the good faith inquiry asks whether the developer acted reasonably, the inquiry already examines whether one party intended to take advantage of the counterparty's lack of knowledge. Judge Posner's discussion of trickery suggests the relevant reasonableness inquiry: did the developer act unreasonably in not informing the finance company of the consequences of its failure to negotiate.

On the one hand, if a reasonable developer would have thought that the finance company knew of the penalty provision, but was for some reason indifferent to the provision, or would not have changed its position had it known of the provision, it would not be unreasonable to fail to inform the owner-finance company of the forfeiture provision. The law does not expect a reasonable person to expend resources when they would not affect another's decisions, and the developer would have understood that the value of the finance company's choices fulfilled the developer's obligations.

On the other hand, if a reasonable developer would have known that the owner-financer did not understand the implications of its decision, and if that decision would have been different had the finance company known, it is arguably unreasonable not to inform the finance company of its misunderstanding. This is so because a reasonable developer would know that he can acquire and transmit the information at little cost, and that the owner-finance company who did not know about the penalty clause would pay a high cost.[22] Moreover, the developer, if reasonable, would have known that the provisions' function was to put a cost on the lessor's failure to negotiate in good faith, but that neither party could have expected the cost to include the cost of remembering that the forfeiture provision was there.

22 Judge Posner noted that the developer knew that the finance company was not paying attention and as the owner of many properties, would have trouble keeping track of all their lease contracts.

One might argue that the finance company should have known about the penalty clause – that, in tort terms, the finance company was contributorily negligent. That is relevant, of course, but in the realm of promising, where the parties already have a cooperative relationship, the institution of contracting is strengthened if one party has the duty to rescue another from the other's own lack of care. More to the point, we can call the developers unreasonable behavior a "trick," just as we could use the word "trick" for any failure to inform someone of important information that can be acquired and transmitted at little cost.[23] But the label adds nothing to the analysis and cannot guide the analysis.[24] Rather, the idea of values-balancing, other-regarding contractual behavior provides the kind of structured analysis that makes the good faith inquiry reasonably determinate.

The kind of reasoning depicted here makes the good faith standard more tractable, predictable, and coherent. It is flexible enough to cover the broad range of circumstances in which the good faith question arises, including, for example, cases in which the defendant has knowingly undercut the benefit of the bargain to the counterparty[25] and cases where an actor has failed to take the effort called for by the contract that was necessary for the counterparty to get its benefit under the contract.[26]

11.3 JUDICIAL INTERPRETATION[27]

Courts and legal scholars have gotten into an arid discussion about the rules that govern contract interpretation, debating whether interpretation should be textual or contextual; whether it should feature form or function.[28] This debate makes the methodological mistake of thinking that there ought to be rules about interpretation – a sort of law of interpretation – and that courts must choose between various modes of interpretation before they undertake the interpretation. This is a meaningless choice, pitting the false predictability of textualism against the supposed indeterminacy of contextualism. It wrongly assumes that judges must be bound by rules in order to correctly determine the obligations of the parties under

23 As Melvin A. Eisenberg has written, *Market Street Associates* can be read to affirm a duty to rescue. Eisenberg (2002) at 667–670.

24 On remand, after a bench trial, the court ruled for the financial company. *Mkt. St. Assoc. Ltd. P'ship* v. *Frey*, 817 F. Supp. 784 (E.D. Wis. 1993), *aff'd* 21 F. 3rd 782 (7th Cir. 1994).

25 *Patterson* v. *Meyerhoff*, 97 N.E. 2d 472 (N. Y. 1912) (actor who agreed to buy real estate knowing that the seller did not own it but was going to buy it at auction, went to the auction, bought the property and thus deprived the seller on the potential profit from the exchange. The buyer had agreed to the burden of refraining from bidding at the auction for the seller's benefit, and may not avoid that burden by buying directly at auction).

26 *Fry* v. *George Elkins Co.*, 327 P 2d 905 (Cal D. Ct of App 1958); *Goldberg* v. *Charlies Chevrolet, Inc.* 672 S.W. 2d 177 (Mo. Ct. App. 1984).

27 This section is drawn from an article coauthored with my colleague, Juliet Kostritsky. *See* Gerhart & Kostritsky (2015).

28 *See, e.g.*, Bagchi (2019).

their contract. And it assumes that the cost of incorrect results from textualism are outweighed by textualism's general predictability, or that the rules can be addressed with rules that modify textualist results. The debate between textualism and contextualism is arid because it creates a false dichotomy, underemphasizing the risks of a textualist interpretation and overemphasizing the risks of contextualist interpretations. The dangers of textualism are that things are not always what they seem on the surface, as we will see shortly. The dangers of contextualism are overrated because properly implemented contextualism does not require an all-things-considered judgment. If grounded in the parties' exchange, contextualism can be implemented efficiently, based on a limited number of contextual features. Interpretation should seek to determine which interpretation best comports with the values-balancing legal reasoning that the parties should implement as they reason about their contractual obligations.

The debate about the rules governing interpretation conflates two matters that ought to be separated: the question of which interpretation best fits the parties' substantive choices, and the question of the information base that courts require before they make the substantive interpretation. Asking a court to choose between methods of interpretation confuses the substantive with the epistemological – it confuses the question of what we want to know with the question of how we get information to know what we want to know. The interpretive goal is to determine the party's obligations based on what they have said and done and our best assessment of the equilibrium of benefit and burdens the parties chose. To be sure, it is relevant to do that with an eye to making the determination efficiently, but courts can conserve litigation resources by making a reasoned assessment of the probable accuracy of the empirical that support the contending claims.[29] The methodology described here does that.

The debate between textualism and contextualism is fueled by the unstated assumption that a straightforward process of reasoning (without rules) will not correctly implement a contract's terms. I dispute that assumption and advance a method of reasoning, based on a decision-tree model, that allows courts to justify an interpretation that upholds the institution of contracting without undue expense, one that respects the contract's text while avoiding mistakes.

Consider the functional framework for interpretive decisions. First, judicial interpretation upholds the institution of contracting by affirming and enforcing each party's exchange obligations and the risk burdens each party has accepted. Second, judicial interpretation provides incentives for the parties to reveal private information during contractual negotiations. In many exchange negotiations, one

[29] The methodology suggested here is to disaggregate the bargaining position of the parties to reflect their divergent, rather than joint positions. Although this distinguishes this approach from that of Listokin, the use of probabilistic, Bayesian decisionmaking to focus the disaggregated issues is consistent with his recommendations. *See generally* Listokin (2010).

party is in a superior position to avoid future disagreements; judicial interpretation ought to provide an incentive for that party to avoid acting opportunistically ex post.

A dispute gets to litigation only because the parties will advance differing interpretations of a contractual term. One of the competing interpretations will accurately reflect the bargain the parties made; the other will be mistaken, or may even be an opportunistic attempt to get an unbargained-for benefit. The competing interpretation may reflect ex post circumstances of a kind not contemplated when the bargain was made, or they may reflect different ex ante assumptions about what the term means. The interpreter must make a decision, and the decision must be geared toward upholding the institution of contracting, which the interpreter can do only by determining the meaning of the term in the context of the bargain the parties made. Because the meaning of the disputed term cannot be known without inquiring into what each party meant the term to mean, one cannot say that because the parties agreed to the term it must have a literal meaning. That assertion conflates the term the parties decided on with the meaning of the term the parties decided on, and the meaning is in dispute.

The interpreter knows that the parties reached a bargain that represents the equilibrium of burdens and benefits the parties agreed to, and it is that equilibrium that the interpreter strives to maintain. The decision-tree methodology simply posits that when the decisionmaker knows the two interpretations the party's present, the decisionmaker can ask what must be true for each of the two interpretations to best reflect the exchange equilibrium the parties chose; the decisionmaker asks what facts and circumstances must be true for the decisionmaker to accept one interpretation as a more plausible account of the parties equilibrium point. The facts and circumstances that make each statement comparatively plausible can then be tested by asking what facts or circumstances must be true for *those* facts and circumstances to be true. This process of reasoning can be separately followed on each branch of the decision tree, as the decisionmaker continually articulates and evaluates what must be true for the hierarchy of statements to be accepted as true. The decisionmaker can then decide which interpretation is best supported by the arguments and whether one party had private information that they should have revealed during the bargaining process.[30]

30 By contrast, a rule-based approach to interpretation often favors generalized empirical assumptions about what method of interpretation most contracting parties would want. Yet that empirical question is impossible to answer with confidence; even if it were measurable it would be unhelpful. The parties control the interpretation by the words they use and by their design of the contract in light of their private projects. If they do not control the interpretation by using undisputable terms, it is because they find it more efficient and effective to allow interpretive disputes to be resolved over time, through adjustments, or by seeking the aid of courts. Moreover, even if we knew that seventy percent of contracting parties say that they preferred a textual reading, a textualist reading would be inappropriate thirty percent of the time, and courts would need to know whether the dispute before them falls into one category or the other. Legal decisionmakers ought to start a case without prejudgments about the weight to give to various factors that might (or might not) become relevant. Instead, they ought to

11.3.1 *The Reading Pipe Example*

Under the decision tree model, each party must state, and justify, the interpretive position they are taking, which requires each party to identify and justify the determinants of their argument. Consider a variation of the issue Justice Cardozo faced in *Jacob & Young Inc.* v. *Kent* (*Reading Pipe*).[31] Assume that the contract calls for Reading Pipe but that Reading Pipe is both a brand name and a generic name for type of pipe. Assume that one party asserts that the term Reading Pipe means genuine, brand name Reading Pipe, while the other asserts that the term means a type of pipe. The buyer would argue that she wanted the genuine article; the seller would argue that the contract specified only the pipe's quality, and not its brand. They cannot both be correct, and one of the parties has knowledge superior to the other about whether there was a misunderstanding.

These two arguments are grounded on the determinants of the contending interpretations,[32] which allows the interpreter to ask what assumptions or assertions support each narrative. The buyer might support their narrative by showing that consumers generally prefer brand name pipe, by alleging that they had special reasons to want the Reading brand pipe, or by offering proof that they made known their preference for Reading brand pipe. They might also allege that the pipe the seller used was, in fact, not equivalent to the Reading brand pipe, so that they suffered an unbargained-for loss if they were to accept this pipe. By contrast, the seller might emphasize that Reading pipe was often used in the trade to denote a type of pipe, that they priced the contract on the basis of the type, rather than the brand, of pipe, that they had no reason to know that the buyer had the genuine brand in mind, and that they saved no money by buying the equivalent pipe from a different source (thus denying any quality shirking). These and other justifications would form the competing narratives about the best interpretation.

The judge must then consider whether any of these justifications raise empirical issues that need to be tried. This depends on a probabilistic assessment of the likelihood that a particular assertion is accurate. The judge need not take evidence

analyze information or assertions about general bargaining strategies as they determine their weight in the context of the dispute before them. The parties' sophistication and contractual complexity become relevant inputs into dispute resolution, rather than the basis for forming rules that can be misapplied in other cases.

31 129 N.E. 889 (Ct. App. 1921). The case questioned the remedy when the breach was negligent, not willful, and when the cost of correcting the breach greatly exceeded the lost market value from the breach. For a comprehensive analysis of the case, *see* Goldberg (2015). Interestingly, the interpretive issue discussed in the text was seemingly addressed in paragraph 22 of the contract, which provided that: "Where any particular brand of manufactured article is specified, it is to be considered as a standard. Contractors desiring to use another shall first make implementation in writing to the Architect, stating the difference in cost, and obtain their written approval of the change." *Id.* at 4. The contractor breached this provision, but only through negligence; this led to the remedy based on the decreased value of the home.

32 *See* Berman & Toh (2013) at 1745 (suggesting the idea of displaying the determinants of a statement to test its validity).

on every assertion the parties make; the judge can, for each assertion, determine whether to accept the assertion as true without taking additional evidence. The court resorts to probabilistic analysis to determine whether it can rule out any determination on a dispositive motion or whether to assign one or more of the competing empirical claims to a fact-finding process.[33]

In other words, an appropriate interpretive methodology entails separating the question of the empirical claims each party is advancing from the question of the information the court uses to test the validity of those empirical claims.

1. Identify, for the two interpretations offered by the parties, the determinants that would justify a finding that an interpretation accords with the equilibrium chosen by the parties, and;
2. Determine, on a probabilistic basis, whether to consider evidence about the empirical claims that justify each party's interpretation.

Notice also that, although this methodology is value-neutral, its conclusions are not. If the buyer advanced the wrongful position that the term Reading Pipe meant brand name pipe, the buyer was attempting to exact an unearned benefit from the seller. On the other hand, if the seller really did gain by not using the Reading brand pipe, or if the seller knew that the buyer actually wanted the Reading brand, then the seller has advanced an interpretation that would allow him to deliver less than he promised. The methodology suggested here identifies which party is using the interpretation for an unbargained-for gain.

This methodology also allows the court to identify which party could produce information valuable to the exchange as least cost (the least-cost information provider) and therefore, by its interpretation, to reward bargaining parties that provide exchange-enhancing information and punish bargaining parties that withhold exchange-enhancing information.

Significantly, this methodology enables courts to avoid relying on the generalities that now plague interpretation. Rather than asking what most parties would expect in the Reading Pipe context, a court would make its decision on the basis of case-appropriate presumptions that can be evaluated by shaping the evidence to assure that the net value of an evidentiary inquiry outweighs the probable cost of foregoing that inquiry. Rather than looking for the intent of the parties, the court would be looking for the bargaining party – the least-cost information gatherer – who had the greatest opportunity to make sure that there could be a meeting of the minds on the disputed term. This methodology focuses on what each party is most likely to have had in mind when using the term Reading Pipe and using the interpretation to force the party who could identify the ambiguity at lowest cost to do so. This methodology therefore leaves room for the buyer with special preferences to contract for them but

33 This methodology disaggregates the bargaining position of the parties to reflect their divergent, rather than joint, positions, and therefore allows courts to use probabilistic, Bayesian decisionmaking. It is therefore consistent with Listokin (2010), although Yair Lostokin focuses on joint expectations.

reduces the chance that a buyer who was unhappy with some other part of the performance would use the source of the pipe term's literal or specialized meaning,[34] or if the seller wanted to create an ambiguity (and later claim that plain meaning of the term applied).

11.3.2 *Allocating Risks*

This interpretive methodology is useful in determining how parties allocated the various risks their collaboration faced. Some risks are naturally associated with one party or the other, depending on their private projects. If the risk is one that affects the private projects of one party and is not influenced by the counterparty's performance, the risk falls naturally on that party. That party is presumably the low cost risk-bearer because that party has knowledge and control over the risk, and can minimize or insure against the risk at the least cost. However, one cannot dismiss the possibility that the party on whom the risk naturally falls will transfer the risk to the counterparty by, in effect, compensation the other party for taking the risk. It is important to know whether this has occurred; the methodology developed here helps in that task.

Consider a garden variety dispute, *Midwest Television Inc.* v. *Scott, Lancaster, Mills, and Atha, Inc.*[35] An advertising agency, the defendant, bought advertising time on the plaintiff's television station on behalf of a client advertiser. When the advertiser went bankrupt and could not pay the television station, the station sued the advertising agency, which defended by claiming that it had bought the advertising time as the agent for the advertiser, its principal, and that because the television station knew the identity of the advertiser the television station could look only to the advertiser, and not the advertising agency, for payment. The ad agency argued that the television station bore the risk of non-payment, a position that was supported by Restatement of Agency, which creates a presumption that, if the agent disclosed the name of the principal, the agent was not responsible for the nonpayment. The television station argued that notwithstanding the Restatement, the ad agency bore the risk because that was consistent with trade usage.[36]

34 The buyer might, for example, have had buyer's remorse for building the house in the first place.

35 252 Cal. Rptr. 573 (Cal. Ct. App. 1988).

36 The court decided that the bargain between the advertising agency and the television station was controlled by usages of trade and that usages of trade revealed that advertising agencies were generally responsible for the money owed by their client to the television station. *Id.* at 579. It also decided not to apply the Restatement of Agency approach, which created a presumption that the agent is not responsible for non-payment by the principal when the agent reveals the identity of the principal to the counterparty, which was surely true in this case. The court called the Restatement rule only a presumption, one that could be overcome by evidence of custom or usage of trade. *Id.* Although the court reached the correct result and was justified in relying on the usage of trade, the methodology I advance shows why it was appropriate to conclude that the usage of trade in fact supported the allocation of risk to the ad agency.

In the advertising industry it is clear why the advertising agency, not the television station, can best address the risk of the advertiser's nonpayment. The advertising agency has a relationship with the advertiser and can adjust to the risk in its contract with the advertiser. This arrangement facilitates payment to the advertising agency, for the advertiser pays the ad agency and the agency deducts its fee and forwards the difference on to the television station. Moreover, the ad agency's contract with the advertiser, which the ad agency drafted, required the advertiser to pay the ad agency even before the advertisement was run so that the ad agency could promptly pay the television station. The advertising agency got the time value of money until they paid the television station. Finally, the contract specified that ad agency would not be financing the advertising services that the advertiser – the client – bought.

If the exchange shifted the risk to the television station, the advertising agency would have had to cover the cost of that risk, which it could do by agreeing to pay the television station more for the advertisements on which the television station took the risk. Although an ad agency might find an additional payment beneficial under some (narrow) circumstances (especially if the ad agency had private information about the risk), shifting the risk would require the ad agency to decrease its profit or become less attractive to clients and potential clients (because of the higher prices). Moreover, because television advertising is usually purchased on the basis of a published price schedule, it is easy to compare the price this advertising agency paid with the price in the schedule to see whether, in fact, the advertising agency had paid more to avoid the risk that would ordinarily maximize surplus. If, in fact, the risk shifted away from the low cost absorber, there would be evidence that the advertising agency could produce.

The decision tree methodology shows why the court rejected the Restatement of Agency. The ad agency functioned as a broker, not an agent. In any event, disclosing the principle's name was a necessary part of the purchase of advertising – the television station could hardly be ignorant of the identity of the advertiser – so the information sharing was not done in a context that suggests that that advertising agency shared the information to shift the risk. Importantly, the facts relevant to this analysis are likely to be undisputed and therefore should not require a trial. Unless the ad agency provides a concrete reason to believe that it shifted the risk to the television station the controversy can be addressed on a dispositive motion.

11.3.3 *Avoiding Textual Mistakes*

Too often the literal text does not identify the equilibrium chosen by the parties; a literal approach leads courts to increase the social cost of interpretation, a cost that could easily be avoided if courts paid attention to inexpensive contextual clues. For example, in *Utica City Nat'l Bank* v. *Gunn*,[37] the defendants were company

[37] 154 N.Y.S. 705 (N.Y. App. Div. 1915).

executives who guaranteed bank loans to their companies if the bank "does make such loans and discounts . . . ."[38] The bank then renewed a preexisting loan that it was about to call and later, when the company defaulted on the loan, sued the sureties under their guarantee. The sureties defended on the ground that the defaulted loan was a renewal of an old loan and not the kind of "loan or discount" for which they gave their surety; for them, the literal meaning of the term "loans and discounts" did not include renewals.

Judge Cardozo refused to follow that literal meaning, and looked instead at the context, saying that "the genesis and aim of the transaction may guide the court's choice." What is striking about this case is how easy it is to decide the dispute correctly because of basic non-controverted information. A bank examiner had told the bank to call the loan and the surety agreement was given to induce the bank not to do so.[39] Under this circumstance, the language of the agreement is less important than the context of the agreement. The facts themselves seemed not to be in dispute; the case arose only because of the formal language of the contract and the force of the plain meaning rule, which sustained this dispute long after it should have been decided for the bank. Yet because of the facial cover that the plain meaning rule gave to the interpretation, the bank had to go through a trial and two appeals before it could get its money – a clear social cost.

The trial court could have disposed of the case definitively and inexpensively. The defendants claimed that their surety agreement applied only to future loans, a claim that would have been plausible if the parties contemplated future loans when they made the agreement. The plaintiff bank claimed that the agreement aimed to forestall the bank from calling the existing loan, which would have been plausible if (a) both parties were made better off by that agreement or if (b) the bank was indifferent to the arrangement but the sureties benefited from it. The circumstances in which the surety agreement was negotiated – which was in the shadow of the bank examiner's direction to call the loan – was not denied by the defendants (nor could it be) and provided a strong possibility that the sureties were guaranteeing the prior, not a future, loan. As for the possibility that the bank would give the company future loans, once that necessary determinant is found to be false or probabilistically unlikely, the court should easily have ruled against the defendants.[40]

38 *Id.* at 706.

39 That is why the agreement was not void for lack of consideration.

40 Other cases in which textualism made easy cases difficult are: *Beanstalk Grp.* v. *AM Gen. Corp.*, 283 F.3d 856 (7th Cir. 2002) (holding that a contract setting royalty amount for independent agent marketing the Hummer brand name did not require the company making the Hummer automobile to pay the licensing fee when the company was sold to General Motors; although Hummer trademark was transferred, it was not the kind of transfer for which the independent agent should have expected payment); *Lippman* v. *Sears Roebuck & Co.*, 280 P.2d 775 (Cal. 1955) (holding that a provision for lease payments geared to monthly sales uses recent sales to determine required payment when store no longer used for retail and that the owner would not have renovated building if tenant could so easily avoid paying rental). Efficient contextualism also allows courts to correctly interpret state law that appears to impose a rule that would reduce surplus. *See, e.g.*, *Baldwin Piano, Inc.* v. *Deutsche*

11.3.4 *Why Contextuality:* Columbia Nitrogen Corp.

Deciding cases on the basis of particular bargaining relationships rather than general beliefs about contracting tendencies will avoid mistakes in difficult cases. Take, for example, *Columbia Nitrogen Corp.* v. *Royster Co.*,[41] a case that has become the poster child for economic (and other) criticism of judicial intervention.[42] At first reading, the contract there appeared to require the buyer to buy a minimum tonnage of phosphate from the seller at a stated price (subject to an "escalation factor up or down" for changes in raw material and labor costs).[43] When the market price "plunged precipitously"[44] the buyer substantially reduced its purchases. Rather than enforcing the contract as if it contained a minimum purchase requirement, the court of appeals overruled the district court and held that extrinsic evidence was admissible, thus allowing the jury to interpret the contract in the light of proffered testimony about the context of the negotiations.[45]

To many, the court appeared to be relieving the buyer of a minimum purchase agreement that the buyer had freely accepted. If the contract did provide, as it seemed to, and as economists have assumed, that the buyer had an obligation to purchase a minimum quality of phosphate, the economic criticism of the outcome is justified.[46] Refusing to enforce the obligation would weaken the contract system by putting courts, rather than parties, in the business of determining obligations in the light of changed circumstances. And if the parties chose terms that disregarded their past dealings, they should not be bound by them.[47]

Why then question the standard economic interpretation of the case? First, contrary to popular belief, the contract did not provide, explicitly, that the buyer would purchase the quantities provided in the contract; the contract was more ambiguous than has been realized and the ambiguity is an important part of the story. The contract stated that:

Wurlitzer GmbH, 392 F.3d 881 (7th Cir. 2004) (although Illinois law governing a trademark licensing contract provided that an unlimited license is terminable at will, court held the rule does not apply to this contract and enforced provision limiting the right to terminate; otherwise trademark would not have been transferable).

41 451 F.2d 3 (4th Cir. 1971).

42 *See* Goldberg (2006) at 162; Kirst (1977); and Duesenberg (1973) (the result "boggles the reasonable mind").

43 *Columbia Nitrogen*, 451 F.2d at 6 n.2.

44 *Id.* at 7.

45 *Id.* at 9.

46 I therefore accept Victor Goldberg's analysis of the outcome of the case had the contract really involved a minimum purchase agreement. If Columbia Nitrogen had, as Professor Goldberg assumed, promised to purchase a minimum quantity there would have been no basis for relieving the company from that obligation. I am, however, challenging his assumption that the contract was, in fact, a minimum purchase agreement. As I discuss in the text, it seems unlikely that Columbia Nitrogen in fact agreed to purchase the quantities specified in the contract.

47 Unlike *Hurst* v. *W.J. Lake & Co.*, 16 P 2d. 627 (Or. 1932) trade usage was not introduced as evidence of the meaning the parties must have attributed to a term they used. Instead, the evidence was produced to show that the buyer never agreed to purchase a minimum amount.

> Contract made as of this 8th day of May between COLUMBIA NITROGEN CORPORATION, a Delaware corporation, (hereinafter called the Buyer) hereby agrees to purchase and accept from F.S. ROYSTER GUANO COMPANY, a Virginia corporation, (hereinafter called the Seller) agrees to furnish quantities of Diammonium Phosphate 18–46-0, Granular Triple Superphosphate 0–46-0, and Run-of-Pile Triple Superphosphate 0–46-0 on the following terms and conditions.[48]

Directly below that language the contract shows the "minimum tonnage per year" of various grades of phosphate. Admittedly, this general language could characterize a minimum purchase agreement, although it is noteworthy that the language did not explicitly refer to minimum purchase requirements. But that reading would require a finding that the contract was unambiguous, and I wonder by what reasoning one could reach that conclusion, given the alternative reading of the contract. The contract could be specifying minimum quantities to be furnished, not quantities to be bought. Immediately below the description of "minimum tonnage per year," the contract provided: "Seller agrees to provide additional quantities beyond the minimum specified tonnage for products listed above provided Seller has the capacity and ability to provide such additional quantities."[49] This makes the meaning of the "minimum tonnage per year" ambiguous because it seems to relate the "minimum tonnage" to the seller's obligations rather than to the buyer's obligations.[50] Taking the two sentences together, the language suggests that the contract obligated the seller to supply the minimum tonnage and to provide additional tonnage if it had the capacity to do so. Under this reading, the seller was guaranteeing a minimum tonnage per year, but the buyer was not agreeing to buy a minimum tonnage per year. So the interpretive question is whether the contract was, in reality, a minimum supply agreement or a minimum purchase agreement, or both.

Given this ambiguity, one cannot approach *Columbia Nitrogen* assuming that the buyer was required to purchase a minimum quantity of phosphate, for that would assume away the interpretive issue in the case. If the buyer was not required to purchase a minimum quantity of phosphate, it would not have breached the contract when it decreased its phosphate purchases. Moreover, the use of contextual evidence to decide what obligations the buyer had undertaken would be perfectly legitimate because it would avoid a mistaken textual interpretation of the contract.[51] And that was all that was at stake in the court of appeals decision.

48 *Columbia Nitrogen*, 451 F.2d at 6 & n.2, 7.

49 *Id.* at 7 n.2.

50 The Fourth Circuit itself noted that the contract refers to products supplied under the contract, not to products (alone) or even products purchased under the contract. *Id.* at 10. The language used is consistent with the idea that this is a minimum supply agreement.

51 The court did not find the ambiguity in the contract that I do; it denied that an ambiguity was necessary before invoking trade usage or course of dealing. Accordingly, the court did not ask, as I do, whether this was really a minimum purchase agreement; the court gave credence to usages of trade to vary what it assumed were the terms of the contract – an approach that was inconsistent with the ideas I advance here.

Consider a factor that has been underemphasized in the literature. Although minimum purchase agreements are normal, they generally occur when the buyer is able to predict its requirements of the product (so that it can manage its risk of over-purchasing), but here the buyer was not buying for its own account but for resale. The buyer, a seller of raw materials, did not make any product that used phosphate; instead, it planned on reselling it, using its contacts in the industry and its brokerage subsidiary to make a market for Royster's phosphate production. It had no assured market and a minimum purchase agreement would have increased its risk substantially,[52] especially because it had a minimum purchase agreement with a different phosphate supplier. The seller knew these facts. Although it is possible that a company that did not use phosphate in manufacturing and could not easily predict its requirements of phosphate would sign a minimum purchase agreement, the probability of that happening is not great unless it received a substantial discount or had inexpensive warehousing capability.[53] Although Columbia Nitrogen's arguments tended to be formal (extrinsic evidence should be allowed) rather than evidentiary (this was not a minimum purchase agreement), its evidence included facts that would support the claim that it did not promise to buy a minimum quantity.[54]

Not only would the buyer have had no reason to sign a minimum purchase agreement, the seller had a reason for signing a minimum supply agreement and for making it look like a minimum purchase agreement. The minimum supply agreement made sense for the seller because, as the buyer certainly knew, the seller had excess capacity and encountered little risk in guaranteeing to make a minimum

52 The fact are from a Joint Appendix the parties filed on Appeal., Joint Appendix on Appeal (Transcript of Oral Argument in District Court, Columbia *Nitrogen Corp.* v. *Royster Co.* 451 F. 2d 3 I4th Cir. 1971) (hereafter Joint Appendix).

53 Although the price specified in the contract was lower than the price specified in the buyer's contract with another supplier, it is not clear that it was lower by a significant amount. The Joint Appendix on Appeal did not disclose the amount of the difference. The Fourth Circuit pointed to other evidence that this was not a minimum purchasing contract. Ordinarily, one would expect a minimum purchase agreement to protect the buyer from price decreases, but this contract "neither permits nor prohibits" the parties from "adjusting prices and quantities to reflect a declining market." *Columbia Nitrogen*, 451 F.2d at 9–10. The seller refused to give the buyer a price protection clause that would be common in a minimum purchase agreement; this is further evidence that the parties did not consider this to be a minimum purchase agreement. Joint Appendix on Appeal at 302. In addition, other terms that one would expect in a minimum purchase agreement were missing. *Columbia Nitrogen*, 451 F.2d at 10.

54 In fact, Columbia Nitrogen argued that this was not a minimum quantity agreement (which it termed a take-or-pay agreement). As Victor Goldberg relates it, Columbia Nitrogen argued that its obligation was only to use its best efforts to sell the quantity in the contract and that Royster appreciated the difference between purchasers for resale, like Columbia Nitrogen, and purchasers for use. Goldberg (2006) at168. In fact, a penalty clause was eliminated from the draft of the contract, which Columbia Nitrogen argued took away the implication that this was a take-or-pay contract for a minimum amount. This too was contained in the Joint Appendix. For Columbia Nitrogen, any implication of a minimum purchase requirement was offset by the implicit price protection that came from prior dealings between the parties, for Columbia's testimony showed that when selling to Royster Columbia has always adjusted the contract price to the market price. Joint Appendix, at 136–137.

quantity available to the buyer.[55] Moreover, the seller was using this agreement to secure financing for the phosphate plant that it was building, so it had an interest in making its banks believe that it had addressed the risk of constructing excess capacity.[56]

Even beyond these basic (and undisputed) contextual facts, the relationship between buyer and supplier was unlike the relationship in the usual minimum purchase contract. The buyer and seller had a working relationship over a number of years, but their normal roles were reversed in the contract under consideration. The buyer under this contract was the seller in their prior dealings and the seller under this contract was the buyer in their prior dealings. The buyer, Columbia Nitrogen, sold raw materials for fertilizer and the seller in this case, Royster, made fertilizer and sold it to farmers. Royster, the seller in this contract, decided to make, rather than buy the phosphate it needed in the fertilizer business, and built in excess capacity to reach an efficient scale; this reduced the cost of the phosphate it used in its business, but only if it achieved the efficient scale of production by selling outside the fertilizer market. Because its expertise was in the fertilizer market not the raw materials market, Royster was happy to sell the excess phosphate to Columbia Nitrogen, which had expertise and markets for selling raw materials. The deal made sense for Columbia because Columbia had recently purchased a broker that, by matching suppliers and buyers, made markets in these raw materials. But Royster continued to be a major buyer from Columbia in other product lines.[57]

In light of this background, was the specification of a minimum tonnage per year an obligation of the buyer or of the seller? Columbia Nitrogen, the buyer, offered proof that the amount of purchases could be adjusted to reflect market conditions, which were highly unstable in the fertilizer business.[58] And because Columbia was asserting no fixed purchase obligation, it was asserting that Royster would renegotiate the price if market prices fell. Under this interpretation, the term "minimum tonnage per year" was the amount that Royster had to be willing to supply. Royster, the seller, asserted that the term "minimum tonnage per year" required Columbia to purchase at least that much each year. How might a court systematically try to determine the obligations of the parties?

If Royster's interpretation prevailed, Columbia Nitrogen would have to pay for that amount of phosphate each year at the contract price (as adjusted, pursuant to the contract, for raw material cost changes). If Columbia's interpretation prevailed, the

55 Joint Appendix, *supra* note 130 at 100, 246.

56 Columbia Nitrogen apparently learned this after the contract was signed. *See* Goldberg (2006) at 170.

57 The fact that the seller, Royster, was also a major buyer from Columbia gave rise to an unsuccessful claim that Royster's purchases were used as leverage to induce Columbia to enter into this contract. Columbia also alleged that it was just that leverage that reduced Royster's incentive to negotiate a fair settlement when market conditions changed. Joint Appendix at 8, 249.

58 According to the testimony, the practice of adjusting the terms of the contract was not only common within the industry but was justified by the frequency and severity of price changes between the time of contracting and the time of performance. Joint Appendix at 102–103, 125–127, 132–137, 286–289.

amount of Columbia's purchases would be unspecified in the contract and Columbia would not have to purchase any particular amount of phosphate at the price called for by the contract, but would be required to use good faith while exercising its option. The contract is allocating one of two risks. If the contract requires Columbia to buy a minimum quantity, Columbia bears the risk that it will not be able to use that quantity productively. If the contract instead provides that Royster must set aside a minimum quantity each year for Columbia, Royster will assume the risk that demand for phosphate will go up and that it would be locked into selling to Columbia Nitrogen when, in fact, it would be better off selling to others.

Royster's interpretation would be correct if Columbia had agreed to assume the risk that it would be required to buy more phosphate than it could sell. It would be plausible to believe that assertion if either (a) Columbia received a price sufficiently below the market price to compensate them for that risk or if (b) Columbia were in a position to minimize that risk by accurately estimating its needs or selling unneeded phosphate on the market. Proposition (a) would be plausible if we could compare the price in the contract with the market price at the time of contracting and if the "escalator clause" allowed the price to stay below market price when prices went down. We have inadequate information about the relationship between the contract price and the market price and about how the "escalator clause" would function.

Proposition (b) would be true if (i) Columbia made products with the phosphate and could reasonably predict its needs for phosphate by reasonably predicting its sales of products manufactured with phosphate or if (ii) Columbia sold in diverse markets that did not move together, so that if Columbia's phosphate sales went down in one market Columbia could sell the phosphate in other markets.

Royster's interpretation would be plausible if: (a) Royster built excess capacity to lower its cost of acquiring phosphate; (b) Royster were not in the business of selling phosphate and faced barriers to getting into that business; and (c) Royster was viewing Columbia as its sales agent or broker. Assertion (a) seems to have been true and admitted by Royster. Assertion (b) would be true if (i) Royster did not have relationships with purchasers of phosphate, and (ii) could not easily build those relationships from the relationships it had. Assertion (c) would be true if (i) Columbia had contacts as a supplier of phosphate to non-fertilizer users that Royster did not have and if (ii) buying Columbia's expertise in non-fertilizer markets would make sense economically, and if (iii) Royster had a reason – a part of its private projects – to make it look as if Columbia has agreed to buy a minimum amount when Columbia did not agree to that.

In summary, the interpretive issue is whether it is likely that Royster was hiring Columbia to function as a broker (in which case the term "minimum tonnage per year" would signify the minimum amount that it guaranteed Columbia) or whether it was selling a fixed amount to Columbia. Although we cannot make any definitive conclusion without considering the evidence in greater detail, the methodology suggested here allows courts to focus on the evidence that is most important to the controversy and to use probabilistic determinations to limit the cost of making the necessary empirical determinations.

11.4 CONCLUSION

In this chapter, I have advanced values-balancing reasoning as a way of interpreting contractual performance obligations. I have claimed that tort law is an integral part of contract law because tort law determines, on the basis of other-regarding reasoning, obligations that are implicit in the decisions made by the parties in a relationship. The tort law category of "special relationships" in fact encompass all relationships in which the parties had an opportunity to bargain but proceeded with their relationship on the assumption that each party would act reasonably. The idea that parties in a relationship implicitly agree to act reasonably then helps us understand the obligation to perform in good faith, as well as about how contracts should be interpreted. When contractual disputes arise, the dueling interpretations allow the interpreter to form a decision tree so that the interpreter can systematically evaluate the assumptions or assertions that must be true in order to choose the interpretation that best reflects the equilibrium of that exchange. The decision tree allows the interpreter to determine which interpretation best fits the empirical assumptions the parties must have made, and the other-regarding reasoning that each party is required to use.

12

Consumer Contracts and Standard Terms

Although contract law often assumes that parties actively bargain over various exchange dimensions, many exchanges are conditioned on one party acceding to the other party's standard terms; sometimes both parties make a bargain contingent on standard terms (which often conflict). Such standard-term transactions seem to challenge the bargaining model, for they appear to leave one party with a take-it-or-leave-it set of terms, giving rise to concerns about contracts of adhesion and unequal bargaining power.[1] Today, this dynamic is being addressed in the context of consumer contracts; various legal approaches are advanced in the context of the proposed Restatement of Law: Consumer Contracts (Draft Consumer Restatement).[2] In this chapter, I demonstrate how other-regarding, values-balancing reasoning can shed light on the role of standard form contracts, and their legal treatment, in the many contexts in which they occur.[3]

12.1 THE DILEMMA

Consumer contracts – purchases for "personal, family, or household"[4] use – present a formidable challenge to the idea of bargaining and mutual assent to be bound. Consumers assent to the basic terms of a seller's offer; they accept price, quality, and delivery terms. But consumers are often confronted with the seller's additional terms that come into play when, or even after, the consumer consents to the core transaction. Although many of these additional terms are benign, or even helpful to consumers, other terms make the product more expensive or less desirable than it

[1] *See generally* Kim (2013), Slawson (1996). Kim (2019) has a fuller treatment of the determinants of consent.

[2] Restatement of the Law: Consumer Contracts (Am. Law Inst., Tentative Draft 2019).

[3] Standard terms raise issues in employment contexts and many exchanges between merchants. Although this chapter addresses consumer transactions only, the mode of reasoning displayed here is, I believe, applicable to exchanges using standard terms more generally.

[4] This definition is similar to the definition of "consumer" in the Uniform Commercial Code §1–201(b)(11) and the draft Restatement of the Law of Consumer Contracts, §1(a)(1).

would be without the terms.[5] Generally, consumers accept such terms without reading them, without comprehending their meaning, or without an opportunity to bargain over them. All sides of the consumer contract debate agree that consumer behavior is unlikely to result in meaningful choices over the standard terms that accompany a transaction. Bounded rationality,[6] information overload,[7] the expense and irritation of reading the standard terms,[8] or the failure to mandate information disclosure,[9] make the cost of consumer self-protection too great to justify an investment in taking greater care. After all, not every consumer expects to have a problem with a product, even though each consumer can expect that some consumer will have a problem with the product. Accordingly, no single consumer has an incentive to invest on behalf of other consumers; high search costs with low projected returns deaden the incentive of any consumer to forgo an otherwise surplus-generating transaction or invest in bargaining just because consumers as a class would benefit. That is true even if the net consumer benefits of bargaining over a term would exceed the value of the term to sellers; even efficient choices will not be made.

Digital communications reduce search costs, of course, but even if competing sellers were to offer diverse standard terms, consumers are unlikely to invest in search and evaluation costs unless the probable value of search information exceeds the cost. Often, search and evaluation costs exceed the value of the underlying consumer transaction. And sellers often fail to provide the different terms that would make consumer choice possible. When a consumer is making a small purchase from the only seller of the product the consumer wants, a consumer faced with the seller's standard terms must make an all-or-nothing decision, which gives the seller power and discretion over the terms of the deal.

Given the challenge to concepts of autonomy and assent when one party is asked to assent to standard terms without knowledge, comprehension, or bargaining, which terms outside the core transaction, if any, should be enforced as part of the exchange? More importantly, is there a way to integrate consumer contracts into a general theory of exchange, or are they destined to be treated as a special case, subject to a different set of determinants? In this chapter, I argue that values-balancing reasoning invites us to broaden our understanding of the dynamics of exchange, which we can do by understanding exchange as a process through which each party takes on an obligation to look out for the well-being of the other party.

5 Standard terms sometimes shift important risks, and therefore important burdens, to consumers, including warranty disclaimers, liquidated damages provisions, exculpatory clauses, indemnification provisions, compulsory arbitration agreements, and choice of law and choice of forum provisions. *See, e.g.*, Lonegrass (2012) at 27–28.

6 Korobkin (2003).

7 Wagner (2019) (noting the strategy of burying crucial provision in a throng of provisions); Becher (2007–2008) (mandated disclosures may weaken consumer decisions by presenting too much information).

8 Lonegrass (2012) at 32–34.

9 Ben-Shahar & Schneider (2014).

Oriented in that way, the problem of standard terms in consumer contracts becomes part of a general approach to the obligations of contracting partners, and we can fruitfully determine an appropriate method of reasoning about standard terms.

12.2 THE DOCTRINAL OPTIONS

Contracts with standard terms pit the idea of choice against the idea of enforceability. One polar position is to say that consumers who assent to the transaction (and its core terms) do not assent to the seller-supplied terms unless a seller allows consumers to pick and choose among them. This "two-contract" or "shared meaning"[10] solution would enforce the core terms of a transaction but not seller-supplied terms over which consumers have no real choice. Those approaches are justified by reference to shifts in contract theory from bargaining to assent,[11] on factors that made these additional terms incomprehensible,[12] and on the impact of certain terms on the nature of the consumer transaction.[13]

The other polar position, the unenforceability option, is to find assent in the consumer acceptance of the standard terms (or the failure to reject the transaction) but to independently determine which of the standard terms are valid and enforceable. Thus, the dilemma: if a consumer assents to the seller's terms, how can the consumer claim that the terms should not be enforced; yet if transacting means consenting to seller terms, the concept of assent has been changed. If contracting is about bargaining or more than a take-it-or-leave it choice, none of the standard additional terms would be enforceable against either party. Yet if standard terms are enforceable in general because contract law endorses such choices, is there any basis for enforcing some terms but not others?

This dilemma is not addressed effectively by referring to contracts of adhesion or even to unequal bargaining power. By itself, the take-it-or-leave-it choice of accepting all the terms or foregoing the transaction does not signal that consumer transactions are unfair; consumers in a store are faced with a similar choice – they either pay the posted price or shop elsewhere. Consumer choice is protected as long as the consumer has a choice among stores which are known to offer different mixes of price and quality (where ancillary terms become a part of quality). Choosing the store in which to shop, when the price and quality of the store's products can be experienced, provides the consumer with choices that keep the market functioning. Similarly, if different sellers are known to offer different kinds of standard terms of known differences, the choice of where to shop provides the consumer with meaningful choice. Take it or leave it deals are hardly sufficient to show whether there is assent unfairness or substantive unfairness.

10 Kar & Radin (2019).
11 Kastner (2010).
12 Slawson (1971).
13 Willis (2015); Gilo & Porat (2005–2006).

Similarly, the dilemma is not really a problem of bargaining power. Collectively, consumers have the bargaining power that would make standard terms fair if consumers could collectively harness their bargaining power. The problem is not bargaining power; it is the collective action problem of organizing consumers to insist on their preferences. Yet the collective action problem is itself a reason for doubting that the market can achieve efficient results.

12.3 THE DRAFT RESTATEMENT

The current draft of the Consumer Restatement would include standard terms as part of the transaction if the consumer had a meaningful opportunity to reject the terms, but standard terms would be invalid and unenforceable if the terms violate notions of abuse of discretion, unconsionability, deception, or attempts to disclaim warranties. Consumers are protected if (1) a court finds that consumers were given insufficient opportunity to assent to the terms, or (2) if a court excludes terms under one of the grounds of invalidity. Clearly, however, the emphasis is on invalidity.

This approach has not silenced critics who continue to insist that if not bargained for, standard terms should be disallowed. But the debate is fueled by confused legal doctrine. The Reporters coded cases that strike down standard terms to show which cases are based on the lack of assent and which on the unenforceability of standard terms.[14] The coding, it is claimed, could not be replicated because the classifications were highly discretionary.[15] This debate is about what courts say they were doing, not about the outcomes. The problem is that courts are faced with a single question – should the term be enforced – but legal doctrine treats it as two questions: Is assent to be bound sufficient and should the term be enforced? Because courts can decide a case under either the assent justification or the enforceability justification, the coding is highly discretionary. The Draft Consumer Restatement would allow courts to go directly to the meat of the problem: the question of enforceability.

The Draft Consumer Restatement is consistent with the relationality of contracts. A consumer transaction flows from a commitment by both parties to the joint seller-consumer collaboration. Because formal assent would impose unnecessary search costs on consumers, the appropriate legal response is to make sellers assume the costs of making reasonable choices for consumers, refraining from suggesting standard terms that would decrease net consumer benefits of the transaction. Sellers ought to be other-regarding by fairly balancing the burdens and benefits of the exchange for both parties. Any terms that do not reflect this other-regarding, values-balancing reasoning are unenforceable.

The Restatement reporters have uncovered an evolutionary legal development that, because of the relationality of consumer contracts, accepts the idea of assent to

[14] Bar-Gill, Ben-Shahar, & Marotta-Wurgler (2017).

[15] Klass (2019); Levitin, Kim, Kunz, Linzer, McCoy, Moringiello, Renuart, & Willis (2019).

be bound for basic terms of the transaction but requires sellers to insert only those standard terms that are reasonable. Although the issue of enforceability is often organized around opaque (or even misleading) words like "unconsionability" and "public policy," the implementation of those terms is fully consistent with the idea of value-balancing, other-regarding contracting. This approach preserves standard terms that are either benign or helpful to consumers, while disallowing terms that are inconsistent with the obligations of an other-regarding seller.

The evolution of the concept of invalid and unenforceable terms is not difficult to trace. Let me briefly describe that evolution before explaining why bargaining over terms is an unessential aspect of contracting. The Draft Consumer Restatement employs the concept of unconsionability to designate unenforceable terms, with a definition similar to the UCC's definition.[16] Although the term "unconsionability," because of its roots, conjures up images of moral failure and exploitation, the term now can be understood as a synonym for terms that add no net consumer burdens to the transaction. The Restatement names three types of unconscionable provisions, each of which is invalid because of its effect on consumers: (1) restrictions on seller's liability or buyer's remedies, (2) the expansion of consumer liability or the seller's remedies against the consumer; and (3) limitations on the consumer's right to seek redress for wrongs. It further explains that a prohibited contract term is one that "potentially undermines the benefit of the bargain [transaction], and for which the businesses cannot show a reasonable business justification."

Prior efforts to authorize courts to make surgical strikes against unreasonable, and therefore invalid, terms were largely unsuccessful but pointed the way. The Restatement of Contracts (Second) attempted to capture the idea of one-sided terms in section 211(3), which would render a term unenforceable if the offeror "has reason to believe that the party manifesting . . . assent would not do so if he knew that the writing contained a particular term . . . ."[17] This provision made surgical strikes against particular terms possible, without undoing the transaction,[18] and focused on a term's acceptability, rather than on assent. It too puts the onus on the proposing party to reason about the counterparty's well-being in a way that evaluates the burdens and benefits of the term for the party to be bound.[19]

16 The UCC's unconsionability provision, §2–302, invites a court to determine whether, in light of the general commercial background and needs of particular trade or case, the clauses involved are so one-sided so as to be unconscionable as of the time of the making of the contract. UCC §2–302, cmt 1 (1952). The Restatement (Second) has a nearly identical provision (Restatement (Second) of Contracts, §208 (1981).

17 Restatement (Second) of Contracts, §211(3) (1981).

18 *See* Lonegrass (2012) at 44. Her contrary reading seems to be unwarranted. Section 211 specifically deals with terms, not transactions. When section 211 (3) refers to "such assent" it seems to be referring to the assent to a particular term, not assent to the transaction, or assent to all the terms. A contrary reading would require a court to nullify a transaction merely because the parties proposed and accepted an unacceptable term.

19 Karl Llewellyn's formulation varied slightly. He would accept the basic obligations of the transaction and other proposed terms that were "not unreasonable or indecent terms the seller may have had in his

The reasons this provision has been ineffective, especially in consumer contracts, are instructive.[20] Judges have routinely conflated the question of assent (*not* the subject of §211(3)) with the question of the term's enforceability (which is the sections subject). Some courts continue to apply §211(3) only if the party seeking to be free of a term has read the term (a holdover of formalism), and other courts give the non-drafting party the burden of showing that the drafter was unreasonable in believing that the term would not be the subject of assent. More directly, the provision presented courts with an unfamiliar standard with no analytical anchor.

A related approach suggests that courts should reject terms that were not within the expectations of the parties when they assented to the terms.[21] This too would be a surgical strike against unacceptable terms. But it hinges on a seemingly empirical inquiry about what consumers actually expect. And courts have no basis for knowing what a consumer expects, especially when expectations are formed by the normal practices of the trade. If the norm to arbitrate disputes were commonly adopted, that norm would become expected. But the question is whether the norm should be created by terms that are not, for normative reasons, acceptable terms of the transaction.[22]

The Draft Consumer Restatement seems to identify the natural next point of this reconsideration of the role of bargaining in promising and contracting, for it recognizes that judges have overcome the formalism of the bargaining model in an effort to make bargaining both efficient and fair. The function of promising and contracting is to determine obligations when bargaining is inefficient, not to make bargaining and bargaining costs the institution's goal. By confirming that the role of courts is to invalidate terms that are unfair to the exchange, the Draft Consumer Restatement has reinforced the idea that promising and contracting are about how actors reason over their treatments of the counterparty, not only about the process by which obligations are determined. Let me turn then to show why the Draft Consumer Restatement approach is consistent with the idea of bargaining and provides a tractable basis for invalidating an exchanges one-sided terms.

12.4 THE BASIS OF EXCHANGE

It is regularly pointed out that standard terms attached to an otherwise enforceable transaction are a departure from the classical bargaining model – the model that assumes that contracts arise from dickering[23] over various arrangements of burdens

form, which do not alter or eviscerate the reasonable meaning of the dickered terms." Llewellyn (1960) at 370.

20 Zacks (2016), the most comprehensive review of §211's implementation, is the source of the information in this paragraph.

21 Slawson (1984).

22 White & Mansfield (2002) 263 predicted that the unconsionability approach would merge with the expectations approach.

23 The term is one of the gifts of Carl Llewellyn. Llewellyn (1960) at 370–371 (contrasting dickered terms with boilerplate terms).

and benefits until the parties determine the equilibrium that jointly satisfies their private projects. That model does not describe, and, because of information costs, cannot efficiently fit consumer contracts. How, then, does the bargaining model serve as the foundation for contract law and simultaneously accommodate consumer market realities?

If we examine why the bargaining model is attractive, we can see a way to reconcile legal treatment of consumer transactions with the bargaining model. Here is how. When we anchor the basis of exchange in the concept of meaningful choice through bargaining, we are recognizing that each party in an exchange takes on burdens so that the other party might benefit. Because that bargaining is driven by the private projects of the parties, each of whom considers several risk-related factors, bargaining may involve several variables that are traded off against each other in various combinations to form an array of burdens and benefits that satisfies each party. Moreover, for bargaining to result in a contract, each party must account for the well-being of the other party to ensure that the benefits and burdens remain sufficient to allow each party to receive net benefits from the transaction (and stay in the relationship). Both parties, in other words, must be reasonably other-regarding. Just as the idea of other-regarding reasoning has illuminated our understanding of good faith, the interpretation of disputed contracts, and implied obligations, it illuminates the obligations of sellers.

Consumer contracts represent a special case of the other-regarding aspects of exchange. Because consumers, by nature of their private projects, do not (and should not be expected to) exercise oversight over the standard terms of a transaction, the seller must do so as a natural application of the general obligation to be other-regarding. Under this view, the seller may add terms to the transaction that meet the seller's desire to make the transaction more attractive and to frame the relationship in ways that reasonably mediate between the interests of seller and consumer. When additional terms are benign or beneficial to consumers, there is no reason to exclude them from the transaction. However, the seller knows that consumers are in no position to pay attention to more than a few of the transaction's terms, and that, in fact, the consumer depends on the seller to make the product reasonably attractive. That means that the seller needs to act in a way that reasonably integrates the seller's private projects with those of the consumer, acting on behalf of the consumer by determining terms for the exchange that add to the value of the product or that provide a consumer benefit that is proportionate to the seller's value from those terms. In words that have come to mark any good relationship, the seller "must think for both of us, for all of us."[24]

The idea that the seller ought to act on behalf of the consumer to reasonably integrate their sometimes-conflicting interests is not foreign to contract law. The

[24] Ilsa to Rick in the movie *Casablanca*. *See* Koch (1972). *Casablanca: Script and Legend* (The Overlook Press 1972).

issue of standard terms in consumer contracts is the mirror image of implied obligations in consumer contracts. Contract doctrine long ago recognized a seller's obligation to provide a level of performance that would deliver net consumer benefits., whether or not the consumer market demanded those benefits. An implied warranty recognizes the dynamics of consumer exchanges – and consumer reliance on the seller to look out for consumer interests – an obligation that is grounded in the dynamics of the consumer exchange. Just as consumer exchanges include an obligation to make sure that a loaf of bread does not have a pin in it, consumer exchanges imply a seller obligation to avoid adding terms to a transaction that unreasonably burden the consumer without an offsetting benefit. Similarly, product liability law requires sellers to anticipate and build into their products, safety features that although expensive, have consumer benefits that outweigh the expense.

The legal imposition of warranties as implied obligations and legal invalidation of a seller's terms both follow the logic of the market. Markets function well when potential transactors have full information about the burdens and benefits of a transaction. Yet because the economics of information create an information asymmetry, the most efficient way for markets to operate is to internalize the information costs to the party that is best able to gather and evaluate the information, the seller. Sellers naturally gather information about consumers and their interests; if sellers are to flourish, they naturally have to put themselves in the shoes of consumers to determine how consumers react to various combinations of quality and price. Sellers gather information, evaluate consumer reactions, and understand what attracts consumers to a transaction. There is no reason that sellers cannot anticipate which terms can be characterized as one-sided or unfair, nor, as I describe in the next section, is there a reason to believe that courts are unable to recognize when sellers have overreached.

Courts perform a legitimate function when they resolve disputes in a way that improves how markets operate, which they do by recognizing the obligation of sellers to make other-regarding decisions. Product liability law and warranty law have done this for decades. Courts have also shown an ability to recognize when reasoning that sellers use to establish the terms of a transaction is not sufficiently other-regarding. As the Consumer Restatement documents, it is as if the courts recognize that it is unconscionable not to be other-regarding.

12.5 THE OTHER-REGARDING CONSUMER TRANSACTION

As we have seen, dispersed and independent consumer choices impair markets in consumer goods. By determining which terms a reasonable, other-regarding seller would add to the transaction, courts can render unenforceable terms that would be inconsistent with the values that sellers and buyers bring to an exchange. Sellers represent the value of offering choices; buyers represent the value of making sure that market choices are efficiently made. Those values can be balanced by requiring sellers to offer choices that do not burden efficient consumer choices.

Under an interpretation of consumer contracts that requires the seller, when setting the terms of the transaction, to account for the well-being of the consumer, the court can avoid standard terms that the seller has reason to know would make the product less desirable than consumer would pay for if consumer collaboration were costless. The Draft Consumer Restatement already identifies several of those terms, including required arbitration where arbitration would serve to limit class actions and thus effectively preclude the consumer from suing, limits on remedies, disclaimers of warranties, or the unreasonable expansion of the seller's remedies.

However, values-balancing reasoning allows the list to expand. In this connection, it is a mistake to believe that the concept of unconsionability is designed just to address cases of egregious exploitation. True, when a seller preys on the vanity and loneliness of a buyer, the behavior is knowingly exploitative.[25] But that does not limit the way that values-balancing reasoning can determine when standard terms are invalid. The outrage at the exploitation is less important than the seller's failure to be other-regarding by making the seller's own goals subservient to the private objectives of the consumer, which he knew to be unobtainable. Focusing on extreme cases should not obscure the fact that courts now employ values-balancing reasoning to render invalid terms that are unreasonable without being morally egregious.

The substructure supporting these examples, which themselves reflect judicial outcomes, seem to embody the following principles. The seller is obliged to know what consumers expect from the transaction, and the seller ought to use that knowledge to put herself in the position of the consumer in order to determine which standard terms are enforceable. If a standard term adds net benefits for the consumer, courts ought to allow it. If the seller benefits from the term but the consumer is not burdened by it, the courts ought to allow it. However, if the standard term adds no consumer benefits, viewing benefits as the consumer would see them, or adds burdens that benefit only the seller, courts should disallow the term. The disallowed terms are ones the consumer would not have freely chosen as a feature of the product if the consumer did not receive an offsetting lower price. For example, in most settings, the seller, behind the veil of ignorance, and not knowing whether she was a seller or consumer, would not choose an arbitration clause because the burden of restricting consumer resort to class actions, would produce no net benefit for the consumer and would benefit the seller only by placing a burden on the consumer. If consumers had effective mechanisms of choice, they would not choose the arbitration remedy as part of the contract.

Under this reasoning, courts have struck down limitations on consequential damages when personal injury is at stake,[26] attempts to limit express warranty

[25] *Bennet* v. *Bailey*, 597 S.W. 2d 532 (Tex. 1980).

[26] *Larsen* v. *Pacesetter Sys.*, 837 P. 2d 1273 (Haw. 1992).

violations claims to product replacement,[27] waiver of class action arbitration,[28] and waiver of class actions lawsuits.[29] Although some of these cases speak in terms of presumptions, it is hard to see how a presumption against such terms can be overcome. What courts seem to be doing is shifting the burden of coming forward with the evidence to the seller. They might, for example, ask sellers to be prepared to show that they accounted for the net consumer benefits of the term before sellers made a particular term a part of the transaction. After all, what courts are reviewing is not just the terms the sellers add to the contract but also the method of reasoning that sellers used to add terms to the contract. It would be consistent with general consumer practice law to ask sellers to reveal their internal discussions about the terms of the transaction so that the court could test the legitimacy of the seller's reasoning.

The other-regarding consumer transaction allows sellers the leeway to offer to reduce the price of the product in exchange for less desirable terms. Within the limits of reasonableness, a lower price in exchange for an undesirable term may allow the consumer to self-insure and get a combination of price and quality that better meets the consumer's needs. In product liability cases, for example, courts recognize that that consumers need not always pay for the highest degree of quality or service if that is not in their interests; consumers are allowed to buy used cars or less safe cars if that is what fits their budget and sellers are not responsible for the costs of those choices. But in such cases, the sliding scale between procedural and substantive unconsionability plays an important role.[30] The consumer must be in a position to evaluate the trade-off the consumer is making, and the seller may not offer varying prices knowing that the buyer cannot afford a better trade-off.

12.6 CONCLUSION

Consumer transactions present unique challenges for contract law. The dynamics of market information impose large and inefficient consumer information costs unless courts internalize these costs to the seller. The law has done that through tort law in the form of seller liability for product defects and negligence liability for service providers. The law has also internalized consumer information costs on the seller through warranty law. The law can do the same for the other terms of consumer contracts, which is what the Draft Consumer Restatement essentially requires. The seller has, or can easily acquire, the information necessary to determine whether the consumer benefits of adding a term to a contract outweigh the costs of those terms to

[27] *Horn* v. *Boston Sci. Neuromodulation Corp.*, 2011 WL 3893812 (S.D. Ga. 2011)

[28] *Discover Bank* v. *Superior Court*, 113 P. 3d. 2100 (Cal. 2005). I am not considering preemption of arbitration provisions under the Federal Arbitration Act.

[29] *Scott* v. *Singular Wireless*, 161 P. 3d 1000 (Wash 2007).

[30] The sliding scale, an attempt to deal simultaneously with the problem of assent and the problem of substantive invalidity was first raised in Leff (1967). Under the view I present, substantive invalidity is sufficient to make a contract term invalid.

the consumer. And the seller can determine whether the benefits of a term for the seller's private projects impose burdens on the consumer.

If the consumer benefits outweigh consumer costs, the term should be enforced. If not, the seller has two choices. The seller can either offer the product at two different prices, with the difference recognizing the consumer losses from less desirable term. That is a satisfactory resolution of the problem of information costs as long as the consumer is fully informed of the implications of the cheaper option. Alternatively, the seller should not adopt the term. And the seller may add terms that benefit the seller without imposing a burden on consumers. These options protect the seller and the consumer and enhance the value of consumer transactions.

13

Excused Performance and Risk Allocation

A contracting party may ask to be excused from her contractual obligations because of ex post circumstances that were seemingly unaddressed in the contract. Alternatively, a party may ask that her obligations be modified because of ex post circumstances, even if the party wants the contract to be binding under modified terms. Legal decisionmakers must deal with post-contract circumstances that make the performance more expensive, less beneficial, or impossible for one of the parties, and the law must determine how those circumstances influence the parties' obligations. These issues, which I will call excused obligation issues, are among the most difficult relational tensions that the parties and courts face.[1]

The challenge to the institution of contracting is significant. The obligations ought to be determined from the parties' exchange (as embodied in the contract), but the parties need to know what to do when ex post circumstances differ from the circumstances that were the exchanges tacit assumptions. The loss must fall somewhere, but if contractual autonomy is to be preserved, the loss ought to be allocated in a way that is consistent with, and honors, the exchange the parties made. How do the parties and legal decisionmakers reconcile ex ante bargains with ex post realities?

Excuse issues are addressed in several doctrinal domains. Modification addresses whether the contract should include or exclude the modified terms. Excusing a party from all her obligations is forced into doctrinal pigeonholes of impossibility, impracticability, and frustration. Legal doctrine does little to help; standards for determining whether the conditions of an excuse exist are particularly opaque.[2] The doctrine governing modifications took a wrong turn, as I will explain below, by asking whether the modification was supported by consideration (the preexisting duty

[1] The historical roots of the doctrine are described in Gordley (2004).

[2] Consider the test from a recent Great Britain case: "Among the factors which have to be considered are the terms of the contract itself, its matrix and context, the parties' knowledge, expectations, assumptions and contemplations, in particular as to risk, as at the time of the contract, at any rate so far as those can be ascribed mutually and objectively ... " *Canary Wharf* v. *European Medicines Agency*, www.bailii.org./ew/cases/EWHC/Ch/2019/335.html. The listed factors are not necessarily irrelevant; they need to be supplemented by a process of reasoning that will give appropriate weight to the factors.

rule); now even legal sources that have abandoned the search for consideration understand modifications only in the amorphous terms of good faith and reasonableness.[3]

But doctrine is troubled by an even deeper problem; doctrine does not attempt to determine explicitly how parties allocated the risks of unaddressed circumstances and is not anchored in the question of whether a party has an obligation in the first place. Without a method of determining how the parties allocated the risks, legal doctrine cannot determine obligations and therefore cannot determine when obligations should be excused. On its face, legal doctrine appears to say that if a condition of excuse is found, the party whose performance is impaired by the condition is excused from its obligations.[4] But that formulation of doctrine assumes that the parties allocated the risk to the party that wants to be excused. That assumption, I believe, is unwarranted. As Victor Goldberg has argued,[5] analysis should not depend on whether a party is able to anticipate future events. Foreseeability is not the issue; responsibility is. We should focus on how parties divided the risks of unassigned circumstances; the party to whom a risk is implicitly assigned is the one responsible for that risk. And if a party has assumed the risk, the party has already been compensated for the risk from unassigned events. Not all future events are known, but people know how to reason about future events that affect their private projects that are unknown, and they know how to protect against those events, even if unknown. They know, therefore, to what extent they should, or should not, count on their contractual counterpart to protect them from unassigned circumstances. We need only ask how the parties who are now disputing their obligations implicitly divided the risks of unanticipated circumstances. That division is the reasonable one.

Accordingly, as I argue in Section 13.1, if a condition of impossibility, frustration or impracticability exists, it tells us that the relationship did not work out because ex post circumstances make the ex ante bargain unworkable. However, the existence of that condition does not tell us where the losses from the failed relationship should fall. The excuse doctrine begs for a method of determining how the parties allocated the risk of loss, for that allocation determines which party should bear the risk. Similarly, as I argue in Section 13.3, doctrines surrounding legal modification cannot be implemented without knowing how the parties allocated the risks of

3 Graham & Peirce (1989) at 12–16 (tracing the rise and fall of the preexisting duty rule).

4 The literal wording of both the UCC and the Restatement (Second) of Contracts suggest that if a condition of excuse is found, the party claiming an excuse is excused from its obligations. Note that comment 8 in the relevant UCC §2–615 suggests that what they call an exemption does not apply "if the contingency in question is sufficiently foreshadowed at the time of contracting to be included among the business risks which are fairly to be regarded as part of the dickered terms, either consciously or as a matter of reasonable commercial interpretation from the circumstances." It continues that a court can find that the parties allocated the risk, which could be found in "the circumstances surrounding the contracting, in trade usage and the like"

5 Goldberg (2010) at 360.

unassigned events. Fundamentally, modification doctrine suggests that a party that bears a certain risk may not seek to reallocate that risk without compensating the counterparty.

Consider a different approach. When seemingly unaddressed ex post circumstances occur, the other-regarding promisor will consider their private projects in relation to the private projects of the counterparty, and will reason about which private projects should bear the burden of those circumstances, taking into account how the parties allocated the risk of ex post unaddressed circumstances. This approach is possible, I will argue, because the contract and its context implicitly allocate the risks the parties assumed ex ante, even if they did not recognize, bargain over, or even contemplate the precise circumstances in which the risk arose. The allocation of risks of unanticipated events follows the division of anticipated risks, given what each party should have known about the private project risks the counterparty faces. This implicit division will reflect the implicit reasoning that led to the bargain; it is the one that reasonable, other regarding contracting parties would use, and that legal decisionmakers can use, to determine which party should bear the risk of loss given how the parties must have viewed the risks to their private projects when negotiating. These points are worked out in Section 13.2.

The analytics of contract modification, a far more prevalent occurrence, follow a similar framework. If a party proposes a contract modification, the counterparty will accept the modifications when the counterparty bears the risks of unassigned circumstances. If the parties reason in an other-regarding, values-balancing way, the modification properly adjusts the party's obligations in the light of unaddressed circumstances; it then preserves the relationship the parties bargained for and should be upheld. On the other hand, when the proposed modification reflects the private projects of only one of the parties – that is, when one party is using its contractual leverage to get more than it bargained for – the modification is not within the implicit contemplation of the parties ex ante. The modification should then be unenforceable.

13.1 THE PROBLEM OF UNADDRESSED CIRCUMSTANCES

Contract doctrine seems to suggest that if a party is able to demonstrate that her performance is impossible, impracticable, or frustrated, the party will be relieved of her obligations. The Restatement (Second) of Contracts, following the UCC, provides if "a party's performance is made impracticable without his [or her] fault by the occurrence of an event the non-occurrence of which is a basic assumption on which the contract was made" the party's performance will be excused.[6] The UCC would excuse a seller's performance if "delivery or non-delivery has been made

[6] Restatement (Second) of Contracts, §261 (1981).

impractical by the occurrence of a contingency the non-occurrence of which was a basic assumption on which the contract was made."[7]

These doctrinal formulations focus on an event and its foreseeability, rather than on how the parties allocated the risks of a seemingly unaddressed event. That is a mistake.[8] When a seemingly unassigned circumstance occurs, the loss must fall somewhere; it cannot be avoided. To excuse the seller is to place the burden on the buyer; to excuse the buyer is to place the burden on the seller. Cases of excuse are, in reality, asking where the risk of loss should fall, which means we ought to focus on where the parties implicitly allocated the risk of loss in the exchange. To make the excuse doctrine work, we need to know how the parties have implicitly allocated the risk of loss from unanticipated circumstances, for if a party has been paid to take a risk it is hard to see how the party can escape responsibility for the risk. Although the words that trigger an excuse (impossible, impracticable, or frustrated) seem to have an objective, acontextual meaning, the background fact that determines the implementation of the excuse doctrine challenges the burdens and benefits that the parties negotiated; it affects both parties because the excuse/no excuse determination allocates the loss to one party rather than another.

Thus far, I have used the term "seemingly unallocated risks" to refer to risks that the contract does not directly address. I now ask whether unallocated risks truly exist. Because each party is using the contract to advance its private projects, each party faces the risks that threaten its private projects, including risks that it believes to be unlikely or cannot even imagine. Those risks exist quite apart from the contract unless a party makes them a part of the exchange. Hence, bargaining starts with the assumption that each party accepts the risks its private projects face, which means that in thinking about the exchange we can think about whether those risks were impliedly shifted as part of the exchange.

I therefore offer a testable hypothesis, which I will explain and illustrate in this chapter. When a seemingly unaddressed ex post circumstance arises, legal decision-makers determine which of the two parties agreed to accept that risk as an implicit part of the exchange. That party must bear the burden of that risk, while the counterparty is excused from its obligations. The doctrines of frustration, impossibility, and impracticability serve to identify excused obligations of the party that did not bear the risk.

As some evidence to support this hypothesis, consider the way in which authorities who carefully articulate the excuse doctrine seem to recognize that excuse doctrine is about ex ante risk allocation, not about the event that provides the excuse. The UCC formulations, for example, prefaces its doctrinal rule with the statement: "unless the parties agree otherwise." This seems to move the analysis of excuse to the implicit exchange obligations. And, the UCC drafters explained the doctrine in

7 UCC §2–615 (2013). A similar provision applies to buyers.

8 Victor Goldberg has shown the incongruity of focusing on whether an event could be anticipated. Goldberg (2010).

a way that seems to turn doctrine from a rule into a workable inquiry into implicit risk bearing. Courts should "use equitable principles in furtherance of commercial standards and good faith in order to determine whether a condition of excuse is implicated."[9] It also allows a court to find a division of risks "in circumstances surrounding the contracting, in trade usage and the like."[10]

Similarly, Professor Eisenberg's formulation of excuse doctrine is carefully crafted to make the risk obligations the fulcrum for excuse, not excuse the fulcrum for obligations. His careful study of excuse doctrines recognizes that obligations can be excused "if the parties shared a tacit incorrect assumption that the non-occurrence of some circumstances during the life of the contract was certain rather than problematic and the incorrectness of that assumption would have provided a basis for judicial relief if the assumption had been made explicit rather than tacit."[11] By focusing on hypothetical explicit ex ante obligations, Eisenberg carefully moves the analysis from the excusing event to the way these parties would have allocated the excusing event had the risk of loss from that event been allocated explicitly.[12]

Hence, the underlying issue is not whether performance is impossible, impractical, or frustrated in a literal sense, for those words simply set up the underlying dilemma of unaddressed circumstances – the dilemma that arises when future events create unaddressed burdens (or lost benefits) that must be allocated. The court must decide which party should bear the loss when performance is rendered more burdensome or less beneficial than was anticipated ex ante, and that decision depends on which party bore the risk, not on the effect of the event. Consider two much-discussed British cases that we will examine again below. In one, a tenant who rented an apartment to watch the coronation of King Edward VII, was relieved of the obligation to pay when the coronation was postponed. In the other, a tenant who rented property to produce crops was not excused from the obligation to pay when the property was confiscated by an army. As we will see below, the different results reflect the different allocation of risks in the two cases not the unaddressed circumstance.

The argument developed here is that a party that bears the risk of loss is not excused from that risk because of unassigned circumstances; the exchange has already compensated that party for the risk the party took. But performance obligations, the obligations spelled out in the contract, do not always coincide with the parties allocation of the risk in the exchange. Excuse doctrine applies only when a performance obligation fails to reveal the party that was paid to take the risk; it was not designed to protect against a risk the counterparty accepted. Hence we need

9 *Id.* cmt 6.

10 *Id.*

11 Eisenberg (2009) at 209.

12 Importantly, this analysis does not ask how a pair of hypothetical bargainers would have divided the risk of loss. It asks, instead, how these bargainers impliedly divided the risk of loss given their private projects and the terms of the contract they did make explicit.

a fuller examination of how contractual exchanges address risk and why risk allocation may differ from performance obligations.

13.2 REASONING ABOUT RISK ALLOCATION

Parties implicitly bargain over the allocation of various risks. For any risk, we can presume that the parties allocate the risk to the low cost risk avoider unless the exchange makes the transfer of risks explicit; doing so minimizes the cost of contracting and maximizes the gains from trade. Each party faces risks to its private projects, risks that will impair its private projects even if the counterparty performs well. Each party is the low-cost avoider of private party risks because they are in the best position to anticipate or insure against the risks they face as part of their private projects. That means that risks, even so-called unforeseeable risks, fall naturally on one party or the other; it also means that the contract is not likely to address the risks that the parties assume to fall naturally, which means those risks are implicit. Although the contract terms often address the risk of a counterparty's nonperformance, generally they do not explicitly address the risks to either party's private projects. It is the implicit division of risks that affect a party's private projects that remain unaddressed because they fall naturally on the party whose private projects would otherwise be impaired.

Consider again the owner of coal who hires a shipping company to transport coal from Norfolk to New York, which illustrated the role of tort law in determining contractual obligations.[13] The contract will determine the price and terms of delivery. The contract, however, is unlikely to cover the risk that the cargo will be lost during an unexpected storm; the parties bargain with the shared understanding that the risk of an unexpected storm is the shipping company's private project risk. The parties are not likely to allocate that risk explicitly because the allocation of risk is a tacit assumption of the bargain. The shipping company "owns" that risk unless it becomes a part of the exchange. That is why tort law feels comfortable in determining whether the shipper reasonably addressed that risk.[14]

Risks, even private party risks, can be made a subject in the exchange, but the party whose private projects entail that risk must make that risk a part of the exchange, in which case they will be addressed directly. And the party that "owns" the risk because it affects their private projects must compensate the counterparty if the counterparty takes over the risk. It is unlikely, however, that the coal company would find that division of risk to be attractive.[15]

[13] *See* Chapter 11.1 ("Performance Obligations: The Values-Balancing Approach").

[14] See the discussion of the way tort law recognized the obligation to act reasonably in *T. J. Hooper*, 60 F. 2d 737 (2d Cir) cert. denied 287 U.S. 662 (1932).

[15] The shipping company has a cost advantage in recognizing and controlling the risk; the shipper would have to go into the weather forecasting business to control that risk. Notice that this result is not changed if the shipper agreed to insure the cargo while in transit. The insurance would cover unexpected storms that could not be addressed at reasonable costs; not harm that could have been

In other words, future events affect a party's private projects. Those risks are generally not articulated in the contract because both parties tacitly assume that each party bears the risks that would otherwise burden their private projects. Although unarticulated, those risks make up a party's obligations just as much as the risks of counterparty non-performance that make up the explicit terms of the exchange.

Implicit and unexpressed obligations are baked into the exchange unless the contract provides otherwise. Courts will not excuse a performance if the risk of loss is already baked into the transaction and falls on the party wishing to be excused. Inherent in the nature of bargaining is that each party understands the burdens and benefits that each party is asking the other to undertake. A seller will ask himself what burdensome price potential buyers will accept, while buyers hope to minimize the price (the benefit) that they give to sellers. Naturally, each party has private information that affects its assessment of the burdens and benefits of any potential transaction. But much information about the incidence of burdens and benefits is given by the market, and the process of bargaining reveals other information. Even when the burdens and benefits of a transaction are not calculated, the determinants of the burden and benefits are. Social and business interactions are possible because persons have experience putting themselves in another's shoes and reasoning as they would reason. Each party also has the ability to make a rough assessment of the options the other party has, which also influences the estimation of burdens and benefits.

Ex ante, the comparative burdens and benefits allow each party to determine which party will bear the risk of unaddressed circumstances, and that will determine which party bears the burden of addressed circumstances. The task is to determine where the risk naturally falls, given the private projects and bargaining strategy of each party. It is to that task that we now turn.

13.2.1 *Paradign*

In *Paradign*,[16] the landlord leased property to a tenant whose private project was to raise crops. When the land was confiscated by one faction in a civil war, the tenant, unable to grow crops, stopped paying the required rent. Although making the obligatory payment was not impossible, farming was and the tenant sought to be excused from his performance obligation. The court held that the obligation to pay was independent of the property's productivity and refused to excuse the tenant from paying. The court effectively allocated the loss from that unaddressed circumstance to the private project of the tenant.

avoided at reasonable expense. Notice also that because the risk of an unexpected storm lies naturally on the shipping company, no one would say that the shipping company is excused from its obligations.

16 82 Eng. Rep 897 (KBD 1647)

Paradign is sometimes cited for the proposition that property law made the tenant's promise independent of the contract. But that reading is implausible, as one can see by asking what the result would be if the owner refused to turn the property over to the tenant, or forcibly removed the tenant from the property. It is unlikely that the tenant's obligations would then be independent of the owner's obligations. In fact, it is more appropriate to view the case as one invoking the excuse doctrine. If we understand the burdens and benefits that each party accepted as part of the risks of their private projects, we can see why the court refused to excuse the tenants payment

The landowner's private project (its benefit from the relationship) was to receive lease royalties; the landowner carried the associated burden of relinquishing, for the period of the lease, the owner's rights to possession. We can assume that the landlord did not have the option of working the property himself; the owner appears to have been an absentee landlord who had neither the inclination nor the capacity to farm. Under this assumption, the owner's private project was to find the tenant who could best reduce the risk of nonpayment. One option the owner could have considered was to find an independently wealthy tenant, one who could make payments whether or not the property was productive. If that was the basis of the exchange, the tenant would have demanded a reduced price as compensation for reducing the landlord's risk of nonpayment and the tenant, having been compensated for the risk of the unassigned circumstance, would not be excused from paying.

But assuming that no potential tenant was independently wealthy, the landlord would choose the highest bidder, after adjusting for the risk that the bidder would not be able to pay, which would depend on the productivity of the property.

Each of the bidders, in turn, had the option of working this particular property or leasing another property; each would weigh the property's anticipated productivity against the productivity of other property it might have leased, given the price. We can assume that the risk of loss from a confiscating army did not distinguish one piece of property from another. The benefit of the contract to any tenant's private projects depended on a tenant's ability to make the property productive. The potential tenants therefore bore the risk that the property would not be sufficiently profitable to afford the rental payment; the tenants' bids would therefore discount the property's expected profitability by accounting for circumstances that would affect the value of the property's output, some within their control and some outside their control.

The tenant would, to complete its private projects, take into account risk factors such as the expected market prices, expected weather patterns, conditions of the soil, and the productivity of the tenant's own labor. The tenant would not necessarily take into account the possibility of losing the property in a civil war; by hypothesis that possibility was too remote. But the tenant would have accepted the risk that it could not make enough money to pay the rent; that was an implied risk of its private projects. When the landlord picked the highest bidder (after discounting for the different expected productivity of various bidders) the landlord would know that the tenant had already figured into the tenant's bargaining calculation the risk-adjusted profitability of the property. The landlord could correctly assume that the risk of inability to pay would be insured by the tenant through the price it included in its bid.[17]

Under this reading, the risk of this kind of unaddressed circumstance would naturally fall on the tenant. Both parties must have made the tacit assumption that the tenant would possess the land, but the risks of the inability to pay the rent for any reason naturally fell on the tenant (unless, of course the contract provided otherwise). Those risks were a part of the tenant's private projects by the nature of the risks that the tenant faced in achieving its private projects.

As the reader can tell, the central issue is not whether the ex post circumstances were unanticipated; the central issue is which party's private projects naturally bore the risk of unaddressed circumstances. A party whose private projects are thwarted by unaddressed circumstances, who did not successfully make that kind of risk a part of the exchange, can hardly attribute that loss to a counterparty that has not promised to accept that risk.

13.2.2 *The Coronation Cases*

In the coronation cases, tenants rented property along the projected route for the coronation of King Edward VII. When the coronation was postponed, the tenant sought to avoid his contractual obligations on the ground that the purpose of the contract was frustrated. The relevant contracts were silent on the allocation of loss from the cancelled coronation.[18] Both landlord and tenant bargained with the tacit assumption that the coronation would take place, but the risk of the nonevent was unassigned.

Considering the party's private projects, the risk of loss was properly associated with the landlords' private projects. Both the landlord and the tenant knew that their tacit assumption was that the coronation would take place. The landlord, in fact, advertised the room for that purpose, and clearly knew that the tenant, who rented the property only for that day, found the property uniquely valuable. Landlord and tenant both knew that the tenant's private projects depended on the coronation taking place. This is not a case, therefore, in which the tenant had private projects that the tenant did not share with the landlord; the law's information forcing function under *Hadley* v. *Baxendale* did not come into play. Still, because the

[17] The tenant could (assuming sufficient bargaining power) protect itself by making its payment obligations depend on certain productivity measures of the property. The burden of unassigned future contingencies would then be explicitly allocated to the landlord, who was paid to take them (but the price would have been high).

[18] Some of the contracts for viewing the coronation route explicitly divided the risk between landlord and tenant, in which event the contractual division of risk prevails. Krell v. Henry, 2 K.B. 740 (1903).

tenant could not use the property if there were no coronation, and the landlord could, why would knowing of the tenant's special use put the risk of loss from the tacit assumption on the landlord?

The landlord's private projects (renting its property) got the value of the tenant's special use for the tenant's private projects. When the tenant was considering his options for viewing the coronation, the tenant knew that each option included a premium for this special use (which the landlord, by the facts surrounding the exchange, also knew). As for the landlord, he knew he had to compete with other landlords on the basis of the special use premium they could charge (after taking into account the relative attractiveness of the properties for the occasion). The landlord's private projects therefore included a premium for owning property along the parade route. That must imply that they, seeking to benefit from the coronation, would also accept the burden if the coronation did not take place. In the terms that helpfully determine the allocation of risk, unless the parties specify otherwise, one whose private projects benefit from a common assumption of the bargaining would bear the burdens of that assumption unless they are made a subject of bargaining.

We might generalize from these examples. The probability of an unaddressed circumstance is the same for each party. But the loss will differ for the two parties, depending on the relationship between the circumstance and each party's private projects. A party who knows the value the counterparty places on their private projects will charge a price that extracts that value, given the counterparty's options. Having extracted that value, the party who extracted the value bears the risk that the value will disappear because of circumstances that could impair that value. Returning to *Paradign*, if the landlord chose a tenant because they were independently wealthy, the tenant will have received the benefit of a lower lease payment and would not be excused from paying because of an unaddressed event. The tenant, having received that benefit, cannot then disclaim the burdens associated with that benefit. If, on the other hand, the landlord chooses a tenant who promised the least risk of nonproductive use of the land (and therefore nonpayment) that tenant has been compensated for that value and must bear the risk of loss if the value does not appear. The risk of loss was then on the tenant, who could not disclaim the obligation to pay. The tenant accepted the risk of loss without regard to what event caused the loss.

Consider another prominent case. In *Taylor* v. *Caldwell*,[19] Taylor rented Surrey Gardens and Music Hall to present a series of summer concerts. When the music hall burned down, both parties accepted the fact that their obligations were excused. The risk of loss from the destruction of the music hall was clearly a part of the private projects of the property owner, and the property owner did not seek to enforce Taylor's obligation to pay. Taylor, however, sued to recover for expenses Taylor had invested to prepare for the concerts. That suit was dismissed. The expenses of preparing for the performance were a part of the plaintiff's private projects and the

19 122 Eng. Rep. 309 (1863).

plaintiff bore the risk of loss of investment from whatever ex post event kept the plaintiff from making money. The destruction of the music hall was equivalent in effect to the same loss the plaintiff would have incurred had the plaintiff sold no tickets. Unless, the plaintiff negotiated to shift that risk to the music hall, the plaintiff bore the burden of the unaddressed risk.

13.3 MODIFICATIONS

Instead of asking to be excused from an obligation, a party may ask that their obligations be modified to reflect unaddressed circumstances that lead to unexpected burdens (including lost benefits), or to breach and the contractual relationship's demise. Often, modifications are undertaken without dispute; as Chapter 8 discussed, the flexibility and accommodation that parties display when adjusting their obligations to unaddressed circumstances exemplifies how contracting parties in successful relationships make other-regarding decisions. Parties will adjust their obligations because they understand the problems the other party faces and are willing to make sacrifices so that the relationship continues.[20] Sometimes both parties adjust their obligations; a buyer may accept a later delivery than the contract calls for; in return the seller may lower the price to compensate the buyer for late-delivery losses. Other-regarding contracting parties, to maintain their relationship, adjust their obligations to preserve the balance of burdens and benefits of the bargain.

Yet contract modifications present contract law with a difficult identification problem. Contract modifications may occur because a party uses its contractual leverage to procure unwarranted benefits under the contract. Those modifications, because they are coercive and wealth destroying, should not be legally enforceable. Yet, in other instances modifications reflect circumstances that might justify a claim of excuse and the end of the relationship. Modifications under those circumstances are wealth producing, reasonable accommodations to circumstances beyond the effective control of either party. Because the two kinds of modifications are superficially indistinguishable, legal decisionmakers need some basis for determining which modifications are legally enforceable and which are not.

The dilemma is illustrated by two venerable cases. In *Lingenfelder v. Wainwright*,[21] an architect defendant designed a brewery for the plaintiff and

[20] Self-interest and other-regarding reasoning do not provide distinct motivations. A party who makes adjustments to preserve a contractual relationship, is motivated by self-interest, of course; the party is accommodating a counterparty to minimize losses given their other options. But that is not a reason to reject other-regarding reasoning as a basis for evaluating the enforceability of the modified obligations. The idea of the other-regarding reasoning does not assume that a party necessarily sacrifices her private projects in order to benefit another party's private projects. The idea reflects that, in the face of unaddressed circumstances, the relationality of contracting requires a party to account for the values represented by both parties.

[21] 15 S.W Rep. 844 (Mo. 1891). These two cases were used by Charles Fried to show the inadequacy of the doctrine of consideration. Fried (1981) at 30.

agreed to supervise the brewery's construction of the brewery. During construction, the architect discovered that the brewery had bought refrigerator equipment from an independent vendor, although the architect owned a refrigeration company that could have supplied the brewery's refrigeration needs. The architect walked off the job until the brewery promised to pay him the profit the architect would have made if the brewery had bought its refrigeration equipment from him. When the brewery subsequently refused to pay the modified amount, the architect sued for breach of the modified agreement. The court held the modified promise to be unenforceable for lack of consideration; the brewery, which was burdened by the extra payment, was given no return benefit by the architect.[22]

Just a few years later, however, a similar-looking case came out the other way. In *Linz* v. *Schuck*, a contractor agreed to excavate a basement for a homeowner. When it turned out that underneath the basement's firm crust the land was swampy, the homeowner agreed to modify the contract to pay the extra cost of excavation. The court held this additional payment to be enforceable, notwithstanding the contractor's preexisting promise to excavate the basement for a fixed price. The requirement of consideration gave way to the modification in light of unaddressed circumstances.[23]

In both cases, a party used its contractual leverage from a threatened breach to induce a contractual modification. In both, a preexisting duty was modified without consideration. Yet the two cases had different outcomes, and one cannot determine by looking at the fact of modification whether the modification enhances or subtracts from the institution of contracting.

13.3.1 *The Doctrine*

The distinction between enforceable and unenforceable modifications is not made easier by the doctrinal framework courts use to address the issue. The early common law addressed these modifications through the doctrine of consideration, reasoning that a modification that added a new obligation to a preexisting obligation had to be met by consideration. Taking on a new burden to please a counterparty that was already under a duty required that the counterparty bestow a reciprocal benefit (the prior-duty rule). This, of course, proved to be a contrivance as courts found that consideration existed when they wanted to enforce a modification and found no consideration when they did want to. This led to the predicament found in the Restatement Second, which, honoring both *Lingenfelder* and *Linz*, maintained the preexisting duty rule,[24] but modified the rule if the circumstances that led to the modification were not "anticipated by the

[22] The court also rejected the architect's argument that the client, having not sued to protect its contractual rights, was now stopped from disclaiming its second promise.

[23] The court was clear that its decision was based on the unanticipated circumstances.

[24] Restatement Second of Torts, §73.

parties when the promise was made" and the modification was otherwise fair and equitable.[25]

The UCC wisely does not make the consideration the touchstone of legal enforceability. Instead, the UCC substitutes the standard of good faith.[26] According to the UCC: "The effective use of bad faith to escape performance on the original contract terms is barred, and the extortion of a 'modification' without legitimate commercial reason is ineffective as a violation of the duty of good faith."[27] How, exactly, is this standard to be implemented? The burden of this section is to determine what good faith and "unanticipated circumstances" mean in this context.

13.3.2 *Modifications and Excuses*

Modification cases are like excuse cases because they often involve unaddressed ex post circumstances that disturb an exchange's balance of burdens and benefits. When modifications benefit both parties, enforcement of the modified obligations is clearly justified. But legal decisionmakers must distinguish between the unlawful use of contractual leverage and lawful modifications that account for unaddressed circumstances. Whether this is characterized as a contest between fairness and the unlawful use of leverage or between welfare-enhancing or welfare-reducing modifications, courts must deploy a methodology that allows them to distinguish the permissible from the impermissible.

Despite this resemblance, modification cases present an added dimension. Modifications do not signify that the original relationship is untenable. Contrary to the assumption sometimes made, a party faced with a request to modify a contract does not face a dichotomous choice of accepting the modification or ending the relationship.[28] She has a third choice; she may accept the modification and continue the relationship, knowing that she can later ask a court to determine that the modified obligations are unenforceable. Acceptance of a coerced obligation does not make the obligation legally enforceable.

The key to resolving modification cases builds on our understanding of excuse cases: The way the parties allocated the risk shows which party assumed the risk of unaddressed circumstances; the party assuming a risk should not seek a modification that imposes the cost of that risk on a counterparty. We ask, in other words, whether a request for a modification is sufficiently (and reasonably) attentive to the private projects of the counterparty (given the way the parties have allocated the risks), or whether, instead, it is designed to consider only the private projects of the party seeking the modification. The risk allocation determines which party implicitly

25 Restatement Second, §89.

26 UCC, §2–209(1): "an agreement modifying a contract within this Article needs no consideration to be binding."

27 UCC, §2–209, cmt. 2.

28 Bar-Gill & Ben-Shahar (2004).

accepted the burden of that risk and thus which party must bear that burden without seeking additional compensation. As a starting point for analysis, the risk of an unanticipated event would be associated with the party whose private projects would be negatively affected by the event; that assignment mirrors the tacit assumption the parties must have made as they negotiated. Identifying which party's private projects naturally bear the risk identifies which party bears the risk unless the risk is shifted as part of the exchange; it therefore determines which party should make that risk a part of the negotiations if they are unwilling to keep the risk.

In other words, the party whose private projects are associated with a particular circumstance, "owns" the unanticipated circumstance and, unless the risk is shifted as part of the exchange, must therefore bear the burden of the unanticipated circumstance. Attempting to shift that burden to another outside of the exchange the parties have made is unreasonable (and therefore coercive). Interpreting the contract to assign the burden to the party that "owns" the risk is reasonable, for then the burdens and benefits of the exchange are aligned with the parties' private projects.

Viewing unaddressed circumstances by asking which party carried the burden of the risk confirms the view of the court in *Lingenfelder*. As others have pointed out, the architect's behavior was extortionate – the architect used its power under the contract to superimpose an extracontractual obligation into the original agreement. The original contract said nothing about the obligation of the client to buy refrigerator equipment from the architect; it was neither an express nor an implied term of the contract. The risk that the brewery would not buy its refrigeration equipment from the architect affected only the architect's private projects, and the modification asked for would have been a burden to the brewery. Had the architect wanted the terms of the contract to include the brewer's obligation to buy the refrigeration equipment, the architect should have made it a part of the bargain. In terms of the other-regarding contracting party, the architect should have known that the burden he was imposing on the other party was a burden that no reasonable person would exact without conferring an offsetting benefit.[29]

Although the judges reached the correct result, the finding of no consideration in *Lingenfelder* was unnecessary and ill fitting. It was unnecessary because the court could have decided the case under the doctrine of duress. By using the doctrine of consideration to decide the case, the judges made any modification of contracts

[29] This analysis illuminates why early courts grasped the doctrine of consideration as the doctrinal home for modifications. Because the architect "owned" the risk but sought to shift the burden of that risk to the brewery, the modification was, in effect, a new obligation, one that would have required a new enforceable exchange. However, that doctrinal approach could not be generalized under the concept of a preexisting performance duty because the assignment of a performance obligation does not necessarily coincide with the allocation of the risks. When the person seeking the modification did not bear the risk of the unaddressed circumstances, the duty to perform diverged from the implicit allocation of the risk. The court confused the duty to complete the contract with the duty to accept the risks in the way the contract allocated them.

subject to the malleable doctrine of consideration, and that doctrine did not adequately disclose the circumstances that determine how the doctrine should be applied. After all, if there had been a reason to enforce the second promise in *Lingenfelder* the court might have said that the return to his supervisory responsibilities was adequate consideration for the second promise. The finding of consideration or lack thereof cannot correctly determine the outcome of modification cases.

The solution, which by now will not surprise the reader, is to assign the loss from the unaddressed contingency to one party or the other based on which party's private projects assume the non-existence of the unaddressed contingency. In *Lingenfelder*, the unaddressed contingency was the obligation of the brewery to buy its refrigerator equipment from the company owned the architect (or at least to pay the opportunity cost of not doing so to the architect). But this contingency was clearly a part of the private projects of the architect, not the private projects of the brewery. True, the brewery knew that it had to buy refrigeration equipment for its brewery, but the success of that private project did not depend on buying the refrigeration equipment from the company affiliated with the architect. Until the architect connected the refrigeration equipment to the architectural services, the risk that the brewery would buy its refrigerating equipment elsewhere was clearly a part of the private project of the architect. If the architect had wanted to make that contingency a part of the exchange, the architect should have made it a part of the original bargain; that is the only way by which the brewery could adequately determine the burdens that it would take on when it bought architectural services from the architect.

In *Linz*, by contrast, the risk-related issue was to determine which party, the contractor or the homeowner, bore the risk that the land under the ground's crust was swampy. Ordinarily, one would associate the risk of higher-than-unanticipated construction costs with the private projects of the contractor. The contractor prepared the bid and had the opportunity and expertise to investigate the potential cost of the excavation. Were there no additional facts, one would assume that the contractor bore the risk, which would have made the buyer's agreement to make an additional payment unenforceable. But additional facts allow us to see that the parties shifted the risk of the swampy land to the homeowner. The parties had considered the condition of the ground to be excavated before the bid was made. The owner took the contractor to a building across the street to inspect the cellar, which showed that "the soil was nice and sound."[30] Further, the owner stated that the contractor "would not have any trouble" in digging out the cellar. Unless the contractor had some reason to doubt the homeowner's assurances, it seems to me that the homeowner's assurances effectively shifted to the homeowner the risk that the excavation would be more expensive than expected. The issue is not which party should have investigated to examine the risk, for either party could have asked the question that would reveal the unaddressed circumstance. The point, instead, is that

30 67 At. Rep at 287.

once the homeowner found out that there was a swamp under the property, the homeowner would have to pay the extra cost of the excavation, whether it paid the plaintiff or someone else. The homeowner could accept the contractor's repudiation but the homeowner could not have avoided the higher cost of the excavation. That cost was unavoidably a part of the private projects of the homeowner. That being the case, modifying that contract to recognize that burden was not unreasonable.

This analysis also allows a legal decisionmaker to take into account the parties' relative opportunity (and obligation) to have anticipated and investigated the otherwise unassigned burden of unanticipated circumstances. When the private projects of one of the parties includes the obligation to anticipate and evaluate information needed to implement the contract, that party will bear the risk if it has done that investigation reasonably. But when the parties consider that risk and it is shifted to the other party, that party bears the cost of the risk, which includes the extra cost of unaddressed circumstances.

This analysis provides a testable hypothesis. A modification should not be upheld when the party seeking the modification bears the risk of unaddressed circumstances. Such an attempt to shift a risk that a party "owns" seeks an unbargained-for benefit and constitutes the unlawful use of contractual leverage. However, when the parties modify the contract in a way that benefits each party (other than by maintaining the relationship) the modification should be upheld because of that mutuality of benefit. A modification should also be upheld if the burden of the unaddressed circumstance falls on the party that was paid to take the risk of the unaddressed circumstance. That solution is "fair and equitable" precisely because it follows the division of risks in the original exchange and the sensible conclusion that this unaddressed circumstance was already priced into the original exchange. Although I do not attempt to prove this hypothesis here, a review of the cases decided under the Restatement Second is consistent with the approach recommended here.[31]

[31] Invalid: *McCallum Highlands, Ltd.* v. *Washington Capital Dus, Inc.*, 66 F.3d 89, 94–95 (5th Cir. 1995) (finding the lender's modification of loan terms to be invalid, because the lender, as part of its private projects, bore the risk that a change in Fannie Mae regulations would reduce the lender's benefit of the transaction); *Margeson* v. *Artis*, 776 N.W. 2d 652 (Iowa 2009) (seller and buyer of weight loss franchise modified contract to increase the purchase price without any intervening circumstance that would justify the modification). Valid: *United States* v. *Sears, Roebuck and Co.*, 778 F.2d 810 (D.C. Cir. 1985) (finding that agreement to modify the imposition of antidumping duties was "fair and equitable" because it recognized the invalidity of an earlier, tentative assessment); *Univ. of V. I.* v. *Petersen-Springer*, 232 F. Supp. 2d 462 (D.V.I. 2002) (finding employee acquiescence in modified duties to be valid as a matter of law); *Quigley* v. *Wilson*, 474 N.W.2d 277 (Iowa Ct. App.), aff'd, 474 N.W.2d 277 (Iowa 1991) (holding that the modification to lower buyer's price was valid, in part because the risk was far greater than anticipated and the seller benefitted from the modification); *Gintzler* v. *Melnick*, 116 N.H. 566, 364 A.2d 637 (1976) (upholding a guarantor's oral modification of a guarantee on a construction contract, because this allocated risk of defect to the guarantor); *Wilder* v. *Cody Country Chamber of Commerce*, 868 P.2d 211 (Wyo. 1994) (involving a former employee hired without written contract, but whose compensation and job protection was later

13.4 CONCLUSION

Promissory transactions are undertaken under conditions of uncertainty that allow post-contracting circumstances to upset the equilibrium of burdens and benefits that flow from an exchange. That uncertainty potentially influences the private projects of one of the parties. It also potentially influences the collaboration. Promissory transactions are therefore undertaken with the implied obligation on each party to reconsider the obligations implied by promising when the facts turn out to be different from the state of the world assumed in the exchange. Successful promising and contracting require the parties to use a method of reasoning about which private projects should bear the risk of the unexpected circumstances. When they do, the parties are able to adjust their obligations in ways that reflect the allocation of risks in the exchange in the fact of changed circumstances.

Sometimes one party will seek more than it is entitled to under the promises that were made. And sometimes the unexpected circumstance makes the continuing relationship impossible, in the sense that no party can achieve the private projects they expected from the exchange. In those cases, the parties, and courts, must assign the loss to one of the parties or determine a method of sharing the loss.

This chapter has outlined an appropriate method of reasoning about the impact of unaddressed circumstances on the obligations of the parties. The party that bears the risk of loss is responsible for that loss. In many cases it is easy to determine where the loss from unaddressed circumstances will fall simply by observing that one of the parties, because of the threat to its private projects, was responsible during the negotiations for pricing that risk into the transactions. But at other times, the parties must reason about how other-regarding, values-balancing parties would allocate the loss. When parties reason successfully about the risk, the relationship can flourish.

reduced to writing, and finding that it was up to jury to decide whether modification was valid); *Roussalis* v. *Wyo. Med. Ctr., Inc.*, 4 P.3d 209 (Wyo. 2000) (modification to the size and cost of a medical facilities construction project was valid because the owner took the risk that costs would go up and the modification benefited the owner's change in plans).

14

Remedies

Remedies are among the most contested and complex issues in contract law. The general objective of a contract remedy is identical to the general objective of a tort law remedy– namely, to make the aggrieved party whole by putting her in the position she would have been in had there been no breach; the remedy is, in other words, to correct the wrong that an unaddressed breach imposes on the aggrieved party.[1] In contract law we call that measure expectation damages; in tort law we call it compensatory damages; they are, I maintain, equivalent terms.[2] What the terms *expectation* and *compensatory* mean, however, is highly contextual and often hotly contested.

Although the basic rules governing remedial obligations are clear, their implementation is subject to gaps and judicial modifications that are both unsettled and unsettling. Expectation damages are thought to reflect the value the contracting party would have received had the contract been fully performed (which can be conceived of as the asset value to the aggrieved party or as a termination fee for ending the relationship).[3] That generally means that the aggrieved party is entitled to recover the difference between the contract price and the cost of a substitute performance – the value of the aggrieved party's self-help performance that is substituted for the promisor's performance. An aggrieved seller may recover the contract's value by selling the wrongfully rejected product and collecting from the buyer the difference between the resale price and the contract price (if any). Aggrieved buyers are allowed to buy the product on the open market and hold the breaching party responsible for the additional price, if any, of the product or service subject to the contract.

1 Under the UCC §1–106, remedies for breach of contract are to be "liberally administered to the end that the aggrieved party may be put in as good a position as if the other party had fully performed." *See also* Restatement (Second) of Contracts §§344, 347(a) (1981) ("The initial assumption is that the injured party is entitled to full compensation for his actual loss").

2 Williston, for one, agrees: "In fixing the amount of these damages, the general purpose of the law is, and should be, to give compensation: – that is, to put the plaintiff in as good a position as he would have been in had the defendant kept his contract." Williston (1920) at 1338.

3 Goldberg (2019).

Under this formulation, the breaching party is seemingly able to buy her way out of her obligations by paying for a substitute performance that makes the aggrieved party whole, a result that economists call efficient because a party will breach when the substituted performance is cheaper than the breaching party's gains. To increase one person's well-being without decreasing the other person's well-being is efficient. The relationality of promising is preserved; the aggrieved party is made whole and the breaching party preserves its freedom to make autonomous decisions to maximize its well-being (contingent on remedying the aggrieved party's loss). Because of its emphasis on efficiency, this basic rule implicates the larger contest between morality and efficiency. If the remedy is to allow for efficient breaches, what happens to the morality of promising; how can paying to get out of a commitment be moral if one has a moral obligation to keep one's commitments?[4]

Many remedial disputes fail to fit the basic rules. The assumptions that justify the basic remedy are strict, contracts allocate various risks in unpredictable ways, new forms of contracting arise,[5] and contextual details matter. Courts encounter contextual variations that make remedial determinations difficult and contested. To the extent that we try to craft acontextual rules to govern remedies, we are bound to do injustice. Because rules do not describe their own domain, or the circumstances that justify their implementation, we need a remedial approach that reflects the parties' exchange, and we seek a method of reasoning about remedial obligations that justifies results when rules run out.

Scholars generally articulate a remedial purpose and then seek to identify a remedy that seems to meet that purpose. Many use the goal of protecting expectations, of course, but often without revealing their method of reasoning about the factors that determine a party's expectations. In his approach, Victor Goldberg suggests that the appropriate remedy is determined by the asset value of the contract on the date of the breach.[6] This is an acceptable goal as long as we recognize that we are looking for the asset value of the contract to the aggrieved party, and that the asset value of a contract to a particular party may differ from market value. Others, like James Gordley, adopt a risk-focused approach, determining how the parties divided the risks and seeking to insure that a party that was paid to accept the risk actually pays for harm from the risks it was paid to accept.[7] This approach provides a method of determining what each party expected as long as we can successfully determine how the parties allocated various risks.

The remedial approach suggested here draws from each of these accounts, but identifies a substructure of reasoning that fits the remedies to an exchange's context. I make two interrelated claims. The first claim rests on a distinction between

[4] Shiffrin (2007).

[5] Remedial gaps often arise because new forms of contracting challenge existing remedial models. *See, e.g.*, Schwartz (2019) (discussing inadequacies of standard remedial models to supply chain contracts).

[6] Goldberg (2019).

[7] Gordley (2020).

contractual surplus and the way the exchange divided the surplus. Each party has a surplus associated with its private projects – the difference between benefits and burdens that party bargained for, which I call private surplus. My first claim is that legal decisionmakers ought to focus directly on the private surplus to which the aggrieved party is entitled, and address remedial issues in a way that protects the aggrieved party's private surplus.[8] This approach follows the idea of protecting expectation value, for the private surplus is precisely what the aggrieved party expected. It is also a compensatory remedy in the tort sense because it is an appropriate measure of what the aggrieved party would lose from the breach. Private surplus identifies the asset value of the contract, for the aggrieved party's asset value is the amount an aggrieved party would have gained had there been no breach.[9] The aggrieved party's private surplus, as the analysis in this chapter will show, also preserves the idea that a party that is paid to take a risk should in fact pay for the harm within that risk.

Most importantly, private surplus also reflects the reasoning of an other-regarding contracting party. Each party understands the private projects of the other party, how the exchange allocated the risks, and a counterparty's risks to its private projects. If a party reasons in the right way about a counterparty's well-being, they will be able to evaluate the lost surplus from the breach.[10]

Importantly, preserving private surplus is the central feature of the standard remedial picture. The aggrieved party is entitled to the equivalent of its private surplus – the net benefits that it would have received had there been no breach. That amount is akin to a forced termination fee, the amount the aggrieved party would charge to let the breaching party out of the breaching party's commitment. The remedy is both fair and efficient. For the reasons articulated below, I believe that it is also moral. From this perspective, the conventional notion that the aggrieved party should get the benefit of the bargain, really means that the aggrieved party should get

8 This suggestion follows Cooter & Eisenberg (1985) at 1439. "The difference between the value that a party places upon what he expects to receive and give up is called surplus. The *lost-surplus formula* awards the victim of breach the surplus that he would have enjoyed if the breaching party had performed" (emphasis in original, footnote omitted). This approach was also foreshadowed in Markovits (2004) (the notion of the benefit of the bargain is formal only, and the actual remedial entitlement "depends on a separate understanding of the content of the bargain whose benefit [the aggrieved party] is to receive.").

9 Because the aggrieved party would have a legal right to this amount, a market in the asset would require the buyer to agree to pay that value (adjusted from the costs of collecting the damages).

10 Fortunately, the determinants of the aggrieved party's private surplus are not difficult to identify. A decisionmaker need only identify the burdens and benefits each party accepted as part of the exchange. The burdens include the aggrieved party's cost of performance, the costs associated with the risks the aggrieved party accepted, and the net lost value the aggrieved party gave up by foregoing other options. The benefits include the breaching party's performance and the benefit of avoiding less desirable options. Note that foregone opportunities serve as both a benefit and a burden, because foregone opportunities include both those that would increase and those that would decrease the value of the party's private surplus. What matters is the net benefits over burdens, which depend on the probability that external circumstances will move in one direction rather than another.

their benefit of the bargain, which is the net difference between their benefits and burdens of the bargain they made.

My second claim is more adventurous: when parties exchange performance obligations, they implicitly choose their remedial obligations; remedial obligations are baked into an exchange by the nature of parties' tacit understandings about their exchange. The contract literature sometimes views remedial issues to be independent of the content of the promises the parties made; it is thought that the parties determine their performance obligations, but courts determine a party's remedial obligations.[11] But why would that be? If the parties, through their exchange, determine their performance obligations, why would that determination not be relevant to their remedial obligations? If the purpose of the remedy is to put the aggrieved party in the position the party would have been in had there been no breach (lost private surplus), how can the nature and contextuality of the exchange not be relevant to the remedy?

Perhaps we have backwards the chicken-and-egg view of performance obligations and remedial obligations. Conventionally, it might be thought that parties bargain in the shadow of remedial doctrines, which courts establish independently of the nature of the bargain. But it could be the other way around. It could be that the law reacts to the exchange the parties have made, and that the law recognizes remedies that reflect the exchange. That, at least, is what I will argue here. Under this view, remedial obligations are determined by the parties and recognized by legal decision-makers. Each party implicitly agrees to perform in good faith, *and* to protect the private surplus of the other party if a breach occurs.[12] Sometimes the remedial obligations are explicit; courts enforce reasonable formulas for determining liquidated damages and parties often include provisions for indemnity or third-party duties. Even when not explicit, remedial obligations reflect a method of reasoning about what the parties must have thought their remedial obligations entailed.

The two claims are related in the following way. An other-regarding contracting party will understand that to increase total contractual surplus, they must be prepared to guarantee the private surplus the counterparty expects from the exchange. Because the law requires each party to be other-regarding, the parties will share the tacit assumption that each will provide the insurance that guarantees the counterparty's private surplus (reducing the risk of nonperformance that contracting otherwise entails and increasing overall contractual surplus). That means that each party must have in mind the burden of guaranteeing the other party's

[11] Fuller & Perdue (1936) at 52 made this assumption explicit ("the parties left it to the courts to effectuate [the contracts] purposes"). Other scholars who appear to view the remedy to be independently determined are Eisenberg, (2013); Martin (2016); Smith (2004) at 388.

[12] As Daniel Markovits argued, two events disrupt the collaborative community at the heart of contract law: by wrongfully getting into the community or by wrongfully getting out of the community. A party that does not fulfill her remedial obligations "nevertheless estranges herself from him, and violates the command that she treat him as an end, because she pursues (through her breach) an end he cannot possible share." Markovits (2004) at 1431.

private surplus when it determines the net benefits of the exchange and compares those benefits to its other options. Each party will build into the burden it carries as part of the exchange the cost of that guarantee, which means that the parties must have the nature and extent of the remedy in mind when they make the contract.[13] If either party is uncomfortable with the cost of the guarantee, that party can make the cost an explicit item of bargaining and can thus reallocate the risk of the counterparty's private surplus. But the risk falls on the party who is paid to accept the risk and, in this way, becomes part of determining that party's contractual surplus.

Under this remedial conception, expectation damages are determined by reasoning about a party's private surplus, rather than through a rule or formula. This preserves that idea that the breaching party may substitute for the private surplus that would otherwise be lost, but it allows that substitute performance to reflect the exchange-implicit remedial obligations of an exchange. It also allows the exchange to recognize an explicit or implicit promise to provide more than substituted performance, including an implied promise of restitution or specific performance. Moreover, by tailoring the remedy to the nature of the exchange, reasoning about the determinants of lost private surplus responds to concerns that expectation damages, because they are contextual, cannot be captured by a single formula.[14]

There is much to be clarified about the method of determining the aggrieved party's private surplus. There is also much to be clarified about the claim that the remedial obligations reflect, and are embedded in, the exchange the parties made. In Section 14.1, I elaborate on the claim that the parties, when they choose their performance obligations, are also choosing (at least implicitly) their remedial obligations. In that discussion, I address the distinction between monetary damages and specific performance, as well as the related question of the moral and efficiency property of remedies. In Section 14.2, I survey some persistent remedial questions to further illustrate and implement my two claims.

14.1 PROMISES AND PERFORMANCE

Under the theory advanced here, when contracting parties are sufficiently other-regarding, their performance obligations impliedly include a remedial promise that legal decisionmakers identify and enforce. That implicit promise is to protect the aggrieved party's contractual surplus. When the parties fulfill that promise they are, I claim, acting morally and efficiently. To demonstrate this point, consider

[13] In this approach, it does not matter that the parties may make a miscalculation. Any miscalculation is no different from any other evaluation they make about the burden and benefits of the exchange. The important point is that each party will know, from the terms and context of the exchange, the kinds of remedial burdens they will face if they want to get out of the exchange. Each will know the termination fee for unwinding the relationship.

[14] Scott & Triantis (2004) at 1430–1431.

substituted performance and various other contract remedies, including specific performance and remedies for willful breach.

The assertion that parties implicitly agree to protect their counterparty's contractual surplus in the event of a breach reflects efficient breach theory. When parties bargain over the sale of a commodity or service subject to a deep market, neither party knows whether the other will breach; nor can either party say with confidence that post-contracting events will not give it a reason to breach. Markets move in both directions, so neither party can predict with any certainty which party will be inclined to breach and which will be the aggrieved party. It is not surprising, then, that both parties would want a remedy that allows them to substitute payment for performance, and it would not be surprising if each understood the preference of the other. Given those assumptions, it would not be surprising if the parties negotiated with the tacit assumption that they could substitute payment for performance. The standard substituted performance remedy seems to be a remedial obligation that reflects the parties' shared assumption about what would happen in the event of a breach. The parties did not promise to perform; they promised to protect the aggrieved party's private surplus.[15]

This view has important implications for both the efficient breach concept, and for our view of the moral obligations of promising. If we accept the moral imperative that "a promisor should keep their promises," and if I am correct that the promise was to protect the aggrieved party's private surplus, then the standard substitute performance remedy is, under the prescribed conditions, a moral remedy.[16] The promises the parties exchanged would include the promise to accept substituted performance for actual performance. It is not immoral to break a promise when the promise includes a remedy in the event of breach and that remedy is provided. Indeed, the reciprocity of the promise to accept substituted performance rather than to insist on actual performance makes the idea of efficient breach also a moral remedy that reflects the moral requirement that parties keep their promises.[17] Not coincidentally, if the parties tacitly agreed on substituted performance as a part of their performance, then substituted performance is specific performance – it is the specific performance the parties agreed to provide.

Moreover, if it is true that the parties can, in light of the shared assumptions generated in the exchange, determine the remedy, the idea of efficient breach becomes not so much an inquiry into efficiency, but an inquiry into what the parties each assumed their remedial obligations to be. Breach is efficient not because the courts choose an efficient outcome, but because an efficient outcome is what the

15 Notice that the tacit understanding I describe is a shared understanding and does not depend on one party bearing a risk (and cost) that the other party does not bear. There is no question about which party should have accepted a risk or made it a part of their exchange, for both parties faced the same, symmetrical risk.

16 This is not a new point. Smith (2004) at 400 (terming obligations to be disjunctive).

17 *Compare* Katz (2012) (arguing that efficient breach is consistent with deontic obligations).

parties impliedly promised each other when they made their bargain. The parties, not the court defined an efficient outcome; the courts recognized it. The parties are naturally efficient because each has an interest in reducing the costs of contracting as a way of increasing surplus. The reciprocal promises to accept, and to pay for, substituted performance reflect the interest each has in reducing the cost of contracting, and their interest ends up with an implicit promise to protect the counterparty's private surplus, but not to do more

But substituted performance is not the only remedy that the parties may accept as an implicit exchange promise; consider the remedy of specific performance. When a buyer values the subject matter of an exchange at more than market value, and the other party knows that, or when there is no market value, the parties are not likely to bargain around an implicit promise of substituted performance. Where no alternative market-based substitute exists, and both parties realize this, it would make no sense for a party to agree to accept substituted performance. A buyer who buys a painting or a house wants the thing bargained for, not the market value of the painting or house. Moreover, when the seller knows that the buyer wants the painting or the house, not a substitute, the seller is likely to receive a price that compensates the seller for the seller's forgone options. The seller is betting that no buyer will come along who puts a higher value on the painting or the house, and the seller should be held to that bet.

Under these circumstances, specific performance is the remedy that best reflects the ex ante exchange the parties implicitly made.[18] And, it is the remedy that an other-regarding contracting party would provide. The aggrieved party's contractual surplus depends on actually receiving the object of the bargaining, while the seller, because of the benefit of that presumably higher value, has given up the option of finding an alternative buyer to get that benefit. Specific performance is, for those reasons, the bargained for (and efficient) remedy.[19]

In light of this analysis, consider how unhelpful legal doctrine is in determining the circumstances under which to invoke a specific performance remedy.[20] The idea that a monetary remedy might be "inadequate" is, by itself, vacuous. The further idea that specific performance is appropriate when the subject matter of the contract is "unique" requires a method of reasoning about "uniqueness." Moreover, it is misleading to repeat the standard statement that specific performance is not the preferred remedy. Specific performance *is* the preferred remedy when that remedy is implied by the parties' private projects and implicit promises. Empirically, circumstances giving rise to specific performance may be infrequent, but if specific

18 *Florida Power & Light Co.* v. *Westinghouse Elec.*, 597 F. Supp. 1456 (E.D. Va. 1984).

19 This point is associated with Tony Kronman's view that specific performance is the remedy the parties would have chosen given their ex ante interests. *See* Kronman (1978) at 365. I extend that idea to suggest that specific performance is the remedy the parties implicitly chose, given what they knew or should have known about their private projects.

20 The doctrine is surveyed in Hecke (1961).

performance is the remedy implied by the promises the parties exchanged, then specific performance is not disfavored. Rather, it is the remedy that is an implied remedial promise that accompanies the performance promises. And, as already implied, if performance (and not substitute payment) is what the parties promised, then that is also an efficient remedy;[21] the remedy the parties bargained for in order to minimize costs.

The uniqueness of a contract's subject matter is one instance in which specific performance is necessary to protect the aggrieved party's contractual surplus. It would be a mistake, however, to think that specific performance is limited to that circumstance. Because specific performance is grounded in protecting the aggrieved party's private surplus and the parties' tacit exchange understanding, specific performance should be the remedy whenever it is necessary to protect an aggrieved party's private surplus. This requires a close examination of what both parties knew about the counterparty's private projects and how the exchange arranged the determinants of private surplus.

City Stores Co. v. *Amermann*[22] illustrates an appropriate analysis. The defendant, a retail mall developer, agreed to lease space as an anchor tenant to the plaintiff, City Stores, and City Stores agreed to help the developer secure necessary zoning changes. Although the developer was free to replace City Stores with a different anchor store, the contract allowed City Stores to match any offer the developer received from a rival anchor store. The developer breached the contract by accepting a rival bid without giving City Stores the opportunity to match the bid. Ordinarily, one might assume that monetary damages would be appropriate. The defendant might have had good reasons to prefer a rival anchor store, which would have made the breach efficient. Although monetary damages (City Store's lost profits) might have been difficult to calculate, that alone would not make a monetary remedy inadequate.

But monetary damages would not have protected City Store's private surplus. Because City Stores was instrumental in helping the developer get needed zoning changes, the contract gave the developer an ancillary benefit that increased City Stores' burden. The parties, if other regarding, must have understood that City Store's private surplus could be protected only if City Stores were given what it had been promised: the opportunity to match a rival bid. The court was justified in thinking that the parties must have contemplated that City Stores would be rewarded with the lease if City Stores matched a rival bidder.[23] Although the subject

21 Kronman (1978) at 363 (because specific performance creates a property rule it is an efficient way to form a remedy when the information available to determine the damages is unavailable or unreliable); Schwartz (1979).

22 266 F. Supp. 766 (D.C.).

23 Naturally, this analysis depends on what the parties knew (or, if suitably other-regarding, should have known) about the private projects of the other party, which implicates the question of whether one of the parties should have disclosed information about their private projects to the other. That is the topic of consequential damages.

matter of the contract (the lease of space to be an anchor store) was not "unique," the circumstances of the exchange were; and those circumstances justified specific performance.

Thus far we have seen that substituted performance and specific performance follow the logic of an other-regarding exchange. Consider also the exchange dynamics that seem to influence a choice between two measures of expectation damages when the seller breaches a contract with an intermediate buyer who planned to resell the goods. The intermediate buyer suffers two sorts of losses: the buyer has to find a substitute product to resell and would lose the profits (with reputational losses) if the resale does not occur.[24]

Steve Thel and Peter Siegelman have explained the theoretical basis for equating expectation damages with lost private surplus in such a case:

> Promisors will get more in exchange for their promises if they can credibly commit not to breach. The level of commitment for which they will bargain depends on the cost to the promisor of avoiding breach. The more costly it is to avoid breach, the more a promisor will charge to accept liability for such breach. When bargaining parties know that a breach will damage the promisee and can be avoided by the promisor at no net costs to the two parties taken together, they will want to permit it. Since a commitment not to breach in these circumstances will be of value to the promisee, the promisor will receive more for her promise when she makes that commitment. Moreover, the promisor will get the premium at no or little cost, since she can, by definition, avoid enhanced liability simply by not breaching willfully.[25]

In other words, a promisee can buy an insurance policy against a promisor's breach. The size of the insurance premium would account for the promisor's cost of avoiding the breach (the amount the promisor must invest or forgo to avoid a breach) and the promisee's benefit from the insurance policy. The promisor is likely to charge less for insurance against a breach that is knowing or voluntary (and hence willful) for that implies that the cost of avoiding the breach is low; the promisor is likely to charge more for an insurance policy against the promisor's negligence, for those breaches would be costly to control. The insurance policy becomes a part of the promisee's contractual surplus and the obligation to protect that surplus becomes part of the promisor's burden. Such a distribution of burdens and benefits can arise implicitly when both parties recognize the conditions for its existence and the fact that the distribution permits them to maximize contractual surplus. It can also arise from a promisor's assurance.

[24] Courts sometimes use the term "willful breach" to describe the choice they have made in cases involving intermediate buyers. This term is highly misleading. Although there can be a negligent breach. many breaches are willful in the sense that the breaching party knows that it is breaching. Indeed, a seller who breaches in order to sell to a different buyer at a higher price is doing so with knowledge of the breach, and therefore willfully. Motivation for the breach is not an occasion to vary the remedy for breach. As the text will show, the term "willful breach" appears to be a label that courts apply in order to choose a remedy that protects the aggrieved party's private surplus.

[25] Thel & Siegelman (2010) at 163 (citing Shavell (1980)) at 467–469.

Assume that an intermediary party has a contract to buy goods that it plans to resell under a separate contract. The intermediate party is protected from the seller's breach, but the buyer may nonetheless suffer reputational damages with its customers if the buyer cannot fulfill that contract. The value of the contract to both parties is increased if the seller can promise not to sell to another buyer for a higher price. To avoid such a breach, the buyer may be willing to buy an insurance policy against a seller's breach, and the seller may be able to increase the price by more than the cost of giving up the opportunity of a better offer. The seller then takes the risk that prices will rise but is compensated for that burden. The buyer accepts the burden of the higher price for the benefit of having the goods available for his customers. On the other hand, the seller is not likely to sell an insurance policy for any reason that could be too costly for the seller. The parties may, in other words, implicitly try to distinguish between breaches that can be avoided at low cost and those that can be avoided only at high cost, which would vary the remedy depending on the seller's cost, and the buyer's benefit, of avoiding breach.

Indeed, when the buyer is an intermediate party, Professors Thel and Siegelman believe that courts recognize this phenomenon. In those cases, the court must decide between two defensible measures of expectation damages: the buyer's lost profit from the resale and the buyer's cost of substitute goods. When a seller breaches because the seller diverts the goods to a higher bidder, courts normally award the buyer the difference between that price and the contract price, which is higher than the expectation damages measured by the buyer's lost profit margin.[26] On the other hand, where the breach seemed to be beyond the seller's control, the buyer receives only the lower lost-profit margin.[27] In the first scenario, where the buyer's contractual surplus can be interpreted to include a promise not to sell to a higher bidder, the remedy reflects that promise. But that remedy is not appropriate in the second scenario; when the cost of preventing a breach is high, it is unlikely that the seller would guarantee against a breach, which makes the lower lost-profit margin the appropriate measure of expectation damages. The damage remedy follows the implicit promises of the exchange.

In this section, we have explored the rationales for substituted performance, specific performance, and remedial choices for the buyer who resells the goods. We have done this to support the idea that the remedy for breach reflects the bargain the parties made, reinforcing the idea that when contracting parties choose their performance obligations they are, by implication, also choosing their remedial obligations. That conclusion reflects the idea that, in order to lower the cost of contracting, promises to do something are accompanied by the implicit promise to

[26] *TexPar Energy Co.* v. *Murphy Oil USA, Inc.*, 45 F. 3d 1111 (1113–14 (7th Cir. 1995); *KGM Harvesting Co.* v. *Fresh Network*, 42 Calif. Rptr 2d 286, 289–93 (Ct. App. 1995); *Tongish* v. *Thomas*, 840 P. 2d. 471, 475–76 (Kan. 1992).

[27] *H-W-H Cattle Co.* v. *Schroeder*, 767 F. 2d 437, 438 (8th Cir. 1985); *Allied Canners & Packers, Inc.* v. *Victor Packing Co.*, 209 Cal. Rptr. 60, 61–62 (Ct. App. 1984).

protect the counterparty's private surplus. Judicial remedies are not independent of the parties' bargain; remedies sit in the domain of contract interpretation. Let us examine how the idea of protecting a party's private surplus implied by the exchange works out in some common remedial controversies.

14.2 SOME COMMON REMEDIAL CONTROVERSIES

14.2.1 *Consequential Damages*

Determining a breaching party's responsibility for consequential damages also requires a legal decisionmaker to determine how the parties to an exchange allocated the risk that such damages would occur. *Hadley* v. *Baxendale*[28] frames the issue. When a lad delivered a shaft to the railroad to be shipped to a repair shop, the lad understood that without the shaft the mill could not operate and would lose profits. Whether the lad told the railroad of this circumstance is disputed, but is arguably irrelevant. As James Gordley has shown, the shaft was shipped under the railroads general pricing schedule, which did not include a premium for the risk of lost operating profits from delayed shipment.[29] The risk of the loss of operating profits, which was a part of the private projects of the milling company, was never priced into the contract and was never shifted, even if the railroad clerk had knowledge of it. Again, remedies follow from our understanding of how the parties, when they are sufficiently other-regarding, would have understood their private projects in the context of the counterparty's private projects.

Contract doctrine is insufficient to determine where the parties impliedly allocated the risk of harm.[30] It should not surprise us that concepts of foreseeability and proximate cause dominate the literature on consequential damages. But foreseeability begs the question of what risks are foreseeable, and to whom, while proximate cause was tort law's way of dealing with the need to identify which risks were one's for which an actor was responsible. The better approach, in both tort law and contract law, is to ask which harm was within the risks that made the defendant's conduct wrongful.[31] In contract law, the answer to that question points directly to the need to determine how the exchange allocated the risk of harm in order to determine which party is responsible for that harm. That cannot be done under a foreseeability analysis or by asking which party caused the harm. The parties allocated the risk and priced the risk into the contract, and the risk allocation should determine which party bears losses from consequential damages.

28 156 Eng. Rep. 145 (Ex. Ch. 1854).
29 Gordley (2002).
30 General doctrinal surveys are in Anderson (1987b) (using foreseeability and "reason to know" as organizing principles) and Turner (2001).
31 Gerhart (2010) at 127–149.

More generally, recovery for consequential damages operates at the intersection of the bilateral obligation to be other-regarding. The buyer can recover consequential damages when the risk of that kind of harm was priced into the contract. This obliges the buyer to give the seller fair notice of the consequences for which the buyer would hold the seller responsible so that the seller can price those risks into the contract. It obliges the seller to understand the buyer's private projects and anticipate the private project risk that the buyer would reasonably expect the seller to cover. Both parties have a role in reducing the risk of harm: the defendant by adjusting the level of care to the risk the defendant is responsible for, and the plaintiff by addressing harm if a breach were to occur. In any dispute, what matters is the relative ability of each party to understand the private projects of the other party in a way that allocates the risks of private project loss in the contract. Without that notice and the implicit allocation of the risk of harm, the bargain does not include those damages. With the notice, the contract does.[32]

Under this notion, the parties negotiate around assumptions that each party is permitted to make about the private projects of the counterparty, and those assumptions determine both what performance obligations are owed and the damages that a breaching party must pay to remedy the aggrieved party's losses.[33] When the assumptions are shared and accurate, the assumptions form the basis of the bargain. When the assumptions are not shared, one party has the more reasonable assumption (given the party's private goals and the exchange context), which puts pressure on the party with the less reasonable assumption to clarify the assumption that should form the obligations (including the remedial obligations) under the contract. Where the seller has no reason to know of the loss the aggrieved party will suffer (that is, where the seller is allowed to assume that a buyer's special need is a part of the buyer's private projects, and therefore not a part of the exchange), the seller is not responsible for that loss. What the parties know or ought to know about the content of the exchange determines the scope of each party's responsibility for damages that the law calls consequential.

A routine case illustrates the way in which obligations for consequential damages reflect the other-regarding contracting party. In *Lewis* v. *Mobil Oil Corp.*,[34] a buyer asked the seller to provide oil that was appropriate to the new equipment the buyer was installing. When the seller-supplied oil impaired the machinery's operation, the buyer sued for property damage and for lost profits from the equipment's reduced productivity. The exchange dynamic that informed that case was the interplay between the seller's advice about the correct oil to use for the machinery, which turned out to be wrong, and the buyers failure to undertake an independent

32 *See generally* Anderson (1987b) (using foreseeability and "reason to know" as organizing principles). *See also* Turner (2001).

33 As James Gordley has said, recovery for consequential damages reflects the idea that no person should gain at another person's expense. Gordley (1997).

34 438 F. 2d. 500 (8th Cir, 1971).

investigation of the problem with the machinery. Because the seller knew of the specific purpose for which the buyer would use the oil, and the buyer relied on the seller's recommendation, the seller had clearly accepted the risk that their decision would be wrong. As the equipment repeatedly broke down, and the equipment manufacturer and seller tried to determine the cause of the equipment failure, the plaintiff's loss of profits was clear to both parties. As to whether the plaintiff should have sought an alternative expert during the two and a half years the parties tried to figure out the problem, the jury found that the plaintiff's continued reliance on the seller was not unreasonable (probably because the seller could also have called in an expert). The buyer could recover the lost profits from the machines malfunction However, the court rejected the plaintiff's claim for lost profits after the problem was fixed. Plaintiff's difficulty in securing financing was not one of the risks that the seller assumed when deciding how much care to invest in addressing the plaintiffs problem; that risk was within plaintiff's control and was not a risk the seller had assumed.

14.2.2 *Restoration Value versus Market Value*

The idea that remedies protect a party's private surplus illuminates the debate about whether the remedy for a broken promise to restore land should be the cost of restoring the property or the diminished value of unrestored property. We take a well-trodden path, although we end up at an unexpected destination. In *Peevyhouse* v. *Garland Coal & Mining Co.*,[35] a landowner leased mining rights to a strip miner, who agreed to restore the land when mining was over. Evidently, the strip miner did little or no restoration work and thus breached the contract. Equally evidently, the miner had to correct the loss from that failure. But should that correction be, as the parties argued, the ex post cost of restoration (claimed to be $29,000) or the property's lost market value from the failure to restore the property (which was $300). Without a doubt, the strip miner saved money, welched on the deal, and imposed a loss on the landowner. But how much the strip mine company saved or the landowner lost depends entirely on what the strip mine company should have done under the contract. What, exactly, was the landowner's lost private surplus?

Framing the issue as ex post restoration cost versus ex post market value is misleading. Courts are confused because they are looking for a substitute remedy where none exists. In the normal breach case, the price term defines the aggrieved party's private surplus. The basic remedy looks to the ex post facts to determine the aggrieved party's ex ante surplus. The aggrieved party is protected from price increases or decreases and that protection makes ex post facts relevant to determining the ex ante private surplus. But in the cases exploring the promise to restore land, the terms do not specify the parties' obligations in a way that allows for ex post circumstances to define the ex ante

[35] 382 P.2d 109 (Okla. 1962).

private surplus. The obligations depend on the determinants of private surplus, which is a contextual and fact-based question and the obligation to restore ex ante is not necessarily measured by the cost of restoration ex post.

Nor is it appropriate to search for a rule that chooses one measure of damages over the other; the ex ante private surplus depends on the facts that determined the content of the exchange. The quest is to determine the remedy needed to protect the landowner's lost private surplus. The owner undoubtedly could have charged a higher price without the mining company's promise to restore the property; the lower return was one of the burdens the landowner bore in order to get the benefit of the mining company's promise to restore the land. It is strange that the court would use ex post figures to determine ex ante commitments. The mining company bore the risk that the ex ante restoration cost would rise ex post, just as the landowner bore the risk that the market or personal value from the restoration would go down ex post. The ex post calculations do not reveal the value of those risks ex ante.

Before addressing the determinants of the landowner's ex ante lost surplus, we can discard several other perspectives. Some might view *Peevyhouse* through the lens of present-day environmental consciousness and see a contest between industrial progress and the natural environment. But the question is not what the strip-mining company should do to be socially conscious; the landowner's lost surplus is a contract issue not an environmental issue. The landowner's bargained-for right to restoration determines the landowner's damages, and given the year of the bargain (1954) that value may not have been great. The landowner's lost surplus must be determined by the landowner's ex ante understanding of the value of the restoration.

Some might view *Peevyhouse* to be a political decision. Indeed, the judges may have minimized the value of restoration because of their prior affiliation with the strip-mining industry.[36] That would influence the value they put on restoration and what they might have assumed about the landowner's expectations. It would not, however, change the fact that the remedy depends on what the landowner bargained for and is not independent of the bargain.

Nor does it help to see *Peevyhouse* through the lens of the efficiency hypothesis. The remedial question is not whether it makes sense to invest in restoration value when doing so minimally increases ex post market value. Although such an investment looks like waste, if it is offset by the landowner's bargained for surplus, it is not waste. Again, the ex post difference between restoration value and market value is irrelevant except to the extent that it provides evidence of the value of the right the landowner purchased in the exchange.

What then are the determinants of the exchange that allow us to assess the landowner's lost private surplus? If data about comparable leases were available from 1954, it would be informative to compare leases that had no restoration requirement to determine the value the landowner gave up over the life of the

[36] Maute (1994). Her work is also the source of many of the facts cited in the text.

contract.[37] As it turned out, the landowner declined a flat payment of $3,000 that was then common in such leases; suggesting that the landowner bargained for a higher valuation. We ought to acknowledge that the landowner is entitled to have any idiosyncratic valuation counted toward his surplus, but only if that valuation was communicated to the lessee and built into the contract. If the landowner's valuation was not idiosyncratic, or was not built into the contract, we can assume that the exchange valued the restoration as the average ex ante cost of restoration, given the parties expectations about how deep the coal would be mined. Accordingly, we might seek to determine the parties' assumptions about restoration costs given their assumptions about how deep the mining would be and the distribution of burdens and benefits if the vein of coal was deeper than expected. We would also want to know whether the lease provided for payments on the basis of a fixed sum or as a percentage of the coal's value. Although the mining company accepted the risk that the vein of coal was deeper than expected, as well as the risk that restoration costs would go up (given the parties' understanding of what restoration meant), that risk would be affected by other contract terms. If the contract was for royalty payments, any increase in restoration costs (from digging deeper) also increased the mining company's benefits, and an implied term of the contract would have justified spending more on restoration. But if the lease was for a fixed sum, the landowner's surplus would have been formed by an expectation about the depth of mining and that would limit the landowner's surplus (just as a shared assumption about the cost of excavation shifted the cost of excavation to the landowner in *Lenz*).

What do these determinants tell us about the landowner's lost contractual surplus? I have already pointed out that ex post restoration costs and market values could not determine the monetary value needed to protect the landowner's ex ante private surplus. Those figures are, however, relevant evidence that the landowner had not bargained for the amount the landowner claimed. Even if this landowner had a specialized valuation on the land as restored, the disjunction between the landowner's claim for restoration costs and the value of the land after restoration makes it unlikely that the landowner bargained for such gold-plated restoration.[38] Indeed, if restoration had a common meaning within the community, then it is likely that the burden would have fallen on the landowner to make his specialized meaning of restoration known to the mining company so that it could be priced into the contract.[39]

[37] Even this figure is difficult to evaluate. In *Peevyhouse*, the landowner was given a premium price for the lease rights, primarily because of the strategic location of the property lines with respect to the seam of coal.

[38] The landowner argued that its subjective value was its attachment to the land as a family farm, and that having restoring the parcel that was mined would make it easier to integrate that parcel into the rest of the property.

[39] The literature contains a number of perspectives on *Peevyhouse* that are consistent with the idea that the jury was enforcing the bargain that the jury felt the parties had made. One perspective is that neither party expected the strip mining to be as deep as it was, and that both parties assumed that the cost of restoration would be de minimis. My reading reinforces the need for judicial interpretation to force the party that can avoid misunderstanding to do so.

In evaluating *Peevyhouse*, then, the question is whether the jury's award of $5,000 as damages was a fair measure of the landowner's lost private surplus. Given all the circumstances, it seems to be. The Oklahoma court's mistake was to allow the issue to be framed as ex post market value versus restoration costs; rejecting the plaintiff's claim for $29,000 may not have been a mistake, but reducing the award to market value ($300) surely was. After all, the ex post decrease in market value from the breach was not likely to have been the basis on which the parties bargained ex ante.

14.2.3 *Seller's Choice of Remedies*

The UCC provides for two seller remedies: the difference between the contract price and either the market price or the resale price. This presents a recurring issue – should the seller have the option to choose the remedy, perhaps speculating on the buyer's account?[40] How should law react when the seller holds onto the goods and sells them later at a profit, a problem sometimes known as the "election of remedies" problem. On the one hand, it is thought that if the benefit of an actual resale is not taken into account the aggrieved seller can receive a windfall by holding the goods until the market rises. On the other hand, it is argued that the seller should have the freedom to choose what to do with the goods the breach frees up, and that it does not stand in the mouth of the breaching party to avoid paying damages if the seller later makes a profit on the resale. Neither the common law nor the Uniform Commercial Code present a definitive answer and courts weigh the conflicting claims in various ways.

Courts should address the question by determining the private surplus that the exchange gave the aggrieved party, which means that they must assess the implicit division of post-breach risks. The choice of remedy is up to the parties, not the courts, which is, I would conjecture, why the UCC leaves the question open. Victor Goldberg has provided a vivid example of how the parties implicitly settle the issue for courts by allocating the risk of post-breach price changes[41] In *Peace River Seed Co-operative Ltd.* v. *Proceeds Marketing, Inc.*,[42] the seller produced and sold grass seed in a market in which wholesalers contracted for the grass seed and resold it to retailers. When the wholesaler-buyer repudiated a two-year obligation to buy the seed, the market price had decreased and the seller was entitled to the difference

40 UCC §2–706(1) allows the seller to recover the difference between the resale price and the contract price (with certain adjustments) and §2–708(1) allows the seller to recover the difference between the market price at the time of breach or repudiation and the contract price. The UCC leaves it to the courts to mediate between these two measures. Justice Peters identified the dilemma. To allow the seller to choose the resale price "is to allow speculation [by the seller] the expense of the [buyer]; forbidding it allows the [buyer] to profit from a substituted transaction which he can neither compel not control." Peters (1963) at 259. Professors White and Summers find that the answer to this question is "not clear." White & Summers (2010).

41 Goldberg (2018) at 7.

42 355 Or. 44 (2014).

between the market price and the contract price. The seller, however, did not sell the grass seed on the market; instead, the seller held onto it for three years, at which time the market price had risen and the seller made a handsome profit on the resale. Naturally, the buyer-defendant claimed that the seller should deduct from its claim for damages the profit it made on the resale.

As Victor Goldberg has pointed out, that issue need not be resolved by a legal rule that is independent of the bargain the parties made; it can be resolved by the way the parties implicitly determined the risk of market fluctuations after the breach or repudiation. In *Peace River* itself, the parties bargained in the light of an industry custom in which the seller and buyer agreed to engage in a "wash" transaction to shift the risk of market fluctuations to the seller. The buyer and seller would engage in a fictitious transaction, the buyer paying at the contract price for seed that the seller never delivered. This meant that the seller was compensated fully under the contract (it received the difference between the contract price and the market price). The agreement to engage in the wash transaction meant that the seller took the risk of market fluctuations after the wash transaction, which implies that the seller, having taken the risk for further market declines, should also reap the rewards of market increases. In that event, the buyer could not benefit from profits that the seller made by holding the goods. The wash transaction was, in effect, an election of remedies that protected the aggrieved party's private surplus.

But the *Peace River* result is not necessarily applicable to other exchanges and we should reject the assumption that the law functions to pick a rule that can settle this choice of remedy issue.[43] After all, in the *Peace River* setting the parties could have agreed that the buyer would bear the risk, and reward, of market fluctuations after a breach or repudiation. *Tesoro Petroleum Corp.* v. *Holborn Oil Co. Ltd.*[44] is one such case. When prices fell, the buyer repudiated the contract. However, the seller was able to resell the gasoline for more than the market price, and the buyer claimed that the appropriate price for determining damages was the resale, not the market, price. The court had to decide whether the buyer or the seller would get the benefit of that higher-than-market price. Noting that a windfall for the seller "could not have been in the contemplation of the parties at the time of their negotiation,"[45] the court accepted the buyer's reasoning and awarded the seller damages based on the difference between the higher resale price and the contract price, which means that the buyer, not the seller, benefited from the seller's ability to sell at above-market prices.

This result seems to be correct. The contract was for specific goods on a specific ship. The parties were frequent exchange partners. The buyer must have known that

43 Professor Goldberg assumes that the law functions to choose the remedial rule that reasonable bargainers would agree to, along with the further assumption that *Peace River* represents that rule. But reasonable bargainers will choose different equilibria in different situations, depending on which party can bear the risk at least cost and, as I show in the text, that will vary with the bargaining context.

44 484 N.Y.S. 2d 834 (Sup. Ct. 1989).

45 *Id.* at 722.

the seller had connections that would allow the seller to resell the gasoline at an above-market-price. Indeed, the buyer may well have bought from the seller because the buyer wanted to take advantage of the seller's connections. Under these circumstances, it is not surprising that the court would interpret the exchange relationship to allow the buyer to benefit from the resale price the seller arranged.

More generally, when the parties negotiate, and do not make the remedial formula clear, they implicitly decide which party will bear the risk (and reward) of market sales that are above or below the market price. The parties are able to include the risk of post-breach/repudiation market fluctuations in their bargain; and that possibility increases the disutility of a law-supplied default rule on the topic. A method of reasoning that enhances a court's ability to determine what the parties implicitly assumed if they were sufficiently other-regarding avoids two kinds of costs: the cost of forcing business people to be more explicit in their bargaining and the cost of imposing remedial obligations that are different from the ones the parties bargained for.[46]

Putting aside the rare instance in which the seller's resale (cover) price is below the market price (in which event the seller will not have mitigated the risk),[47] a legal decisionmaker can look to a number of factors to determine whether the seller or the buyer took the risk of a change in the market price after the date of the breach. The key inquiry is why a seller's resale price would differ from the market price. A seller with a unique opportunity in the resale market that the buyer is not aware of may well bargain with the expectation that they (the seller) should benefit from the unique opportunity by not revealing that information to the buyer. Or the seller could use that information to increase the value of the transaction to the buyer by minimizing the risk of a drop in prices. The assumption that a buyer would want the certainty of fixed damages at the time of repudiation might not reflect reality. A buyer who is especially confident in a rise in the market price may bargain with the expectation that even if the buyer cannot use the goods, the buyer will get the advantage of rising prices after the contract is repudiated. Just as a course of dealing in the grass seed market demonstrated how sellers would be able to speculate in market price changes after the breach, a course of dealing might show that buyers want to take the risk of post-beach price changes. It all depends, and because "it all depends" the assignment of the risks and benefits of post-breach price changes is best

46 In other words, the reasonable bargain approach assumes, wrongly, that there is a "right way" for the parties to arrange their post-breach obligations. It also assumes that there is an "efficient way" of arranging obligations (including post-breach obligations). The better view is that obligations are efficient if they reflect the way the parties arranged them. Accordingly, the remedial obligations must be determined as terms that are inherent in the exchange the parties made and can be found in the nature of their exchange.

47 As unlikely as this scenario is, we might imagine an instance in which the seller was barred from a market and was therefore unable to sell at the market price, as well as an instance in which the seller held onto the goods into a rising market but could not unload the good fast enough when the market fell.

determined contextually, based on our best estimate of the implicit exchange terms that affect a party's private surplus.

14.2.4 *Lost Volume Sellers*

A hotly contested issue is whether an aggrieved seller may collect damages for the profits the seller would have made had the seller not lost the profit on the sale to the breaching party. This so-called lost volume recovery occurs when the seller has enough inventory to have made the sale on the contract the buyer breached and an additional sale. An approach that recognizes the position of the parties at the time of exchange, and the seller's lost contractual surplus, would provide a better fit between the remedy and the parties' ex ante understanding.

Under the lost profit rule of UCC § 2–708(2), the seller is entitled to lost profit on the sales the seller would have made but for the breach; lost profits serve as an alternative or supplement to the normal substituted performance remedy. Similarly, the Restatement (Second) suggests that the seller has lost the profit the seller would have made under the contract if the buyer had fulfilled the contract.[48] Under these approaches, the resale of the product the buyer bought would provide the seller's substitute performance if the resale price was below the contract price, but the seller would still lose the profit that it would have made if the seller had sold both the product under contract and another product.

Respected scholars have lined up on either side of the issue. To Professors White and Summers, the lost profit should be a common remedy in any situation in which the seller is not limited in the amount the seller could sell, for the breach deprives the seller of the profits on a sale the seller would have made.[49] Not all agree. Professor Goldberg suggests that the aggrieved party is entitled to a termination fee, but nothing more,[50] and Professor Gordley agrees but argues that the termination fee would be zero because, in a competitive market, buyers would not pay for the termination fee and sellers would not be able to charge one.[51] The notion that remedies should protect the aggrieved party's private surplus suggests that generally the rule allowing recovery for lost profits is the correct one.

Consider how the buyer and seller, if other-regarding, would have thought about the division of contractual surplus between them, For the seller, the contractual benefit is to spread the seller's cost of doing business over a greater volume, which reduces the seller's burden of per unit inventory and marketing costs. The seller's private projects, I would argue, include the cost of being in a position to make the sale, which was the general overhead costs the seller expended. Spreading that cost

48 Restatement (Second) of Contracts §347.

49 White & Summers (2010) at 381 (lost profits as "the recovery which all right-minded people would agree the lost volume seller should have."); Childress & Burgess (1973); Anderson (1987a).

50 Goldberg (2017) and Goldberg (2018).

51 Gordley (2020).

must be included as part of the seller's contract surplus because a single sale was not made in isolation. The seller sold (and the buyer bought) not just the product but the seller's ability to be in the position to make the sale in the first place. The buyer surely recognized that once the sale is make the seller is burdened by giving up the opportunity to sell from its inventory at a higher price.

From the buyer's perspective, the contractual benefit is, by securing the contract price, to avoid the risk of having to pay a higher price. It is also the benefit of having a seller who can supply the product when the buyer wants it (the burden that the seller absorbed). The buyer's burden includes foregoing a lower price, of course, but something more. The buyer carries the burden of regret risk; the risk that post-exchange circumstances would make the purchase less valuable than the buyer expected. In one oft-cited case, *Neri* v. *Retail Marine Corp.*,[52] the buyer bought a boat from a retail dealer and six days later found that he needed to have surgery and would be in the hospital for four months. This was a part of the private projects of the buyer, not the seller, and the exchange would, under ordinary circumstances, be priced on the assumption that the buyer carried the burden of that risk.

Under this analysis, it is difficult to escape the conclusion that the seller's private surplus included the profit from the lost sale occasioned by the breach. If the buyer did not want the risk of buyer's regret, the buyer should have asked for a termination option, which would have decreased the seller's surplus unless the seller was compensated for it. The absence of a termination option is one of the benefits that increased the seller's private surplus and the seller would have charged a higher price if the buyer had wanted the benefit of a termination option.

Victor Goldberg would challenge this conclusion by suggesting that the seller could protect their contractual surplus by charging a termination fee, and that the fee would measure the seller's loss. But this does not address the question of why the risk of termination should be on the seller and not the buyer. The seller might have given the buyer the option to terminate in order to get an additional sale, but the termination fee would have then become a part of the exchange. Professor Goldberg seems to think that a nonrefundable deposit is a proxy for a termination fee,[53] but I doubt it; the nonrefundable deposit might simply protect the seller's investment in serving that buyer. A genuine termination fee would be quite high; the seller would want the termination fee to reflect the seller's lost profits and protect against the buyer's false claim of a justification for breaching. The premium for insuring against termination would, because of moral hazard, be quite high, varying only with the seller's prediction of the probability of the buyer exercising the right. Given the divergence of interests between buyer and seller, a deposit does not a substitute for lost profits.

52 30 N.Y. 2d 393 (1972).
53 Goldberg (2017) and Goldberg (2020).

James Gordley's conclusion, mimicking Fuller and Purdue,[54] that the seller "lost nothing" reflects the belief that in a competitive market, competing sellers would drive the price of termination down to zero, and that the seller's contractual benefit was in not having to sell at a lower price. I have a different understanding of how markets address risks. If I am correct that risk of regret falls on the buyer, then markets would price that risk separately only if the buyer made it a part of the transaction. Given the assurances of the bargain, a termination fee is not costless and if sellers do not offer a termination fee it is because they do not expect to benefit from one. And if I am correct that the seller benefits from both the insurance against having to sell at a lower price *and* the sale's contribution to overhead, then the seller suffers a real loss once the exchange is created and then breached, the same as any other disappointed party.

14.3 CONCLUSION

What makes remedial obligations for breach of contract difficult is that the standard remedy, substituted performance, is quite common, but does not cover, or respond to, the contextuality of promising. It does not provide courts with a workable idea of remedial obligations when substituted performance does not reflect the exchange's contextual details that matter. The idea that courts should look for an efficient remedy requires courts to determine how the parties allocated the burdens and benefits of the exchange, and outside of the standard case, this is not obvious. By understanding the determinants of substituted performance, this chapter has offered a new way of understanding remedial obligations.

Because, as I have argued, the parties in an exchange have an obligation to look out for the well-being of their counterparty, each party, if making reasonable bargaining decisions, will have an expectation about post-breach remedies if one of the parties breaches its performance obligations. Accordingly, the parties have implicit remedial obligations in mind in the event of a breach, and the search for those implicit obligations should guide courts to a remedy that is consistent with the exchange the parties made. For this reason, remedies are inherently contextual and require a court to understand the party's private projects, allocation of risks, and understanding of each other's private projects.

The expectation that ought to guide the court in designing a remedy is the lost private surplus of the aggrieved party, who is entitled to the surplus of benefits over burdens that the aggrieved party bargained for. Accordingly, in fashioning a remedy courts need to take into account the burdens and benefits that the parties allocated

54 Fuller & Perdue (1936). Their challenge to expectation damages was that an expectation is something a person never had, which is a strange foundation for damages. Yet, in my view, once the contract is signed, the seller has something of value; and the purpose of a contract is to protect that which is valuable. Accordingly, protecting the private surplus of the seller is protecting the seller's reliance interest.

through the exchange and fashion a remedy that protects the aggrieved party's private surplus. The standard remedy allowing substitute performance does that, which is why it is the appropriate remedy in a large number of commercial cases. Yet in appropriate circumstances, the goal of protecting a party's lost private surplus will lead to other remedies, like specific performance and forms of monetary compensation that deviate from the idea of substituted performance.

References

Adler (2010): Barry E. Adler, *Contract Law and the Willfulness Diversion*, in Omri Ben-Shahar and Ariel Porat (eds.), FAULT IN AMERICAN CONTRACT LAW (Cambridge University Press 2010).

Alexander & Sherwin (2001): Larry Alexander & Emily Sherwin, THE RULE OF RULES: MORALITY, RULES, & THE DILEMMAS OF LAW (Duke University Press 2001).

Anderson (1987a): Roy Ryden Anderson, *Damages for Sellers Under the Code's Profit Formula*, 40 SW L. J. 1021 (1987).

Anderson (1987b): Roy Ryden Anderson, *Incidental and Consequential Damages*, 7 J. LAW AND COMM. 327 (1987).

Atiyah (1981): P. S. Atiyah, PROMISES, MORALS, AND LAW (Oxford University, Clarendon 1981).

Atiyah (1986): P. S. Atiyah, ESSAYS ON CONTRACT (Oxford University, Clarendon 1986).

Ayres & Gertner (1989): Ian Ayres & Robert Gertner, *Filling Gaps in Incomplete Contracts: An Economic Theory of Default Rules*, Vol. 99 YALE L.J. 87 (1989–90).

Bagchi (2018): Aditi Bagchi, *Contract and the Problem of Fickle People*, 53 WAKE FOREST L. REV. 101 (2018).

Bagachi (2019): Aditi Bagchi, *Risk-Averse Contract Interpretation*, 82 L. AND CONT. PROB. 1 (2019).

Baird, Gertner, & Picker (1994): Robert G. Baird, Robert H. Gertner, & Randal C. Picker, GAME THEORY AND THE LAW (Harvard University Press 1994).

Baird (2013): Douglas G. Baird, RECONSTRUCTING CONTRACTS (Harvard University Press 2013).

Baker, Gibbons, & Murphy (2002): George Baker, Robert Gibbons, & Kevin J. Murphy, *Relational Contracts and the Theory of the Firm*, 117 O. J. ECON. 39 (2002).

Balganesh & Parchomovsky (2015): Shyamkrishna Balganesh & Gideon Parchomovsky, *Structure and Value in Common Law*, 163 U. PA. L. REV. 1241 (2015).

Bar-Gill & Ben-Shahar (2004): Oren Bar Gill & Omri Ben-Shahar, *The Law of Duress and The Economics of Credible Threats*, 33 J LEG. STUD. 391 (2004).

Bar-Gill, Ben-Shahar, & Marotta-Wurgler (2017): Oren Bar-Gill, Omri Ben-Shahar, & Florencia Marotta-Wurgler, *Searching for Common Law: The Quantitative Approach of the Restatement of Consumer Contracts*, 84 U.CHI. L. REV. 7 (2017).

Barnett (1986a): Randy E. Barnett, *A Consent Theory of Contracts*, 86 COLUM. L. REV. 269 (1986).

Barnett (1986b): Randy E. Barnett, *Contract Remedies and Inalienable Rights*, 4 SOC. PHIL. & POLICY 179 (1986).

Barnett (1996): Randy E. Barnett, *The Death of Reliance*, 46 J. LEG. ED. 518 (1996).

Barnett & Becker (1987): Randy E. Barnett & Mary E. Becker, *Beyond Reliance: Promissory Estoppel, Contract Formalities, and Misrepresentations*, 15 HOFSTRA L. REV. 443 (1987).

Becher (2007–2008): Shmuel I. Becher, *Behavioral Science and Consumer Standard Form Contracts*, 68 LA. L. REV. 117 (2007–2008).

Ben-Shahar & Porat (2010): Omri Ben-Shahar & Ariel Porat, FAULT IN AMERICAN CONTRACT LAW (Cambridge University Press 2010).

Ben-Shahar & Schneider (2014): Omri Ben-Shahar & Carl E. Schneider, THE FAILURE OF MANDATED DISCLOSURE (Princeton University Press 2014).

Berman & Toh (2013): Mitchell N. Berman & Kevin Toh, *Pluralistic Nonoriginalism and the Combinability Problem*, 91 TEX L. REV. 1739 (2013).

Benson (2001): Peter Benson, *The Unity of Contract Law*, in Peter Benson, THE THEORY OF CONTRACT LAW: NEW ESSAYS (Cambridge University Press 2001).

Bernstein (1992): Lisa Bernstein, *Opting Out of the Legal System: Extralegal Contractual Relations in the Diamond Industry*, 21 J. OF L. STUD. 115 (1992).

Bernstein (2016): Lisa Bernstein, *Beyond Relational Contracts: Social Capital and Network Governance in Procurement Contracts*, 7 J. L. ANAL. 561 (2016).

Binmore (2005): Kenneth Binmore, NATURAL JUSTICE (Oxford University Press 2005).

Bix (2012): Brian Bix, CONTRACT LAW: RULES, THEORY, AND CONTEXT (Cambridge University Press 2012).

Bolton & Dewatripont (2005): Patrick Bolton & Mathias Dewatripont, CONTRACT THEORY (MIT Press 2005).

Bratman (2015): Michael Bratman, *Shared Agency: A Planning Theory of Acting Together*, 172 PHIL. STUDIES 3375 (2015).

Braucher (2012): Jean Braucher, *The Sacred and the Profane Contracts Machine: The Complex Morality of Contract Law in Action* 45 SUFF. L. REV. 666 (2012).

Bridgeman (2020): Curtis Bridgeman, *Twenty-First Century Contract Law Is a Law of Agreements, Not Debts: A Response to Lewinsohn*, 129 YALE L. J. 535 (2020).

Brudner and Nadler (2013): Alan Brudner & Jennifer M. Nadler, THE UNITY OF THE COMMON LAW (Oxford University Press 2013).erns

Burton (1980): Steven J. Burton, *Breach of Contract and the Common Law Duty to Perform in Good Faith*, 94 HARV. LAW REV. 369 (1980).

Burton (1981): Steven J. Burton, *Good Faith Performance of a Contract Within Article 2 of the Uniform Commercial Code*, 67 IOWA L. REV. 1 (1981).

Burton (1984): Steven J. Burton, *More on Good Faith Performance of a Contract: A Reply to Professor Summers*, 69 IOWA L. REV. 497 (1984).

Chen-Wisehart (2013): Mindy Chen-Wisehart, *In Defense of Consideration*, 13 OXFORD U COMMONWEALTH L. J. 209 (2013).

Childress & Burgess (1973): Robert Childress & Robert K. Burgess, *Seller Remedies: The Primacy of UCC 2–708 (2)*, 49 N. U. L. REV. 833 (1973).

Cohen (2011): George M. Cohen, *Interpretation and Implied Terms in Contract Law*, in Vol. III (The Regulation of Contracts) Encyclopedia of Law and Economics, 2d ed. (Edward Elgar Press; Gerrit De Geest ed. 2011).

Connelly, Crook, Combs, Ketchen, & Aguinis (2018): Brian L. Connelly, T. Russell Crook, James G. Combs, David J. Ketchen, Jr. & Herman Aguinis, *Competency and Integrity Based Trust in Interorganizational Relationships: Which Matters More?* 44 J. MGT. 919 (2018).

Cooter (1982): Robert Cooter, *The Cost of Coase*, 11 J. OF LEGAL STUDIES 1 (1982).

Cooter (1984): Robert Cooter, *Prices and Sanctions*, 84 COLUM L REV. 1523 (1984).

Cooter and Eisenberg (1985): Robert Cooter & Melvin Aron Eisenberg, *Damages for Breach of Contract*, 73 CAL. L. REV. 1434 (1985).

Corbin (1917–1918): Arthur Corbin, *Does a Pre-Existing Duty Defeat Consideration*, 27 YALE. L. J. 362 (1917–1918).
Crawford (1982): Vincent P. Crawford, *A Theory of Disagreement in Bargaining*, 50 ECONOMETRICA 607 (1982).
Crawford (2013): Vincent P. Crawford, *Boundedly Rational Versus Optimization-Based Models of Strategic Thinking and Learning in Games*, 51 J. ECON. LIT. 512 (2013).
Dixit & Skeath (2004): Avanish Dixit & Susan Skeath, GAMES AND STRATEGY (W. W. Norton, 2nd ed. 2004).
Dobbins (2005): Teri J. Dobbins, *Losing Faith: Extracting the Implied Covenant of Good Faith from (Some) Contracts*, 84 OR. L. REV. 227 (2005).
Dubroff (2006): Harold Dubroff, *The Implied Covenant of Good Faith in Contract Interpretation and Gap Filling: Reviling a Revered Relic*, 80 ST. JOHN'S L. REV. 559 (2006).
Duesenberg (1973): Richard W. Duesenberg, *General Provisions, Sales, Bulk Transfers, and Documents of Title*, 28 BUS. LAW. 805 (1973).
Dworkin (1986): Ronald Dworkin, LAW'S EMPIRE (Harvard University Press 1986).
Dworkin (2011): Ronald Dworkin, JUSTICE FOR HEDGEHOGS (Harvard University Press 2011).
Dworkin (2013): TAKING RIGHTS SERIOUSLY (Harvard University Press, 2d ed. 2013).
Eggleston, Posner, & Zeckhauser (2000): Karen Eggleston, Eric A. Posner, & Richard Zeckhauser, *The Design and Interpretation of Contracts: Why Complexity Matters*, 95 NW. L. REV. 91 (2000).
Eisenberg (2001): Melvin A. Eisenberg, *A Theory of Contracts*, in Peter Benson (ed.), THE THEORY OF CONTRACT LAW: NEW ESSAYS (Cambridge University Press 2001).
Eisenberg (2002): Melvin A. Eisenberg, *The Duty to Rescue in Contract Law*, 71 FORDHAM L. REV. 647 (2002).
Eisenberg (2009): Melvin A. Eisenberg, *Impossibility, Impracticability, and Frustration*, 1 J. OF LEG. ANALYSIS 207 (2009).
Eisenberg (2013): Melvin A. Eisenberg, *Conflicting Formulas for Measuring Expectation Damages*, 45 ARIZ L. REV. 369 (2013).
Ellickson (1994): Robert C. Ellickson, ORDER WITHOUT LAW (Harvard University Press 1994).
Farber & Matheson (1985): Daniel A. Farber & John H. Matheson, *Beyond Promissory Estoppel: Contract Law and the "Invisible Handshake,"* 52 U. CHI. L. REV. (1985).
Farnsworth (1963): E. Allen Farnsworth, *Good Faith Performance and Commercial Reasonableness under the Uniform Commercial Code*, U. CHI. L. REV. 666 (1963).
Farrell (1987): Joseph Farrell, *Information and the Coase Theorem*, 1 J. ECON. PERSPECTIVES 113 (1987).
Feinman (2015): Jay M. Feinman, *The Duty of Good Faith: A Perspective on Contemporary Contract Law*, 66 HAST L. J. 937 (2015)
Finnis (1980): John Finnis, NATURAL LAW AND NATURAL RIGHTS (Oxford University, Clarendon 1980).
Fried (2012): Barbara Fried, *The Limits of a Nonconsequentialist Approach to Torts*, 18 LEGAL THEORY 231 (2012).
Fried (1981): Charles Fried, CONTRACT AS PROMISE: A THEORY OF CONTRACTUAL OBLIGATION (Harvard University Press 1981).
Frydlinger, Hart, & Vitasek (2019): David Frydlinger, Oliver Hart, & Kate Vitasek, *A New Approach to Contracts: How to Build Better Long-Term Strategic Partnerships*, SEPTEMBER-OCTOBER HARVARD BUS. REV. (2019).
Fuller & Perdue (1936): Lon L. Fuller & William F. Perdue Jr., *The Reliance Interest in Contract Damages*, 46 YALE L.J. 52 (1936).

Fuller (1941): Lon L. Fuller, *Consideration and Form*, 41 COLUM. L. REV. 779 (1941).
Geis (2008): George S. Geis, *Economics as Context for Contract Law*, 75 CHI L. REV. 569, (2008).
Gergen (1992): Mark P. Gergen, *The Use of Open Ended Terms in Contracts*, 92 COLUM. L. REV. 997 (1992).
Gerhart (2010): Peter M. Gerhart, TORT LAW AND SOCIAL MORALITY (Cambridge University Press 2010).
Gerhart (2014): Peter M. Gerhart, PROPERTY LAW AND SOCIAL MORALITY (Cambridge University Press 2014).
Gerhart & Kostritsky (2015): Peter M. Gerhart & Juliet P. Kotritsky, *Efficient Contextualism*, 76 U. PITT L. REV. 509 (2015)
Gil & Marion (2013): Richard Gil & Justin Marion, *Self-Enforcing Contracts and Relational Contracting: Evidence from California Highway Procurement*, 29 J. L. ECON. & ORG. 239 (2012).
Gilmore (1974): Grant Gilmore, THE DEATH OF CONTRACT (Ohio State University Press 1974, with 2d ed. in 1995).
Gilo & Porat (2005–2006): David Gilo & Ariel Porat, *The Hidden Rules of Boilerplate and Standard Form Contracts: Strategic Imposition of Transaction Costs, Segmentation of Consumers and Anticompetitive Effects*, 104 MICH L. REV. 983 (2005–2006).
Gilson, Sabel, & Scott (2013): Ronald J. Gilson, Charles F. Sabel, & Robert E. Scott, *Contract and Innovation: The Limited Role of Generalist Courts in the Evolution of Novel Contractual Forms*, 88 N.Y.U L. REV 170 (2013).
Goetz & Scott (1980): Charles J. Goetz & Robert E. Scott, *Enforcing Promises: An Examination of the Basis of Contract*, 89 YALE. L. J. 261 (1980).
Goetz & Scott (1981): Charles J. Goetz & Robert E. Scott, *Principles of Relational Contracts*, 67 VA. L. REV. 1089 (1981).
Goldberg (2006): Victor P. Goldberg, FRAMING CONTRACT LAW (Harvard University Press 2006).
Goldberg (2010): Victor P. Goldberg, *Excuse Doctrine: The Eisenberg Uncertainty Principle*, 2 J. LEGAL ANALYSIS 359 (2010).
Goldberg (2015): Victor P. Goldberg, *Rethinking Jacob and Youngs v. Kent*, 66 CASE W. LAW. REV. 111 (2015).
Goldberg (2017): Victor Goldberg, *The Lost Volume Seller, R.I.P.*, 3 CRITERION JOURNAL OF INNOVATION, 205 (2017).
Goldberg (2018): Victor P. Goldberg, *Reckoning Contract Damages: Valuation of the Contract as an Asset*, 75 WASH. & LEE L. REV. 301 (2018).
Goldberg (2019): RETHINKING THE LAW OF CONTRACT DAMAGES (Elgar Press 2019).
Gordley (1997): James Gordley, *Contract and Delict: Toward a Unified Law of Obligations*, 1 EDIN. L. REV. 345 (1997).
Gordley (2001): James Gordley, *Contract Law in the Aristotelian Tradition* in Peter Benson (ed.), THE THEORY OF CONTRACT LAW (Cambridge University Press 2001).
Gordley (2004): James Gordley, *Impossibility and Changed and Unforeseen Circumstances*, 52 AM. J. COMP. LIT. 513 (2004).
Gordley (2012): James Gordley, *Consideration* in Jan M. Smits (ed.), ELGAR ENCYCLOPEDIA OF COMPARATIVE LAW (Elgar 2nd ed. 2012).
Gordley (2020): James Gordley, *The Myth of "Expectation Interest,"* 52 U. PAC. L REV. __ (2020).
Graham & Peirce (1989): Daniel A. Graham & Ellen Peirce, *Contract Modification: An Economic Analysis of the Holdout Game*, 52 LAW AND CONT. PROB. (1989).
Hart (1961): H. L. A. Hart, THE CONCEPT OF THE LAW (Oxford University Press 1961).

Hart (1994): H. L. A. Hart, THE CONCEPT OF THE LAW (Oxford University Press 2d ed. 1994).
Hart (2017): Oliver Hart, *Incomplete Contracts and Control*, 107 AM. ECON. REV. 1731, (2017).
Hartsad & Selten (2013): Ronald M. Harstad & Reinhard Selten, *Bounded-Rationality Models: Tasks to Become Intellectually Competitive*, 51 J. ECON. LIT. 496 (2013).
Hecke (1961): M. T. Van Hecke, *Changing Emphasis in Specific Performance*, 40 N. CAR. L. REV. 1 (1961).
Hershkovitz (2014–2015): Scott Hershkovitz, *The End of Jurisprudence*, 124 YALE L.J. 1160 (2014–2015).
Hillman (1997): Robert A. Hillman, THE RICHNESS OF CONTRACT LAW: AN ANALYSIS OF CRITIQUE OF CONTEMPORARY THEORIES OF CONTRACT LAW (Springer 1997).
Hirschman (1970): A. O. Hirschman, EXIT, VOICE, AND LOYALTY: RESPONSES TO THE DECLINE IN FIRMS, ORGANIZATIONS, AND STATES (Harvard University Press 1970).
Holmes (1881): Oliver Wendell Holmes, THE COMMON LAW (Little, Brown, and Co. 1881).
Holmes (1897): Oliver Wendell Holmes, *The Path of the Law*, 10 HARV. L. REV. 457 (1897).
Hume (1739): David Hume, A TREATISE ON HUMAN NATURE, BOOK III, Pt. II, Ch 5. (1739) (Dover Ed. 1960).
Jennejohn (2018): Matthew Jennejohn, *The Architecture of Contract Innovation*, 59 BOSTON COLLEGE L. REV. 71 (2018).
Kant (1785): IMMANUEL KANT, GROUNDWORK FOR THE METAPHYSIC OF MORALS (H. J. Paton, trans., Harper and Row 1964 (1785).
Kaplow (1992): Louis Kaplow, *Rules Versus and Standards: An Economic Analysis*, 42 DUKE L. J. 557 (1992).
Kar (2016): Robin Bradley Kar, *The Empowerment Theory of Contracts*, 83 U. CHI L. REV, 759 (2016).
Kar & Radin (2019): Robin Bradley Kar & Margaret Jane Radin, *Pseudo-Contracts and Shared Meaning Analysis*, 132 HARV. L. REV. 1135 (2019).
Kastner (2010): Tal Kastner, *The Persisting Ideal of Agreement in an Age of Boilerplate*, 35 LAW & SOC. INQUIRY, 793 (2010).
Katz (2012): Avery Katz, *Virtue Ethics and Efficient Breach*, 45 SUFF. L. REV. (2012).
Kaczorowski (1990): Robert J. Kaczorowski, *The Common Law Background of Nineteenth Century Tort Law*, 51 OHIO ST. L. REV. (1990).
Kelson (1945): Hans Kelsen, GENERAL THEORY OF LAW AND THE STATE (Harvard University Press 1945).
Kennedy (1976): Duncan Kennedy, *Form and Substance in Private Law Adjudication*, 89 HARV. L. REV. 685 (1976).
Kim (2013): Nancy S. Kim, WRAP CONTRACTS: FOUNDATIONS AND RAMIFICATIONS (Oxford University Press 2013).
Kim (2019): Nancy S. Kim, CONTESTABILITY: CONSENT AND ITS LIMITS (Cambridge University Press 2019).
Kimel (2014): Dori Kimel, *Personal Autonomy and Change of Mind in Promise and Contracts*, in Gregory Klass, George Letsas, & Prince Saprai (eds.), PHILOSOPHICAL FOUNDATIONS OF CONTRACT LAW (Oxford University Press 2014).
Kirst (1977): Roger W. Kirst, *Usage of Trade and Course of Dealing: Subversion of the UCC Theory*, 1977 U. ILL. L. FORUM 811 (1977).
Klass (2008): Gregory Klass, *Duty, Power, and Compound Rules*, 83 N.Y. U. L. REV. 1726 (2008).
Klass, Letsas, & Saprai (2014): Gregory Klass, George Letsas, & Prince Saprai (eds.), PHILOSOPHICAL FOUNDATIONS CONTRACT LAW (Oxford University Press 2014).

Klass (2019): Gregory Klass, *Empiricism and Privacy Policies in the Restatement of Consumer Contract Law*, YALE J OF REG. BLOG (2019), http//yalejreg.com/nc/empiricism-and-privacypolicie-in the-restatemen-of-consumer-contract-law.

Koch (1972): Howard Koch, *Casablanca: Script and Legend* (The Overlook Press 1972).

Knapp (1998): Charles L. Knapp, *Rescuing Reliance: The Perils of Promissory Estoppel*, 49 HASTINGS L.J. 1191 (1998).

Korobkin (2003): Russell Korobkin, *Bounded Rationality, Standard Form Contracts, and Unconsionability*, 70 U. CHI L. REV. 1203 (2003).

Korsgarrd (1996): Christine M. Korsgaard, CREATING THE KINGDOM OF ENDS (Cambridge University Press 1996).

Kostritsky (1987): Juliet P. Kostritsky, *A New Theory of Assent-Based Liability Emerging under the Guise of Promissory Estoppel: An Explanation and Defense*, 33 WAYNE L. REV. 895 (1987).

Kostritsky (2018–2019): Juliet P. Kostritsky, *A Bargaining Dynamic Transaction Cost Approach to Understanding Framework Contracts*, 68 AM. U. L. REV. 1621 (2018–2019).

Kostritsky (2007): Juliet P. Kostritsky, *Plain Meaning vs. Broad Interpretation: How the Risk of Opportunism Defeats a Unitary Default Rule for Interpretation*, 96 KY. L. J. 43 (2007–2008).

Kraus (1993): Jody S. Kraus, THE LIMITS OF HOBBESIAN CONTRACTUALISM (Cambridge University Press 1993).

Kraus (1997): Jody S. Kraus, *Political Liberalism and Truth*, 5 J. LEGAL THEORY 45 (1997).

Kraus (1997): Jody S. Kraus, *Legal Design and the Evolution of Commercial Norms*, 26 J. L. STUD. 377 (1997).

Kraus (2000): Jody S. Kraus, *Reconciling Autonomy and Efficiency in Contract Law: The Vertical Integration Strategy*, PHILOSOPHICAL ISSUES, SUPPLEMENT TO NOUS, VOL. 11. ISSUE 1 (2000). https://onlinelibrary.wiley.com/doi/10.1111/j.1758-2237.2001.tb00052.x.

Kraus (2007): Jody S. Kraus, *Transparency and Determinacy in Common Law Adjudication: A Philosophical Defense of Explanatory Economic Analysis*, 93 VA. L. VA. 287 (2007).

Kraus (2008): Jody S. Kraus, *From Langdell to Law and Economics, Two Conceptions of Stare Decisis in Contract*, 94 VA. REV. 157 (2008).

Kraus & Walt (2000): Jody S. Kraus & Steven D. Walt, *In Defense of the Incorporation Strategy*, in THE JURISPRUDENTIAL FOUNDATIONS OF CORPORATE AND COMMERCIAL LAW (Cambridge University Press 2000).

Kreitner (2011–2012): Roy Kreitner, *On New Pluralism in Contract Theory*, 45 SUFF. U.L. REV. 915 (2011–2012).

Kronman (1978): Anthony T. Kronman, *Specific Performance*, 45 CHI. L. REV. 351 (1978).

Leff (1967): Arthur Leff, *Unconsionability and the Code – The Emperor's New Clause*, 115 U. PENN. L. REV. 485 (1967).

Levitin, Kim, Kuntz, Linzer, McCoy, Moringiello, Renuart, & Willis (2019): Adam J. Levitin, Nancy S. Kim, Christina L. Kunz, Peter Linzer, Patricia A. McCoy, Juliet M. Moringiello, Elizabeth A. Renuart, & Lauren E. Willis, *The Replication Crisis of the Draft Restatement of Consumer Contracts*, YALE J. OF REG. AND BLOG (2019). http//yalejreg.com/nc/the-replication-crisis-of-the draft restatement of consumer contracts.

Lewinsohn (2020): Jed Lewinsohn, *Paid on Both Sides, Quid Pro Quo Exchange and The Doctrine of Consideration*, 129 YALE L.J. 690 (2020).

Listokin (2010): Yair Listokin, *Bayesian Contractual Interpretation*, 39 J. LEGAL STUD. 359 (2010).

Listwa (2019): D. B. Listwa, *Cooperative Covenants: Good Faith for the Alternative Entity*, 24 STAN. J. OF L. BUS. AND FIN. 137 (2019).

Llewellyn (1960): Karl N. Llewellyn, THE COMMON LAW TRADITION: DECIDING APPEALS (Little, Brown & Co. 1960).

Lonegrass (2012): Melissa T. Lonegrass, *Finding Room for Fairness in Formalism – The Sliding Scale Approach to Unconsionability*, 44 LOY. CHI. L. J. 1 (2012).

Macaulay (1963): Stewart Macaulay, *Non-Contractual Relations in Business: A Preliminary Study*, 28 AM. SOCIOL. REV. 55 (1963).

Macaulay (1985): Stewart Macaulay, *An Empirical View of Contract*, 1985 WIS. L. REV. 465 (1985).

Macneil (1977–1978): Ian R. Macneil, *Contracts: Adjustment of Long-Term Economic Relations under Classical, Neoclassical, and Relational Contract Law*, 72 NW U. L. REV. 854, 905 (1977–1978).

Markovits (2003–2004): Daniel Markovits, *Contract and Collaboration*, 113 YALE L. REV. 1417 (2003–2004).

Martin (2016): Jennifer S. Martin, *Opportunistic Resales and the Uniform Commercial Code*, 2016 U. ILL. L.REV. 488 (2016).

Maute (1994): Judith Maute, *Peveyhouse v. Garland Coal & Mining Co. Revisited: The Ballad of Willie and Lucille*, 89 NW. L. REV. 1341 (1994).

Mischkowsky, Stone, & Stremitzer (2019): Dorothee Mischkowsky, Rebecca Stone, & Alexander Stremitzer, *Promises, Expectations, and Social Cooperation*, 62 J. L. AND ECON. 687 (2019).

Moore (1990): Michael S. Moore, *A Theory of Criminal Law Theories*, 10 TEL AVIV U. STUD. IN L. 731 (1990).

Muris (1980): Timothy J. Muris, *Opportunistic Behavior and the Law of Contracts*, 65 MINN. L REV. 521 (1980).

Nance (2006): Dale A. Nance, *Rules, Standards, and the Internal Point of View*, 75 FORDHAM L. REV (2006).

Note (1999): Note, *Sympathy, Community, and Promising: Adam Smith's Case for Reviving Moral Consideration*, 66 CHI L. REV. 213 (1999).

O'Neill (1989): Onora O'Neill, CONSTRUCTIONS OF REASON: EXPLORATIONS OF KANT'S PRACTICAL PHILOSOPHY (Cambridge University Press 1989).

Peters (1963): Ellen A. Peters, *Remedies for Breach of Contracts Relating to the Sale of Goods under the Uniform Commercial Code: A Roadmap for Article Two*, 73 YALE L. J. 199 (1963).

Posner (1977): Richard A. Posner, *Gratuitous Promises in Economics and Law*, 6 J. LEGAL STUD. 410 (1977).

Posner (1985): Richard A. Posner, *The Law and Economics of Contract Interpretation*, 83 TEX. L. REV. 1581 (2005),

Rabin (2013): Matthew Rabin, *Incorporating Limited Rationality into Economics*, 51 J. ECON. LIT. 528 (2013).

Rakoff (2006): Todd Rakoff, *Good Faith in Contract Performance: Market Street Associates, Ltd. v. Frey*, 120 HARV. L REV. 1187 (2006).

Rawls (1971): John Rawls, A THEORY OF JUSTICE (Harvard University Press 1971).

Raz (2009): Joseph Raz, BETWEEN AUTHORITY AND INTERPRETATION (Oxford University Press 2009).

Sanga (2018): Sarath Sanga, *Incomplete Contracts: An Empirical Approach*, 34 J L. ECON. AND ORG. 650 (2018).

Scanlon (1990): Tom Scanlon, *Practices and Promises*, 19 PHIL. & PUB. AFF. 199 (1990).

Scanlon (1998): Tom Scanlon, WHAT WE OWE EACH OTHER (Cambridge University Press 1998).

Scanlon (2001): T. M. Scanlon, *Promises and Contracts*, in Peter Benson (ed.), THE THEORY OF CONTRACT LAW: NEW ESSAYS (Cambridge University Press 2001).

Schilke & Cook (2005): Oliver Schilke & Karen S. Cook, *Sources of Alliance Partners Trustworthiness: Integrating Calculative and Relational Perspectives*, 36 STRATEGIC MANAGEMENT J. 276 (2015).

Schilke & Lumineau (2018): Oliver Schilke & Fabrice Lumineau, *The Double-Edge Effect of Contracts on Alliance Performance*, 44 J. MGT. 2827 (2018).

Schwartz (1979): Alan Schwartz, *The Case for Specific Performance*, 89 YALE. L. J. 271 (1979).

Schwartz (1993): Alan Schwartz, *The Default Rule Paradigm and The Limits of Contract Law*, 3 S. CAL. INTERDICS.L. J. 389 (1993)

Schwartz (2019): Alan Schwartz, *Keynote Address: Modern Supply Chains and Outmoded Contract Law*, 68 AM. U. L. REV. 1503 (2019).

Schwartz & Scott (2003): 113 Alan Schwartz & Robert E. Scott, *Contract Theory and the Limits of Contract Law*, YALE LAW J. 541 (2003).

Schwartz & Scott (2016): Alan Schwartz & Robert Scott, *The Common Law of Contract and the Default Rule Project*, 102 VA. L. REV. 1523 (2016).

Scott (1990): Robert E. Scott, *A Relational Theory of Default Rules for Commercial Contracts*, 19 J. LEG STUD. 597 (1990).

Scott & Leslie (1993): Robert E. Scott & Douglas L. Leslie, CONTRACT LAW AND THEORY (Michie & Co. 1993).

Scott & Triantis (2009): Robert E. Scott & George G. Triantis, *Embedded Options and the Case against Compensation in Contract Law*, 2004 COLUM. L. REV. 1429 (2004).

Shavell (1980): Steven Shavell, *Damage Measures for Breach of Contract*, 1 BELL J. ECON. 466 (1980).

Shapiro (2011): Scott J. Shapiro, LEGALITY (Harvard University Press 2011).

Shell (1991): G. Richard Shell, *Opportunism and Trust in the Negotiation of Commercial Contracts: Toward a New Cause of Action*, 44 VAND. L. REV., 221 (1991).

Shiffrin (2007): Seana Shiffrin, *The Divergence of Contract and Promise*, 120 HARV. L. REV. 708 (2007).

Simon (1996): Herbert A. Simon, THE SCIENCES OF THE ARTIFICIAL (MIT Press 1996).

Slawson (1971): David W. Slawson, *Standard Form Contracts and Democratic Control of Lawmaking Power*, 84 HARV. L REV, 529 (1971).

Slawson (1984): David W. Slawson, *The New Meaning of Contract: The Transformation of Contracts Law by Standard Forms*, 46 U. PITT. L. REV. 21 (1984).

Slawson (1996): David W. Slawson, BINDING PROMISES: THE LATE TWENTIETH CENTURY REFORMATION OF CONTRACT LAW (Princeton University Press 1996).

Smith (1758): Adam Smith, THE THEORY OF MORAL SENTIMENTS (D. D. Raphael and A. L. Macfie (eds.) (Liberty Classics 1982).

Smith (1762–1763): Adam Smith, LECTURES ON JURISPRUDENCE (R. L. Meek, D. D. Raphael, & L G. Stein (eds.), (Liberty Classics 1982).

Smith (2012): Henry E. Smith, *On the Economy of Concepts in Property*, 160 U. PENN L. REV. 2097 (2012).

Smith (2004): Stephen A. Smith, CONTRACT THEORY (Oxford University Press 2004).

Steinman (2013): Adam N. Steinman, *To Say What the Law Is: Rules, Results, and the Dangers of Inferential Stare Decisis*, 99 VA. L REV. 1 (2013).

Stone (2016): Rebecca Stone, *Economic Analysis of Contract Law from the Internal Point of View*, 116 COLUM. L. REV. 2005, (2016).

Stone & Stremitzer (2019): Rebecca Stone & Alexander Stremitzer, *Promises, Reliance, and Psychological Lock-In* (December 2, 2019). UCLA School of Law, Law-Econ Research Paper No. 15–17. Available at SSRN: https://ssrn.com/abstract=2660949

Summers (1968): Robert S. Summers, *Good Faith in General Contract Law and the Sales Provisions of the Uniform Commercial Code*, 54 VA. L. REV. 195 (1968).

Summers (1982): Robert S. Summers, *The General Duty of Good Faith – Its Recognition and Conceptualization*, 67 CORN. L. REV. 819 (1982).

Taylor & Plambeck (2007): Terry Taylor & Erica Plambeck, *Supply Chain Relationships and Contracts: The Impact of Repeated Interaction on Capacity Investment and Procurement*, 53 MANAG. SCI. 1577 (2007).

Thel and Siegelmen (2010): Steve Thel and Peter Siegelman, *Willful Breach: An Efficient Screen for Efficient Breach*, in Omri Ben-Shahar and Ariel Porat (eds.), FAULT IN AMERICAN CONTRACT LAW (Cambridge University Press 2010).

Turner (2001): Paul S. Turner, *Consequential Damages: Hadley v. Baxendale Under the Uniform Commercial Code*, 54 S.M.U. L. REV 655 (2001).

Villanueva (2002): Enrique Villanueva (ed.), LEGAL AND POLITICAL PHILOSOPHY: SOCIAL, LEGAL & POLITICAL PHILOSOPHY 385 (Rodopi Phil. Studies 2002).

Wagner (2019): Wendy E. Wagner, INCOMPREHENSIBLE (Cambridge University Press 2019).

White & Mansfield (2002): Alan M. White & Kathy Lesser Mansfield, *Literacy and Contract*, 13 STAN. L. & POL'Y REV. 233 (2002).

White & Summers (2010): James J. White & Robert S. Summers, UNIFORM COMMERCIAL CODE 6TH ED. (West Academic Publishing 2010).

Willis (2015): Lauren Willis, *Performance-Based Consumer Law*, 82 CHI. L. REV. (2015).

Williamson (1975): Oliver Williamson, MARKET AND HIERARCHIES, ANALYSIS AND ANTITRUST IMPLICATIONS (The Free Press 1975).

Williamson (1985): Oliver E. Williamson, THE ECONOMIC INSTITUTIONS OF CAPITALISM (Free Press 1985).

Williston (1920): Samuel Williston, THE LAW OF CONTRACTS (Baker, Voorhis, & Company 1920).

Yee (2001): Woo Lei Yee, *Protecting Parties' Reasonable Expectations: A General Principle of Good Faith*, 1 OXFORD U. COMMONWEALTH L. J. 195 (2001).

Zacks (2016): Eric A Zacks, *The Restatement (Second) of Contract §211, Unfulfilled Expectations and the Future of Modern Standardized Consumer Contracts*, 7 WM. & MARY L. REV. 733 (2016).

Index

Lightning Source UK Ltd.
Milton Keynes UK
UKHW022021250321
381016UK00006B/81

9 781107 136762